To North India With Love

A Travel Guide for the Connoisseur

To North India With Love
Edited & with contributions by Nabanita Dutt
Photography by Nana Chen

To Asia With Love series created by Kim Fay
Cover and book design by Janet McKelpin/Dayspring Technologies, Inc.
Copy-editing by Elizabeth Mathews
Book production by Paul Tomanpos, Jr.

Please be advised that restaurants, shops, businesses, and other establishments in this book have been written about over a period of time. The editor and publisher have made every effort to ensure the accuracy of the information included in this book at the time of publication, but prices and conditions may have changed, and the editor, publisher, and authors cannot assume and hereby disclaim liability for loss, damage, or inconvenience caused by errors, omissions, or changes in regard to information included in this book.

For information regarding permissions, write to:
ThingsAsian Press
3230 Scott Street
San Francisco, California 94123 USA
www.thingsasian.com
Printed in Singapore

ISBN-13: 978-1-934159-07-1
ISBN-10: 1-934159-07-7

Table of Contents

Introduction

Imagine that on the eve of your upcoming trip to North India, you are invited to a party. At this party are dozens of guests, all of whom live in or have traveled extensively through the country. Among this eclectic and well-versed group of connoisseurs are contributors to acclaimed travel guides, popular newspaper writers, veteran gourmets, and pioneering adventurers. As the evening passes, they tell you tales from their lives in these exotic places. They whisper the names of their favorite shops and restaurants; they divulge the secret hideaways where they sneak off for an afternoon or a weekend to unwind. Some make you laugh out loud, and others seduce you with their poetry. Some are intent on educating, while others just want to entertain. Their recommendations are as unique as their personalities, but they are united in one thing ... their love of North India. If you can envision being welcomed at such a party, then you can envision the experience that *To North India With Love* aspires to give you.

Kim Fay
Series Editor, To Asia With Love

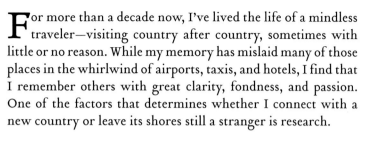

For more than a decade now, I've lived the life of a mindless traveler—visiting country after country, sometimes with little or no reason. While my memory has mislaid many of those places in the whirlwind of airports, taxis, and hotels, I find that I remember others with great clarity, fondness, and passion. One of the factors that determines whether I connect with a new country or leave its shores still a stranger is research.

By research I do not mean reading guidebooks and drawing up busy itineraries full of popular tourist sights. That's a bit like going to the Louvre and leaving after having seen only the *Mona Lisa*—an awful waste of a trip. To get your finger on the pulse of a country and to know its rhythm, you have to do spontaneous things like eat at seedy restaurants with no English-language menus, explore forgotten old neighborhoods that tourists never get to see, rummage in poky little shops for great bargains, and deal with rapscallion taxi drivers with the authority of a resident.

For seemingly insignificant little experiences like these, I depend on a combination of serendipity and the recommendations of other travelers who have gone that way. With their enthusiastic suggestions—my version of research—they infuse life and energy into a new country until it ceases to be a mere squiggle on the map but rather a warm, three-dimensional entity I can almost touch and feel even before I arrive. I look out for the pitfalls they warn of and borrow freely from their adventures. The successes of their journeys become a starting point from which I begin my own.

While editing *To North India With Love*, I envisioned my readers to be travelers just like me—people inspired by a little mystery, an out-of-the-way tip, a morsel of insider information—and tried to put together a collection exclusively for them. I assumed that their queries about India and their interest in all things Indian would have no boundaries. And I hoped that this book would help to spark a lifelong obsession with the country in at least some of them.

The recommendations in this book will prove particularly useful on your India visit because the country does not sell itself very well. Unlike Thailand, Singapore, and other Asian hotspots, the Subcontinent has not grabbed a significant share of the tourism market by packaging itself as the ultimate tourist destination. It's an old country that goes back five thousand years, and like its elephants, it is too large and unwieldy to turn this way and that to easily show off its best angles to the world. No wonder then that the Taj Mahal continues to be such a stereotype of tourism in India.

If you consider the diversity of experiences our contributors have written about, the travel possibilities here are enough to boggle any visitor's mind: mountain adventures in the Himalayas; dreamlike spectacles of a barren, lunar landscape in Ladakh; desert escapades and royal tours in Rajasthan; spiritual tranquility and Buddhist routes to enlightenment in Dharamshala; and ayurvedic and yogic practices in Rishikesh. As well, you will find temple pornography, camels, peacocks, tiger reserves, Kashmiri banquets, tandoori chicken, silk carpets, hand-blocked textiles ... And we're just in the northern part of the country.

To North India With Love introduces you to a group of writers who have spent a significant amount of time in this country. With the ease of locals—along with those writers who *are* locals— they have eaten rice with their hands, smoked local tobacco stuffed in tubes of dried leaves, and ridden in autorickshaws with half their body hanging off the seat. Their time in North India has included stomach bugs and nightmarish bus rides, interspersed with life-changing encounters and unexpected spiritual awakenings. In the end, they all fell in love with the mad, capricious, overpopulated entity that is India.

Read about their travels and share their excitement. Use the nuggets of precious information they offer to prepare for the holiday of a lifetime—a journey launched by their enthusiasm and culminating in an experience that is uniquely Indian ... and uniquely yours.

Nabanita Dutt
Editor, *To North India With Love*

How This Book Works

A good traveler has no fixed plans, and is not intent on arriving.
~Lao Tzu

To North India With Love is a unique guidebook with chapters organized by theme as opposed to destination. This is because it focuses foremost on the sharing of personal experiences, allowing each place to serve as the colorful canvas on which our writers overlay vivid, individual impressions. Within each themed chapter you will find the recommendations grouped by states and then cities or areas within each state. Chapters begin where most travelers start their journeys, in New Delhi. From here, the essays travel alphabetically throughout the states of North India. For attractions or experiences by destination, a complete index of cities can be found at the end of this book.

Each recommendation consists of two parts: a personal essay and a fact file. Together, they are intended to inspire and inform. The essay tells a story while the fact file gives addresses and other serviceable information. Because each contribution can stand alone, the book does not need to be read in order. As with an old-fashioned miscellany, you may open to any page and start reading. Thus every encounter with the book is turned into its own distinctive armchair journey.

Additional information and updates can be found online at www. TOASIAWITHLOVE.COM/NORTHINDIA. Keep in mind that *To North*

India With Love is selective and does not include all of the practical information you will need for daily travel. Instead, reading it is like having a conversation with a friend who just returned from a trip. You should supplement that friend's stories with a comprehensive guidebook, such as Lonely Planet or Frommer's.

Confucius said, "A journey of a thousand miles begins with a single step." We hope that this guide helps you put your best foot forward.

KEY TERMS AND IMPORTANT INFORMATION

DELHI: The official name of India's capital city is New Delhi, but it is often just called Delhi, although New Delhi is preferred for correspondence and official documents. Both are used throughout this book to refer to the same place. You will also find mention of Old Delhi, which is a neighborhood within New Delhi.

DIRECTIONS: In most fact files, you will find basic "getting there" information. If that information is not included, it is because the city is large and easy to reach. Again, please note that we recommend using a standard guidebook—containing details about transportation, hotels, etc.—for your travels.

METRIC SYSTEM: Although we are an American publisher, we have used the metric system for all measurements. For easy conversion, go to WWW.METRIC-CONVERSIONS.ORG.

PHONE NUMBERS: Phone numbers change rapidly in India, with many establishments using personal cell phones. Because of this, we have not included phone numbers in our fact files.

STATES AND UNION TERRITORIES: India's landscape is divided into a combination of states and territories. All essays in this book are located in various states, with the exception of New Delhi, which is in the National Capital Territory of Delhi.

MOVEABLE FEASTS

A tasting menu of exotic flavors

If you're the sort of Indian food junkie who's in constant need of a garam masala fix, I have splendid news for you. You will eat something during your India trip that you have never eaten before: real Indian food! I kid you not, curry addicts. I'm afraid the "authentic" Indian restaurants in your neighborhood have been keeping secrets from you. Reading their predictable little menus, it's no wonder you have never guessed there's more to Indian cuisine than just samosas and tandoori chicken. A whole lot more.

Every Indian state, in fact, has a native cuisine of its own. Barring a few common ingredients, they don't resemble each other. The desert food of Rajasthan, for instance, is not even a distant cousin of the fresh fish delicacies from riverine Bengal. The aromatic meat grills from the royal kitchens of Hyderabad are perfect strangers to Kerala's simple coconut-based dishes.

The list of delicious culinary contrasts and counterpoints goes on and on ... until it finally reaches New Delhi. It is here that all the regional cuisines meet and quietly coexist, waiting to be discovered by foodies and travelers like yourself. New Delhi, without doubt, is the food hub of India. It's a shameful waste of an opportunity not to taste the diversity of Indian food while you're in the city. Because of this, most of the essays in this chapter focus on some of the great meal experiences to be had in New Delhi. From *biryani* to Kobe steak to a uniquely Indian Chinese dish, these essays succeed in covering a lot of ground in the capital.

Naomi Naam has us salivating with his account of *kakori*, a melt-in-the-mouth kebab whose secret recipe is known to only one family of chefs in India. Avirook Sen gives us a first taste of Bengali food, a homemade cuisine that is rarely to be found in restaurants. Amiya Dasgupta shares his rediscovery of *momos*—steamed dumplings of Nepalese origin that he loved and thought he had lost at the age of nine. And Dipanwita Deb

introduces us to Chicken Manchurian, India's most popular Chinese dish—unknown in China! There are also revelatory essays as well, such as Anupam Tripathi's unofficial exposé on Indian "lamb" and "beef" and David Dorkin's candid evaluation of Indian spirits.

The New Delhi recommendations are followed by a few gems in the rest of North India and a sampler of the best restaurants and don't-you-dare-miss-this local specialties that our writers have discovered on the tourist trail. All in all, I think this chapter does a fine job of introducing India's mixed bag of cuisines to travelers who may be caught off guard by its unexpected variety. So prepare your appetite for the medley of food experiences ahead. Savor the anticipation of new flavors, and plan to eat your way through North India like the unapologetic, epicurean pleasure seeker you are. For remember, once you're back home from your trip, it's hello again to samosas and tandoori chicken at your neighborhood Indian restaurants. While they may be good, they won't seem so "authentic" anymore.

NEW DELHI

Naomi Naam encounters Delhi's king of all kebabs

For weeks before I landed in Delhi, I had to put up with a bunch of foodie friends in London, who believed my impending India trip would be wasted without a proper education about the pros and cons of Indian food. Did I, for example, know that every Indian state had a different cuisine? Was I sufficiently knowledgeable about the many facets of Indian food to fully appreciate its diversity? Perhaps they should make it "easy peasy" for me by drawing up a list of good restaurants to eat at in Delhi.

Now this was ridiculous! Wasn't I a Brit as much as these guys? Knowing a thing or two about Indian food is in our genes. Even if my early experiences were predicated on entirely inauthentic vindaloos and Madras curries, I pride myself on being able to recognize the real thing.

So, I made up my mind. A "real thing" was exactly what I was going to track down in Delhi. Something traditional and truly authentic that none of these guys had even heard of. I would return from India only after having made this amazing culinary discovery. And I would be the toast of curry-loving London.

I arrived in Delhi armed with a long list of foodie contacts. On my first day in the city, I asked one of them if he could think of some dish that would have my friends back home regarding me with a new respect. My acquaintance had many suggestions. Cutlets made from animal brains. Whole lamb's testicle cooked in a creamy gravy. He also knew a restaurant that did amazing things with liver. This was interesting to me, but frankly, it was too obvious. There is nothing more awful than the Offal Bore—the sort of chap who brags about eating parts of the animal that most people throw away. I wanted a dish that was relatively common in India, but was virtually unknown in England.

Finally, my acquaintance came up with something. What about a *kakori* kebab?

I'd never heard of it.

"You'll see," he said mysteriously, and he bundled me into his car.

We drove for fifteen minutes through residential Delhi before arriving at an ordinary-looking restaurant where a large man was contemplating a charcoal grill. This man, said my new friend, would cook me an amazing dish that was truly worth bragging about.

The restaurant didn't have much by way of décor or ambience to recommend it. A few tables had been arranged around an open kitchen, and diners could watch their meats and breads being cooked in a huge clay oven called a tandoor. We grabbed a table by the window and ordered Thums Up, a popular local cola that probably did better business in India than Coke and Pepsi.

The *kakori* kebab arrived in due course, garnished with sliced onions and served with an herby green chutney. I confessed to a certain feeling of disappointment. "But this is just a *sheekh* kebab!" I complained.

"Try it," commanded my host.

I did.

He was right. Was he ever right!

It's difficult to explain the taste of a *kakori* kebab to someone who has never tried one. It is made of mincemeat and has the tubular shape of the *sheekh*. But the texture is completely different. When I took my first bite of *kakori*, the kebab melted on my tongue, and the flavor coated my whole mouth. There was none of that strong spiciness that people often associate with Indian cooking. I sensed delicate herbs lurking within the meat. My mouth was in thrall.

"Why have I never heard of this?" I asked, accusingly.

My host offered an interesting explanation. A *kakori*, he told me, is extremely difficult to make. It's a dish that is pretty much "owned" by the Qureshis, a family of celebrated chefs in India. A *kakori* chef is usually a member of the Qureshi family. Or at the very least, trained by one of them.

To make a *kakori*, the chef minces meat and fat, taken from the kidney region of the goat. The ratio of meat to fat is a secret that remains within the Qureshi family. After adding

spices, the chef sets aside the *kakori* mixture for a few hours to tenderize the meat. Then, the mixture is pressed into a tube shape, threaded onto a skewer, and grilled over an open fire. The trick lies in getting the tubes firm enough to stay on the skewer. Lesser chefs get the ratio of mince to fat wrong. So when the fat starts to melt, their *kakori* simply breaks and falls off.

I ate four *kakori* kebabs that night. Two, the following night. Three, the night after that. Though I was told that a chef from the Qureshi family worked for the expensive Dum Pukht restaurant at the ITC Maurya hotel, I was quite satisfied with my unpretentious little hole-in-the-wall and its *kakoris*.

I kept an eye on the contemplative man working the grill, and when I finally got to explain the *kakori*-making process to my mesmerized audience of foodie friends in London, I mimicked his arm movements. A brief silence fell over the crowd as I finished describing the incredible sensation of biting into the silky-soft tubes he gently coaxed off the skewer.

"What was that name again?" asked one of my friends, his voice strained by an intense burst of lusty, gastronomic envy.

"*Kakori*," I said, and then added, smugly, "To make it easy peasy for yourselves, just call it the King of Kebabs."

New Delhi's best kakori

The *kakori* is a specialized dish, and you will not find it on the menu of most kebab restaurants in New Delhi. Aside from the city's many hole-in-the-wall venues, two of the best places to try it are Bukhara and Dum Pukht in the ITC Maurya hotel.

Diplomatic Enclave
Sadar Patel Marg
New Delhi

www.starwoodhotels.com

Andrew Soleimany traces the biryani's royal heritage in Delhi

As a child visiting the Middle East for the first time, I recall drooling over the "fragrant mountains of *biryani*" touted on an Arab airline's poster for its opulent first-class cuisine. Sadly, when I finally tasted it in Arab cafeterias, the dish called *biryani* turned out to resemble an oily pilaf, spotted with chunks of heavily spiced, yet still gamy goat or camel meat. My dejected young taste buds gave up on *biryani*.

Later in life, as my travels took me farther eastward, I rediscovered *biryani*: that is, the true, regal Indian incarnation. My first encounter with the Subcontinent's most famous rice dish came late one night in Delhi, after I had been partying with a bunch of Indian friends. Many beers down and somewhat the worse for wear,

we decided that we were in serious need of solid nourishment.

We had, or so I was told, two options at that hour. We could go to one of those all-night coffee shops at an international hotel and eat a bland club sandwich. Or, if we were willing to drive out a little bit farther, we could end up with *biryani*. I've had more club sandwiches in my travels than I care to remember, so with great presence of mind, I gave *biryani* a second chance to court my palate.

The restaurant we went to was a humble establishment with a few wooden tables and rickety cane chairs squeezed into a small room. There was no reason to give us a menu. Everybody came here for one thing and one thing only: the *biryani*. Once the waiter had taken our orders of soft drinks, he went away to tell the kitchen to send us enough *biryani* for four people.

When he returned, he held a large metal urn heaped with yellow rice, chunks of meat still on the bone, and shards of golden fried onions scattered on top. As accompaniments, we had raw sliced onions, wedges of lemon, and a thick yogurt chutney that I learned was called a *burhani raita*. The chutney was used like a sorbet—it cut through the richness of the *biryani* and cleared the palate between bites, so that we could eat more.

Now, I've been around. I've eaten risottos with saffron in the center of Milan, can see the point of Japanese glutinous rice, and am familiar with the aromatic pilafs of the Near East. But nothing was quite like this *biryani*. With the first mouthful, I was hooked on the taste of the slightly spiced buttery rice and impossibly tender meat. It was, if I am allowed to exaggerate a little, the essence of Indian food and all the flavors I associate with the country distilled into a single dish.

Like many Westerners, I had first thought that the *biryani* was a clever variation of the pilaf and perhaps had been brought to India by Muslim invaders in the Middle Ages. In fact, as I later read, *biryani* is a peculiarly Indian invention, mixing the principles of the pilaf with the method of *khichri*, an Indian rice dish that is at least two thousand years old. Scholars regard the *biryani* as an example of India's ability to take foreign influences and make them her own. In a country that prides itself on Hindu-Muslim unity, the *biryani* is a symbol of religious integration: the Muslim pilaf marrying the Hindu *khichri*.

My appreciation for *biryani* grew, and in my quest for the ultimate *biryani*, I ended up at Dum Pukht at the Sheraton's ITC Maurya hotel, one of Delhi's more expensive restaurants, where I was served a dish called *dum-biryani*. By then, I thought I knew my *biryani* well enough, and so was greatly surprised to see the waiter bring an individual portion to my table in a ceramic bowl with its lid sealed with a layer of dough. I cut through the flour-based covering, and my nostrils were assailed by the aroma of basmati rice, saffron, cloves, fried onion, and what smelled to me like cinnamon.

I called my waiter over. Could he please explain the dish to me? It was quite simple, he said. Then he got technical. The *dum biryani* I was eating was a product of the tradition of Dum cooking that began in the Mughal courts several centuries ago. The principle was that all food would be tightly sealed in cooking vessels (hence the seal of dough) so that no steam escaped. It was then slow-cooked for hours with the cooking heat coming not so much from the fire as from the steam that was trapped inside the vessel.

"Try it, sir, you will taste the difference," he urged. He couldn't have been more right. It was nothing like the other *biryanis* I had eaten at more modest establishments. For a start, the rice was very nearly white. It was only when I put it in my mouth that I realized the color was misleading. Each grain was coated with far more flavor than the regular yellow *biryani* I had consumed on the streets of Delhi. How did your chef manage that? I asked the waiter. He smiled mysteriously and said, "All Dum cooking, sir, simple Dum cooking." (Ask a Dum question, get a Dum answer.)

My adventures with *biryani* suggest that it is that rare phenomenon, a royal dish that is also enjoyed by common people. At cheaper restaurants *biryani* is made in volume, and it is actually possible to buy it by weight. At more expensive places, the meat content is increased and rice quantity lowered to indicate that a lot of money was spent on the making of the dish. I found every variation to be delicious in its own way.

When it was finally time for me to say goodbye to India and return home to America, a couple of Indian friends—knowing about my obsession with the *biryani*—presented me with ready-to-eat packages of the dish. The brand name, I remember, was Kitchens of India, and while they were not nearly as good as the freshly made thing, I fondly recalled all my *biryani* experiences every time I heated one up in the microwave.

Biryani on the cheap

Some of the best *biryani* to be had in Delhi is at Zahid Qureshi's. Qureshi descends from a family of butchers, and he knows the best cut of meat for *biryani*. He uses only marrow bones, which enrich the rice and produce a well-balanced *biryani* with no trace of excess oil or spicing. Until recently, Qureshi was selling his *biryani* only by the *haandi* (big cooking pans in which the *biryani* is sealed and cooked). Each *haandi* costs about $20 and contains approximately ten large portions. Now, he is operating on a larger scale and has opened a restaurant in Sadar Bazar called Zahid Food Plaza, where his *biryani* can be bought by the plate. Sadar Bazar is located in Old Delhi. Local autorickshaw drivers are your best roadmap to this rabbit warren of an area and can help you find this place.

Dum Pukht

See fact file for previous essay.

Kitchens of India

Kitchens of India is part of the same company that owns Dum Pukht restaurant. On its website you will find lists of stores where you can buy Kitchens of India dishes, as well as descriptions of regional cuisines, explanations of Indian cooking utensils, a glossary of Indian food terms, and many more Indian culinary tidbits.

www.kitchensofindia.com

Dave Prager speaks frankly about tandoori bakra in Delhi

The name of one Delhi's oldest restaurants reverberates across the local expat circuit, with every veteran asking every newcomer the same question: "You haven't been to Karim's yet?"

Visiting this Old Delhi institution is a rite of passage. And finding it without having to ask directions qualifies you for legitimate bragging rights, because its unmarked alley entrance ensures that you can never stumble upon Karim's—you have to be seeking it out. You have to be in the know. Old Delhi's twisting lanes hold a million secrets we foreigners will never unearth, but to visit Karim's is to discover at least one of them. This defines the restaurant's allure.

This, and the kebabs.

Ducking our heads to walk through the narrow entrance on our first visit, my wife, Jenny, and I followed the alley just south of Jama Masjid mosque as it opened into a bustling plaza encircled by Karim's multiple dining rooms. Each dining room was overseen by a uniformed headwaiter, and each headwaiter beckoned urgently for us to enter as if they were all in competition with each other.

But we couldn't choose one and sit down just yet—we were still coping with the sensory overload. Kebab guys wrapped ground meat around skewers that oozed grease into the coals and spewed smoke across the plaza; bread makers sat cross-legged in an alcove, slapping dough into balls and pulling puffy white naan out of the ovens; busboys balanced more dirty dishes on one arm than we thought a human bicep could manage; motorcycles honked and wove through what was not just the middle of the restaurant but also an active thoroughfare. We gaped until one of the headwaiters finally commanded our attention, pulling our sleeves and leading us to the particular dining room over which he stood sentry.

Some people had told us that Karim's is the oldest restaurant in Delhi. Others told us that Karim himself invented Mughal-style food. We never really knew, and it never really mattered, because the mystique of Karim's is as satisfying as the food.

Every time we went to Karim's, our appreciation grew. That first visit was one of simple culinary discovery— that chicken curry could be so succulent, that mutton kebabs could be so juicy. During our next visit, we learned that Karim's vegetarian curry, with cottage cheese cubes, dates, and a cashew-based gravy, is the stuff of dreams. On one of our last visits, we found out that the quarter inch of oil puddled atop every bowl of curry isn't supposed to be eaten, but is there to show that the food is so well cooked, the fat has liquefied. Diners should drain it into a separate dish.

Then there was the time we got to the truth about the most tantalizing item on offer, the name of which glistens on the laminated menu cards with the greasy prints of a thousand other patrons who have rested their fingers on it in wonder: "The tandoori *bakra*, only 4,500 rupees ($92). Please order twenty-four hours in advance."

On a menu where the average dish costs one-fortieth of that price and arrives at the table in five minutes, the description had us salivating. With roasted mutton chops this good, what must Karim's tandoori *bakra* be like? Never mind that I had to ask myself: what the hell's a *bakra*?

On one fine November evening, while Jenny stayed home to avoid what she rightly anticipated to be a vegetarian's worst nightmare, I descended on Karim's with thirty-five other people, our appetites whetted and our order placed twenty-four hours ahead of time. We sat, we chatted, we waited, we grew ravenous, we cast increasingly anxious glances toward the kitchen, we listened to our growling stomachs echo off the greasy ceiling, and finally we cheered at the sight of the legendary tandoori *bakra*: a whole goat, stuffed with rice, eggs, and almonds, slow cooked, and presented on a silver platter.

My heart leapt with the appearance of the men bearing the mutton, followed by other men bearing comically tiny knives for us to carve with. Hunger and excitement overcame our table manners: greedy hands sawed and pulled and jerked flesh off the bones and onto our plates. We became the piranhas I had seen in a nature documentary: within moments, we reduced the poor animal to his very bones.

The juicy piece of midsection that landed on my plate looked like heaven. But in my mouth, it was tandoori-flavored chewing gum. I worked at it for minutes. The rice, mixed with boiled eggs and spices, was spectacular. The bread melted on my tongue. The side dishes—various curries and kebabs—were as good as ever. But the *bakra* itself, it turned out, should have remained a mystery.

This is the curse facing inquisitive tourists: Some things are better imagined than experienced. Sometimes, it is more rewarding to peer through latticed windows of ancient mansions, wonder about the fascinating lives being led beyond the cloudy glass, and then just walk away. Because the truth that lies inside—as we discovered somewhere in South India, waved into a Chettinad-style mansion by its smiling owner—is often no more intriguing than the reality of a couple of bored kids watching cartoons on television.

The same, alas, goes for Karim's. While the food at Karim's is a treasure and the atmosphere is an experience not to be missed, its deepest secret would be so much more satisfying if only I had let it stay that way.

Karim's

Karim's is located on Gali Kababian opposite Jama Masjid mosque near the Dariyaganj Market. But this direction is really of no help at all when you're trying to find your way through Old Delhi. This is a crazy neighborhood with alleys and lanes, traffic jams, donkeys, and a million people. Old Delhi is amazing to photograph but HELL to negotiate. Rather than try to locate this place on your own, ask your taxi or autorickshaw driver. They all know where Karim's is.

Helene Shapiro sidesteps dangerous spices with the dosas of Delhi

An Indian dinner invariably gives me heartburn at two in the morning. It's the spices. My system can't deal with them. For this reason, I abstain from Indian food even though I love the taste.

But I was on summer holiday in India, and delicious-looking local food like I had never seen in New York was everywhere. Not sampling any of it was breaking my heart and taking some joy out of the traveling. Resolutely, I soldiered on with my no-Indian-food rule in Agra and Varanasi. The maitre d' at the Taj Lake Palace hotel in Udaipur offered to have a spice-free Indian meal especially cooked for me, but I thanked him and chose the Italian buffet instead. And like the plague I avoided Delhi's Parathe Wali Gali (Street of Fried Bread) with its enticing, spice-tinged aromas, and took the roundabout route to my favorite silver jewelry shop in the area.

This went on until I set out one evening to have dinner with Sarita, my journalist friend in the capital. We were going to Moets restaurant complex to eat sizzlers—dishes that are served sizzling hot in an iron pan on a wooden tray. I sat in Sarita's car, sandwiched between a pile of news magazines and a gym bag, crabbing all the way about my need to make non-Indian food choices. Sarita listened intently to my diatribe and then gave me an endearing little head waggle. She had a solution. We wouldn't go to Moets, but to a South Indian restaurant called Sagar Ratna.

"Indian spices don't agree with me," I protested.

"It's okay; you'll be okay. Trust me."

It wasn't, I couldn't be sure that I would, and I honestly didn't trust her on this matter.

But Sarita was offering me a cop-out. "If you're unsure about the food, I promise we'll go to Moets. It's next door."

That sounded fair. Throwing caution to the winds, I decided to live dangerously. For just one night.

We reached Sagar Ratna at around ten, and the place was still busy with late-night diners. A queue had formed outside the door, and a sweating gentleman, inappropriately dressed for the Delhi summer in a heavy suit and bowtie, was trying to control the crowd. "This place looks popular," I said, lining up in the queue. "How long do we have to wait?"

"The restaurant is like a cafeteria," Sarita said. "People come, eat, and quickly leave. This is the best South Indian food in the city. If they want ambience, they go next door to take their time at Moets."

We were ushered inside in exactly five minutes. Sarita was right. The place indeed looked like a busy cafeteria. But it was clean and blessedly cool with the strong aroma of sweet aniseed—the Indian version of an after-dinner mint—wafting in the air. A waiter materialized from nowhere and whisked us off to our table. He gave us menus, set down a bunch of cutlery, and stood with his pen poised to take our order.

The service wasn't rude; it was just swift and matter-of-fact. Given the huge turnover, the restaurant had to operate with the efficiency of a factory assembly line. And the guests and staff seemed to work together to keep things moving smoothly. No guest, for example, wasted much time browsing the choice of dishes. I guessed people came here already knowing what they wanted and passing around the menu was just a formality.

Sarita quickly placed our order, and the waiter went away. Within a couple of minutes, he was back, carrying something humongous and unidentifiable high above his head. When he laid it down on our table, I could see it was a wafer-thin sheet of fried, crispy dough, rolled into a tube. The tube was three feet long at least, sticking out from the plate quite a ways. I peered into the tube. It was empty inside.

"It's a *dosa*," Sarita said. "A savory pancake made out of a rice-and-pulse batter. I didn't order the one with curried potato stuffing. There's no spice in it. Try it."

I broke a piece off one end and put it in my mouth. I was blown away. It was heavenly, the way the *dosa* crumbled in my mouth, leaving a delicious aftertaste of clarified Indian butter. Two small bowls accompanied the *dosa*: a coconut chutney and a South Indian dal. Sarita encouraged me to dip pieces of my *dosa* into both. According to her, the spice in this particular dal actually helped with digestion. She had also ordered some *rasam* for me, a drink that resembled the dal in flavor.

The waiter came back again, this time with three fluffy white rice cakes. These were *idlis*, made by steaming rice-and-lentil batter. Silky soft, with just a hint of sourness in the taste, they were as good as the *dosa*. I sat dipping and eating, and thinking how

incredible this meal had turned out to be. Picking up the menu, I discovered there were many versions of *dosas* and *idlis*, made with cheese, tomato, onions, etc. Plus there were other fermented batter dishes, like the doughnut-shaped *vadas* and the thick, flat, pan-fried cakes called *uttapam*.

Despite all that I ate and all I had discovered, we were done with dinner and out of Sagar Ratna in fifteen minutes, chewing sweet aniseed as we walked back to the car. We fixed up to meet the following evening at Moets, and Sarita dropped me off at my hotel.

The night passed without interruption. The spices in the South Indian dal and *rasam* slept peacefully in my stomach, and I woke up feeling refreshed and excited about the fact that there would be a slight change in our evening plans. We wouldn't go to Moets, but next door to Sagar Ratna. Again. After all, I had to find out what the *vadas* and the *uttapams* were all about.

Sagar Ratna

18, Defence Colony Market, A Block
New Delhi

www.sagarratna.in

Moets

This multirestaurant venue includes a popular bar. Well-heeled residents of south Delhi hang out here, and it's fairly crowded most evenings.

50, Defence Colony Market, A Block
New Delhi

www.moets.com

Parathe Wali Gali

The Street of Fried Bread is a historical food destination in Delhi's Chandni Chowk area. Parathe Wali Gali gets its name from the *paratha*-sellers here, who specialize in more than twenty-five different kinds of fried bread.

Amiya Dasgupta reunites with his Nepalese roots in Delhi

My first *momo* experience came out of my mother's kitchen when I was about nine.

"You're probably not going to like this," she said, handing me a plate heaped with crescent-shaped pouches of dough.

The dough looked wet and raw, like she had forgotten to bake or fry it. Still, I was willing to give it a try. It was a Nepalese delicacy after all, and for me, Indian born and raised in Nepal, Nepal was the coolest place in the whole world. We lived in Kathmandu at the time, but I was about to be sent off to boarding school in India, and I was already feeling homesick for my birth country.

I blew on a hot crescent and gingerly took a bite. The doughy skin broke easily, releasing a warm, soupy juice. Bits of ground-meat stuffing spilled out, and I crammed the whole thing into my mouth to avoid making a mess.

Mmmm ... delicious! The clean taste of fresh garlic lightly flavored the meat. Crunchy bits of onion and cilantro gave it texture. The aftertaste lingered in my mouth with a richness that made me want to eat more.

I reached out for another *momo*. Mom watched me with suspicion. "You don't really like it," she said. "You're just pretending, to please me."

I wasn't. True, my heart was breaking right then at the thought of parting from her, and I was being particularly clingy. But this strange *momo* thing she had cooked was really very good.

"The raw dough is kind of weird, but in a *nice* sort of way," I said, trying to justify my liking for this unfamiliar food. "Can we have some more before I leave?"

"It isn't raw. It's steamed," my mother said. She cooked another batch the night before my departure, but this time she fried them. I loved the fried version, but I craved another taste of what I still thought of as the raw version.

Thereafter, I moved to boarding school, where I did not encounter a single *momo*. In fact, I forgot all about this Nepalese delicacy until I moved to New Delhi many years later. One evening, I was walking through my neighborhood Defence Colony Market in south Delhi, when I saw a big banner advertising the opening of a new restaurant. The sign said

"Humro Momo," which means "our *momo*" in the Nepalese language.

It couldn't be!

But it was, and right next to the Arabian Nights restaurant where I often bought *shwarma* rolls.

Now, if you have ever rediscovered a food you once loved and lost, you'll perfectly understand the elation and joy that was racing through my heart at that time. I almost ran the last hundred yards, stumbling to a halt in front of Humro Momo.

A Nepalese boy was tending to a huge metal steamer in the front. The place, I saw, was not actually a restaurant but a takeaway food joint that did Chinese as well as *momos*. Breathlessly, I asked for a menu. The boy handed me a card and a takeout leaflet. The *momo* section was right at the top, listing chicken, pork, mutton, vegetable, and *paneer* (an Indian variation on cottage cheese) *momos*. Steamed and fried. For a little less than $1 for eight pieces.

I bought a portion of each and ran straight home to my kitchen. The *momos* were hot, and it was several minutes before I could tear open the paper bags they were packed in. The vegetarian *momos* were shaped like balls, while the ones with meat resembled my mother's half-moon crescents.

In my haste, I mixed up the meat *momos* on my plate and couldn't tell the mutton from the pork. But that was okay. I wasn't eating. I was gorging on the *momos*, and knowing which kind of meat I was chewing on seemed like an unimportant detail. The *momos* more than lived up to my memory of them.

They were juicy and packed with flavor. With just a touch of garlic, onion, and cilantro and no other spicing.

Humro Momo and my reunion with the nearly forgotten *momo* were definitely the food highlight of my first year of living in Delhi. As I became more familiar with India's capital city, I came to realize that *momos* were not as uncommon here as in the rest of India. My *momo* obsession took me to other Nepalese-run takeout joints in the neighborhood markets of south Delhi, and I even discovered some posh and pricey restaurants doing *momos* as well.

The *momo* experience in high-end eateries was frankly quite disappointing. In the hands of seasoned chefs, the dish somehow got complicated and began to look like fancy dim sum with thin dough skins. Thinning out the dough, in my opinion, is a vain attempt at sophistication. *Momos* are a simple dish made by simple Himalayan people. They are supposed to be thick, warm, and rustic. Either you go to the House of Ming restaurant on Mansingh Road for some of the best dim sum available in Delhi, or you head for the nearest Nepalese takeout place and enjoy the *momo* for what it is.

Momos in New Delhi

Following are just a few of our favorite *momo* restaurants in the city.

Humro Momo

Defence Colony Market, Block A
New Delhi

Momo Mia

Stall No. 6, Dilli Haat
Opposite INA Market
Aurobindo Marg
New Delhi

Momo's Point

Shop No. UB-27
Ground Floor, Jawahar Nagar
Kamla Nagar (near University of
Delhi)
New Delhi

Dim Sum in New Delhi

House of Ming

The Taj Mahal Hotel
1, Mansingh Road
New Delhi

www.tajhotels.com

Avirook Sen discovers his mother's Bengali cuisine in Delhi

When it comes to my native cuisine, I confess I'm the stereotypical Bengali mama's boy. Like millions of other men, born and raised in the East Indian state of Bengal, I too believe that nobody can cook Bengali food as well as my mother.

As our food has always been a homemade cuisine, it was easy to hang on to this conviction. No accomplished chef with a sophisticated restaurant kitchen at his disposal had ever challenged my mother's dexterity with the *khunti*, that iron spatula used to cook Bengali food. That is, until Anjan Chatterjee—a fellow Bengali—decided to steal our mothers' best recipes and put them on the menu of a Bengali restaurant in Delhi called Oh! Calcutta.

Steal is a word I use advisedly to convey the outrage most Delhi-based Bengalis felt when we first heard of Oh! Calcutta's opening in 2006. I mean, who in their right mind would ever go to a Bengali restaurant, when the finest food was being cooked by our mothers according to traditional family recipes passed on by generations?

Well, I did.

I went to Oh! Calcutta to vindicate my position that the restaurant would fail, fail, fail. I believed Anjan Chatterjee—a restaurateur with enough chutzpah to open a Chinese restaurant in China—had hopelessly miscalculated with this one. I wanted to be able to tell my friends how the food was crap and how I had predicted right at the start that the restaurant would bomb.

Well, I was wrong.

I loved Oh! Calcutta. It proved to be a culinary ode to our home cuisine. Anjan Chatterjee was presenting Bengali food as authentically as possible, without trying to reinvent anything. And Delhi residents were tucking enthusiastically into *macher jhol* (fish curry) and *mochar ghonto* (spiced banana flowers), dishes many of them had heard of but few had had the opportunity to taste.

My first experience of eating at Oh! Calcutta was a pleasurable combination of elegant surroundings, piped instrumental Bengali music, a friendly staff, and fabulously cooked food. The menu is pretty easy to negotiate because the items are broadly divided into everyday food and banquet food. There is also a selection of dishes that pleased the British palate and became popular with the sahibs (white men) who made Bengal their base during the era of British rule.

Fish is the undisputed royalty of Bengali cuisine, and emperor among them is *hilsa*. If you're a fish lover, you really must try this rich and flavorful seafood. Its silky meat falls right off the bones and literally melts in the mouth. *Shorshey*, a mustard marinade, is another Bengali specialty, which best showcases itself in Oh! Calcutta's prawn selections. Yet another favorite is a coconut-based dish we Bengalis make with prawns called *malai* curry. Coconut milk is not a common ingredient in Bengali cuisine, and one theory goes that the dish was brought back by laborers who had been sent to Malaysia to work on the rubber plantations. The *malai* in *malai* curry is merely a corruption of the word *Malay*.

I also recommend the mutton curries at Oh! Calcutta. Believe me when I say that mutton is something one should *never* attempt to eat outside of India. If you have had mutton elsewhere and hated it, give it just one more try at this restaurant. You'll change your mind. Until you leave India, of course. After that, you'll begin to hate it all over again.

As for those non-meat eaters, the menu is full of vegetarian options. If you're not averse to a bit of deep-frying, you might want to try the veggie fritters covered in crispy chickpea batter. Puts the best tempuras you have ever eaten firmly in the shade.

Wrap up your meal with a selection of Bengali desserts. Given how recently Bengal's food heritage has been "discovered" by the rest of the country, it is interesting that the desserts from this state have long been a pan-Indian delicacy. It isn't at all unusual to see passengers at Kolkata airport lugging huge clay pots full of *mishti doi* (jaggery-sweetened yogurt) onto flights as carry-on luggage. Bengal's variety of cottage-cheese-based sweet treats is probably the best India has to offer.

After almost two years of eating regularly at this restaurant and recommending it all to my friends, I recently had the opportunity to interview Anjan Chatterjee. I heard the passion of a crusader in his voice as he described ambitious plans to popularize his native cuisine. Anjan touched his heart to show me the place where Oh! Calcutta was born. And yes, he proved his credentials as a true-blue Bengali mama's boy when he confessed that the menu was inspired by the best Bengali cook in the world—his mother.

Oh! Calcutta

Oh! Calcutta is easy for a traveler to miss. It is in the bustling Nehru Place business district, far from the tourist trail. More confusingly, it is at the back of the InterContinental New Delhi Nehru Place hotel, but is reached without entering the hotel.

International Trade Tower
E-Block, Ground Floor
Nehru Place
New Delhi

www.speciality.co.in/calcutta.php

Dipanwita Deb investigates India's favorite Chinese dish in Delhi

The Chinese cuisine I remember from my early childhood had the floury pastiness of Cantonese and Peking styles, but then, sometime at the beginning of the 1980s, Sichuan chefs landed on our shores, bringing the fiery flavors of their native Sichuan peppers with them. As far as spice-crazy Indians were concerned, there couldn't be a better cuisine to import. It was tangy, and it went well with rice. We simply adored Chinese food in its Sichuan incarnation. Our favorite dish was Chicken Manchurian.

Do you know about Chicken Manchurian? Balls of batter-fried chicken in a hot, peppery sauce?

It's okay if you don't.

Nobody in China does either!

It comes as a huge shock to Indians when they first learn that Chicken Manchurian isn't an authentic

Chinese dish at all. For decades now, one chef in India of Chinese origin has been fooling us with a food he made up in his restaurant and passed off as "Manchurian." Little did he know that his creation would take on a life of its own and become one of the most popular Chinese dishes in India. That Chinese restaurants all over the country would devote a whole section of their menus to his "Manchurian" technique—Chicken Manchurian, Vegetable Manchurian, Chow Mein Manchurian, and so on.

The man isn't sorry for this elaborate Manchurian trick he played on us, either. Nelson Wang's only regret is that he didn't call his dish Chicken Nelson. "At least then, I would have become immortal!" says this genial raconteur.

My search for Nelson Wang had taken me to China Garden, a swish restaurant and bar that he runs in Delhi's upmarket GK II neighborhood. At the time of my visit, the lower level was still under construction, but Nelson sat me down in the fully functional restaurant upstairs and proceeded to order half the menu for me.

I tucked into a delicious fish ball soup and dim sum, while Nelson took charge of the conversation, charming me with his self-deprecating humor and hilarious anecdotes from his early career as a limbo dancer. By the time the main courses started to arrive, Nelson was talking about his greatest contribution to the country's culinary traditions: Manchurian.

When I charged him with inauthenticity, he agreed happily. "Nobody in China had heard of my dish. In China, Manchurian means 'mad.' That's why I call it Chicken Manchurian."

"Huh?"

Proudly, he explained, "I made the dish up, so it was like a joke name, you see. In the 1970s, the Taj Mahal hotel in Mumbai decided to bring in chefs from Sichuan because Indians wanted spicy Chinese food." Here, Nelson paused to laugh. "At the time, I was working for a cheap restaurant located right behind the Taj. But I had 'ears' in the Taj kitchen, and hearing of this Sichuan idea, I wanted to try it myself. I told my cooks to make up a spicy dish and to say it is called Manchurian."

Bit by bit, the whole story came out. Nelson had been the manager of a restaurant called Frederick's. After the Taj Mahal hotel opened a genuine Sichuan restaurant, his patrons began to ask for similarly spicy food. Nelson, like most Chinese-Indian restaurateurs, had spent three generations in India. He had no clue where Sichuan was. He knew even less about its cuisine.

So he improvised. Knowing how Indians love fried food, he deep-fried the chicken. Then he got his cooks to take local spices like curry powder and heat up the sauce. "Really, the dish has so little to do with Chinese food that if Chairman Mao had tasted it, he would have shot me on the spot." Nelson collapsed in giggles.

Clearly, the man still thinks of his impulsive creation as something of a joke. When the dish proved to be an instant success, he says, nobody was more surprised than he. Within a year, Chicken Manchurian was on every Chinese restaurant menu in Mumbai. Within two years, it had become the centerpiece of Indian-Chinese cuisine. Now, pizzerias offer a Chicken Manchurian pizza and McDonald's has a Chicken Manchurian burger at its Indian outlets.

This is an interesting bit of food history to know when you order your first Chicken Manchurian in India. And order it you will, because Manchurian is as ubiquitous as tandoori. But make sure you try the real thing and book a table at the China Garden restaurant in Delhi—here you will have the dish prepared in the master's own kitchen. If Nelson is in a chatty mood, he will probably come to sit at your table. He loves an eager audience, and if you seem interested, he'll share many tips about Chinese cuisine. How to eat Peking Duck, for example, without the crepes and hoisin sauce. Not only will you have the chance to compliment the chef, you will get to know the father of India's Manchurian cuisine himself.

China Garden
M-73, M Block Market
Greater Kailash II
New Delhi

www.chinagardenindia.com

Nilanjan Mukherjee sneaks a bite of Kobe steak in Delhi

Deep in the heart of Delhi is a small slice of Tokyo. It's called The Metropolitan Hotel New Delhi. Although it tries to be as international as possible, it drops all pretense of being anything but Japanese at Sakura, its signature dining venue. Possibly, Sakura is the only authentic Japanese restaurant in all of North India.

The interior—with plain, wooden tables and chairs and a few screened-off private dining rooms—is not designed to attract an Indian clientele. If you have been to Tokyo, then Sakura's décor will remind you of all the anonymous *udon* and sushi bars you have eaten at in one of the city's small neighborhoods. Few Indians can understand the ordinariness of the surroundings, especially in light of the prices, which are also authentically Tokyo. Most days, as a result, you'll be hard put to find a single Indian eating there. The guests are Japanese, more Japanese, and the occasional Korean.

For many years, The Metropolitan Hotel was managed by a division of Japan Airlines, and Sakura used this connection to its advantage. By flying in fish from Tokyo's Tsujiki market four times a week, the restaurant quickly built a reputation for the freshness of its ingredients. When the master chef cut into the fatty belly of a tuna, diners knew that the fish was probably swimming peacefully off the coast of Japan just the day before yesterday.

Naturally, sushi and sashimi are the highlights of the menu. Just as naturally, Japanese high rollers order the *toro* sashimi because it is the most expensive item. But I have two other favorites at Sakura. The first is a flaky, buttery Japanese cod that melts in the mouth and which the restaurant offers to pair with a bottle of cold Chablis. The second is Sakura's little secret.

Because Delhi has funny laws pertaining to the serving of beef, Sakura does not advertise the fact that it is one of the few restaurants in India that serves the world's most expensive variety: *wagyu*. *Wagyu* is flown in from Kobe, Japan, every two days or so, and I'm told that rich Japanese expats living in Delhi trek to Sakura regularly—and openly—for their Kobe beef fix.

The ordering of the Kobe beef at Sakura is an event in itself, as I found out during my first dining experience there. Two waitresses in kimonos appeared at my table with a huge silver salver of raw Kobe, thinly sliced and set on a bed of onions, peppers, and shiitake mushrooms. The Japanese master chef then appeared and bowed deeply several times. He produced a blowtorch, with which he proceeded to sear the beef before my very eyes.

I was intrigued. I asked the chef to explain the process. But he merely bowed again in acknowledgment of my query, smiled grimly, and continued concentrating on my beef. At this stage, I realized that the only words of English he was comfortable with were *rare* and *medium rare.*

When the beef was ready, he put away his blowtorch, and the two waitresses arranged the salver in front of me. They offered three different sauces, which of course I refused because meat of this quality could require no accompaniments.

On my second visit to Sakura, the chef's demeanor cracked slightly. I was thrilled that he remembered me, but I later worked out that he probably served only four or five non-Japanese guests in an average week. It was no surprise that I had made an impression. The chef advised the manager in Japanese to tell me that even if my steak was rare, Kobe fat tasted best when cooked well done. So he would cook two different parts of my steak in two different ways, and I would be offered red wine for the lean meat and white wine for the fat.

When it comes to food, I usually rely on my own tastes and refuse to be led, preached at, or patronized. On this occasion, however, I wouldn't dream of leaving the fat on the side of my plate like I usually do. I would eat every well-done bit of it, and as the chef suggested, wash it down with a glass of white wine.

From my previous experience at Sakura, I knew this man wasn't just a great chef, but the absolute king of subtlety. You would never do something so crude as to "eat" his food. You "tasted" the amazing morsels of fish, meat, and vegetables he carefully laid on your plate. I would be a fool to taint this unique experience by trying to do things my way.

When I walked out of Sakura that second time, I left a little light in the head from all the different wines and far lighter in the wallet. I was sure my bill equaled the gross national product of a struggling Third World country. So, were my great Kobe experiences worth it? Let me put it this way: Those bite-size pieces of beef play a starring role in all my subsequent food fantasies. I suspect I will have to go back several times before I can even begin to work this Sakura-inspired Kobe madness out of my system.

Sakura

The Metropolitan Hotel New Delhi
Bangla Sahib Road
New Delhi

http://hotelmetdelhi.com

Debasish Bhaduri finds jolly old England in a Delhi food court

It's the utter corniness of Piccadelhi that gets you first.

A token red telephone booth confronts you as soon as you walk through the door. There is a double-decker bus. There are all the expected London underground symbols painted bright and large on the walls. Each section of the food court is named after a neighborhood in the British capital, and to round things out, the Drunken Duck is your typical English pub.

Once you get past the bad-taste décor, though, there's much to admire about this food court in the city's central Connaught Place district. The service is always excellent, and some of the food puts to shame many a deluxe establishment in the city. Piccadelhi serves Indian Chinese, which is fine if you like that sort of thing. There's also Italian in the Little Venice section, which is acceptable enough in a fast food sort of way. Surprisingly, the standout areas are those that serve Indian food.

Here I have eaten Delhi's best *keema paratha* (a flaky bread stuffed with ground meat). I have discovered a canteen dal that closely approximates the flavor of good dal at the best local canteens. The *chaat* (snacks) from Gujarat and Delhi are remarkably authentic, and there is regional Indian food of a caliber you rarely find at this price: the spicy, deep-fried Chicken 65 from the southern state of Andhra Pradesh and a juicy, spicy fried fish from India's west coast.

Strangely, there is not as much British food here as I had expected. When I asked one of the waiters why this was so, he pulled out his pen and drew for me a five-legged octopus on a piece of napkin. Got it. London's Piccadilly Circus, the famous junction where several of the city's major thoroughfares converge.

The waiter was impressed with my knowledge of the London road system. "Exactly, sir!" he said. "Piccadilly Circus is a great symbol of London's multicultural identity. In London there is Soho for Chinese food, Southall for Indian food, and so on. We are presenting a bit of everything to reflect the city's cultural mix."

I wanted to argue with him there. Indian food was clearly over-represented, and it was tipping Piccadelhi's balance. But I let it go. He was dressed like a London policeman, and I didn't want to risk being marched off to King's Bench or some other faux London prison set up somewhere at the back. Besides, I had a pretty good idea of what his counterargument would be.

"What is UK's most popular food item, sir?" he would ask.

"Chicken tikka masala," I would grudgingly admit.

"There you go, sir. The British favor Indian food over any other foreign cuisine. Some of the best Indian restaurants in the world are in London. That's just how it is, sir."

The waiter clicked his heels and did a fine approximation of the Buckingham Palace guard's glassy-eyed stare. We shared a laugh at the silliness of it, and I went to check out the dessert counters while he cleared my table. I chose a gelato and a truffle pastry and ate them with great relish before heading out into the bustling shopping district of Connaught Place. The sky had darkened while I was at lunch, and I wondered if I should go back into the food court and borrow an umbrella. If Piccadelhi was indeed a slice of London, surely there were some brollies set aside for a typically English rainy day.

Piccadelhi
H-Block, Inner Circle
Plaza Cinema Building
Connaught Place
New Delhi

Anupam Tripathi exposes goat in sheep's clothing in Delhi

An English friend phoned me at the end of his first week in India. We spent a few minutes exchanging polite pleasantries, and then he got to the point of his call. "Why do you Indians like your loins tender?" he asked.

Given that my friend had arrived after a fortnight in the fleshpots of Thailand, I imagined that there was some sexual subtext to his query. But no, he was talking about food. At every restaurant he went to, he explained, the menu contained something called "tenderloin." At a Chinese restaurant, it would be "tenderloin with bamboo shoots." At a French restaurant,

"tenderloin in red wine sauce." What was going on?

I took a deep breath. "The problem," I explained hesitantly, "is that the law prevents restaurants from serving beef in Delhi for fear of offending Hindu religious sensibilities. So restaurants don't use the word *beef* on the menu."

My friend sounded relieved. I had finally cracked the code for him. "That means every time I want to order beef I just need to ask for tenderloin, right? They serve it, but I should just use the euphemism. That's what you're saying?"

"Er, not exactly. Tenderloin is not exactly beef."

"Well, what is it then?"

"Water buffalo," I confessed.

Silence on the other end. "Thanks," he said finally. "I'll just stick to the lamb."

"Now that you bring it up, it's not actually lamb either. When the menu says lamb or mutton, what you're really getting is goat."

This was the end for him. "If nothing I order is really what I order, then what in the world should I order?"

"Well, this is the land of vegetarianism ..."

Actually, you can get perfectly good chicken in India. And our fish is among the finest in the world. So there's no need to turn vegetarian just to keep yourself fed. But if you are a fan of red meat, it's good to know in advance that you will be tasting some different animals on your visit here. Because everywhere you go in India, you will find

NEW DELHI

restaurateurs trying to keep the truth from you.

I've lost count of the number of foreign visitors who've looked at me horrified when I've explained that beef in India is actually water buffalo and lamb is goat. No matter what soothing explanations I trot out, most Westerners get queasy at the thought of eating unfamiliar meats that are in fact quite similar to those they take entirely for granted at home.

To an extent, I can understand the water buffalo/beef fiddle. Given that the Hindu religion forbids the consumption of beef, restaurateurs risk losing Hindu customers if they baldly announce bovine delicacies on their menu. It's the reluctance to own up to goat that frankly confounds me, since none of our many religions—at least, as far as I know—has any injunctions against slaughtering this creature.

So why hesitate to call a goat a goat? And why pussyfoot around the sheep-versus-goat issue in front of foreign tourists, when it comes to a matter of taste? Indians dislike the strong, fatty flavor of lamb meat. Goat is perfect for most Indian meat dishes. The best *biryanis* and kebabs are made with goat meat, and that's a well-established fact. Foodies who take their Mughal-style cuisine seriously would sooner go vegetarian than eat the "inferior" chicken versions of goat dishes.

You don't have to take my word for it. You can take the popular Khan Chacha "roll test" instead. I know of many seasoned expats who routinely take foreign guests to Khan Chacha

for a Goat Initiation right at the start of their India tour.

Khan Chacha is a guy who runs a tiny stall in south Delhi's popular Khan Market. He wraps chicken and goat kebabs in pan-fried flat bread, and these rolls are the stuff of dreams. He does an excellent job with both his chicken and goat meat rolls, but if you take a bite out of each, you can compare and see how much more flavorful the goat version is.

This little experiment will cost you $3 for two rolls. And it will clear up all your goat-related doubts forever. Armed with newfound love for this red meat, you will stretch your gastronomic boundaries and enjoy the whole gamut of North India's nonvegetarian dishes. As for me, I will get to rest my case.

Khan Chacha

75 Middle Lane
Khan Market
New Delhi

David Dorkin cautions against local liquor in Delhi

When a couple veteran traveler friends of mine heard that I was heading for India, they had two bits of advice. Don't drink the water, and steer clear of the liquor.

The first I could understand. We all know about the effects of water-borne bacteria that our systems aren't used to. But liquor? What kind of trouble—other than the obvious—could a shot of vodka possibly get me into? Three days of drinking and some insight from Indians in the know finally clarified this caution. Now it is also my advice to you: avoid local liquor at all costs.

Here's why. When you drink whiskey, gin, or vodka in India, you are in fact drinking something called Indian Made Foreign Liquor (IMFL). In layman's terms, this is industrial alcohol flavored with artificial syrups. So the gin and the vodka will consist of the same alcohol base, only one will have a synthetic gin flavor and the other will have a synthetic vodka flavor.

The surprise and shock of this unpleasant industrial alcohol is difficult to handle if you're not accustomed to it. My own first encounter with IMFL vodka left a burning sensation lingering somewhere at the back of my throat for days. Small wonder then that wealthy Indians refuse to partake of the domestic product. There is a huge market in bootlegged Scotch whiskey—the rich Indian's spirit of choice.

As for those of us who do not have access to bootleggers, are smart enough to avoid IMFL, and are unwilling to pay the 200 percent import duty imposed on foreign booze, what can we drink? I think the best bet is beer. After four days of research, I decided that Indian beer is on par with the world's best.

The first Indian beer I ever had was a brand called Cobra. This was in London, at an Indian restaurant, and I remember the sommelier urging us to choose Cobra over all his wines. There was even a fancy version called King Cobra that came in a champagne bottle. It paired well with the food, and I was hoping to drink a lot of it with my meals when I was in India.

Sadly, for some reason Cobra didn't seem to be available at the time. But I quickly got over my disappointment because I had tracked down three other brands that had the same bite I now associated with the taste of Indian beer. I liked Kingfisher, which was easy drinking and satisfyingly rich in malt. There was one called Royal Challenge, whose extralong brewing cycle gave it body. But the beer I drank most often was Kalyani Black Label, India's oldest lager with lots of flavor and a surprisingly sweet aftertaste.

My local friends ragged me constantly about my preference for Kalyani Black Label whenever I went bar hopping with them. Apparently, it was an "old man's beer," and the only way to drink it was leaning on a walking stick. "Kalyani Black Label is totally *uncool*, man," Ajay, a club deejay, would grumble. "In these trendy Delhi watering holes all the girls associate the brand with their fathers!"

The choice was easy. I would be an uncool American dude and drink all the Kalyani beer I could. It was a fantastic brew, highly hopped and satisfyingly strong. And for me, at least, it was the perfect club drink.

After a bottle or two, it made Bollywood music bearable.

Popular Delhi watering holes

Agni

You can eat an amazing Indian fusion meal at FIRE in The Park, New Delhi hotel, and then ignite the rest of your evening at this dramatically designed, flamingly hot nightclub.

The Park, New Delhi
15, Parliament Street
New Delhi

http://newdelhi.theparkhotels.com

Howzatt

At this cricket-themed microbrewery at the Galaxy hotel in Gurgaon, you can sample a variety of different beers before making your final choice. Gurgaon is a glitzy satellite city full of Western-style malls and fancy office buildings. Once upon a time Gurgaon was considered a trek from central New Delhi. An eight-lane expressway now connects New Delhi to Gurgaon. Because of its pretty residential neighborhoods, many Delhiites are moving there and commuting.

NH-8, Exit-8, Sector-15, PART-II Gurgaon

www.galaxyhotel.in

Shalom

This Mediterranean lounge bar and restaurant in south Delhi's posh GK I market is a popular hangout for the capital's media crowd.

N-18, N Block Market
Greater Kailash I
New Delhi

www.facebook.com/shalomexperience

SRINAGAR

Robert Granger feasts at a Kashmiri banquet in Srinagar

I had never heard of *wazwan* until a local Kashmiri gentleman I befriended at a carpet shop in Srinagar spontaneously extended an invitation to his daughter's wedding. "Please come," he said. "There will be a *wazwan* after the wedding, and you will get a chance to enjoy proper Kashmiri hospitality."

Wazwan, I suspected, had to be a feast of some sort, but I did not grasp its scale or importance until two friends forced me to cadge invites for them and their three European companions as well. Michael and his partner, Lizzie, were fellow Americans who had taken seasonal jobs as ski instructors in Kashmir, and as such, had a better understanding of the local culture than I, a mere traveler trying to get to know India in six weeks. This would probably turn out to be *the* gastronomical adventure of my life, they said, and there was no reason why I shouldn't share the moment with them.

Lizzie happily informed me that *wazwan* was the traditional Muslim banquet of Kashmir, hosted to celebrate the most auspicious occasions. Huge ceremony surrounded the *wazwan*, and Kashmiris considered its presentation to be nothing less than an art. There would be thirty-six courses at the very least, if the host was to hold his head up high in society. Of that basic minimum number, around thirty would be various preparations of meat. A respectable Kashmiri wouldn't dream of including too many vegetarian dishes, as that would make him look cheap.

The day of the wedding dawned at last, and our group trooped over to our host's residence, a good hour or so early. He seemed to understand our enthusiasm and did not mind the six of us milling around the kitchen, fingering the rice, chatting with the vegetable boys, and generally getting into everybody's way.

Preparation of this banquet had started a couple of days in advance, and now the *waza* (the expert *wazwan* cook) was ordering his minions about with the urgent authority of a war commander. The job of mincing and grinding began in earnest, with chunks of mutton thrown on chopping stones, and wooden pestles beating it into an elastic mush. We

were informed that most of the *wazwan* dishes require minced meat, which is rolled into balls and put into different sauces. Beating the mutton took up a fair bit of time, and the onslaught of the raw meaty odor, thickened by the smell of freshly cut onions and garlic, was soon making me feel queasy.

More guests began to pour in not long afterward, and we thankfully escaped from all the chopping, slicing, cutting, and roasting to mingle. The groom's party arrived, amid a lot of noise and cheer, and then it was time to eat. But what about the wedding? We were a little disappointed to learn that the ceremony itself had taken place a day earlier. Today's focus was the big *wazwan* occasion, and the banquet was the whole point of the gathering.

Along with all the other *wazwan* guests, we followed the host, who led us into a large room where the banquet would be served. Metal plates the size of an average car wheel had been arranged in rows on the floor, and the six of us were instructed to sit around one. As the other invitees did the same, I heard Lizzie's horrified whisper. "Oh God, all of us have to eat off the same plate!" She had issues about hygiene and hadn't quite managed to give herself over to the Indian experience with the same abandon as the rest of us.

Meanwhile, a huge mound of rice was placed in the center of the plate, a few kinds of meat were arranged around the edges, and our host was urging us to dig in. We hadn't encountered this kind of communal eating anywhere else in North India, but as we observed the other guests, we saw they did the job rather cleanly. Each person had his slice of the rice, which he carved out with his fingers without venturing into anybody else's territory. Gingerly, we tried doing the same.

Knowing that I was vegetarian, the host thoughtfully placed several meatless preparations in front of me consisting of potatoes, aubergines, and lotus roots. My vegetarian share of the feast was something to definitely write home about. It was more rich than spicy, and I could taste the various expensive nuts and fruits that had gone into making the sauce. The meats, from what the others told me, were unusually tender and flavorful. But by the sixth course, they confessed they couldn't tell their dishes apart and were just eating whatever was within easy reach. Halfway through the meal, they declared they'd had enough, and the last eighteen courses or so were a spectator activity for us, as we watched the rest of the guests continue to tuck in and wondered where all that food was going.

After the banquet was over, there wasn't a whole lot to do. The male guests scattered into little groups, smoking and drinking tea, while the women started to disappear somewhere inside the house. We decided it was also time for us to leave, and after thanking the host profusely, we made our way back to the hotel.

A few days later, as my flight from Srinagar took off and I settled into my seat to watch spectacular scenes of

mountains and meadows float past my window, my thoughts returned to the feast. The gods of the Kashmir Valley must have sensed my disappointment at not getting another taste of *wazwan* before I left, because as soon as the seat belt signs were switched off, the lunch trolleys came out with *nadir yakhni* as the vegetarian option. I remembered *nadir yakhni* very well—it had been my favorite dish in the *wazwan* lineup. I delightedly took my tray and then spent a long time over the meal, relishing every creamy mouthful of the lotus root curry. I couldn't have asked for a better parting gift.

Wazwan in Srinagar

In recommending restaurants, we would like to point out that these places are where readers can get a taste of *wazwan* cuisine. As for all of the pomp and ceremony described in Robert's essay, you will need to befriend a local and hope you are in the right place at the right time to experience a *wazwan* feast.

Mughal Durbar

Residency Road
Srinagar

www.mughal-darbar.com

Ruby Restaurant

Lambert Lane
Srinagar

Wazwan in Delhi

Chor Bizarre

Hote Broadway (near Delhi Gate)
4/15A, Asaf Ali Road
New Delhi

www.chorbizarrerestaurant.com

UDAIPUR

Maurice Young binges at a thaali restaurant in Udaipur

I tried to share as many meals as I could with local people while I was in India. Sitting at the same table with them gave me a chance to closely observe what a fellow Australian traveler called "Great Indian Fingerwork"—the custom of eating with the hand. A bit of bread is broken off, swirled around in a bowl of dal (lentil broth), and then wrapped expertly around a piece of vegetable or meat before being folded up and placed in the mouth.

This may sound easy, but believe me, a lot of practice is required to be able eat like that and not embarrass oneself. I tried hard to copy the way Indians use their fingers to eat rice and curry, and by the end of the trip I believe I had mastered the art well enough to find more rice in my mouth than around my plate and on my lap.

During a debate on the practicalities of adapting this custom to the Australian way of life, and perhaps even eschewing knives and forks altogether, the aforementioned traveler, a film site locator I met at my hotel in Udaipur, happened to mention a unique kind of restaurant he had encountered recently in the local bazars. It was called *thaali*, he said, and if I were to go to a *thaali* restaurant, I would get a fantastic meal and a ringside seat to watch Great Indian Fingerwork at its best.

Thaali restaurants, according to him, had no menus. A multicourse meal was prepared each day and then served course by course to a batch of diners. Once these diners had finished eating, a fresh batch of people took their place and the same service started all over again. The food was hygienically cooked, and the staggering variety of dishes more than made up for the fact that it was all vegetarian.

That was all the encouragement I needed to go in search of a *thaali* lunch the very next day. Walking down the busy road running parallel to the Udaipur City Palace, I saw a large hand-painted board that said "Gujarati Thaali." Following the directions marked with arrows, I climbed up a narrow staircase, which opened into a large hall on the first floor. Rows of long tables and benches covered this whole area, and several dozen diners were tucking into a hearty lunch. Food servers darted from table to table

RAJASTHAN

carrying a quaint contraption that held four long tubes filled with curries. Other attendants distributed hot fluffy breads out of huge wicker baskets. The aroma of ghee (clarified butter) and pickles was thick in the air, and the busyness of the scene reminded me of an Indian railway station.

I joined the crowd loitering around the manager's desk and waited for the current service to end. When it was over, the tables were quickly cleaned and prepared with fresh platters and glasses, and then we were asked to sit. I quickly found myself a place at the nearest table, and like everybody else, looked impatiently in the direction of the kitchen for the first course to arrive. After several hours of sightseeing and sailing on Lake Pichola, I was tired from all the sun and heat and feeling extremely hungry.

We were first served a yogurt drink, richly flavored with piquant berries called *kokum* and laced with subtle spices to aid digestion. Its sweet-salty taste was quite refreshing, and no sooner had I drained my glass than somebody came along to fill it. Then the food started to appear, beginning with fried and roasted flat breads to be eaten with three kinds of vegetable curries and dal . *Poppadom* crisps came along next, as well as countless varieties of spicy and sweet pickles, and several savory snack items. My platter, which had earlier seemed unnecessarily large, was now heaped with food, and no sooner would I finish a bread or a curry than some more would be piled on my plate.

Straightening up my spine, I pushed my shoulders back in the *padmasana* yoga pose, hoping to readjust the contents of my stomach and create more free space. But before I could do a few rounds of deep breathing, the second onslaught started with rice cooked into two different kinds of pilafs. The rice course even came with its own selection of curries and savories.

I could only graze at this point, so I tried to taste everything on my platter, and I managed to do some justice to the desserts afterward as well. But by the time the meal was finally over, I was almost groaning with the effort to breathe. I canceled my afternoon plans, lay in bed until the sun disappeared behind the hills, and could only face food a good twenty-four hours later in the form of a simple sandwich.

And yet, after giving you an account of what must sound like an ordeal, I am recommending the *thaali* meal as something every visitor with an interest in local food must try. Just keep in mind the cardinal rule of *thaali* that I had foolishly ignored: Pace yourself. Choosing variety over volume and trying to taste everything that is served is the way to go.

Thaali meals include many unusual "homestyle" dishes that you won't find in any other kind of restaurant. I discovered, for example, a Rajasthani desert vegetable called *sangri*. It had a wild sort of flavor that is pleasing on the tongue but impossible to describe. As I ate it, I remembered having had the same sensation when I first tasted a truffle. Later, I ordered *sangri* wherever I went in Rajasthan, but none of the preparations were quite as good as when it was part of a *thaali* menu.

As for a handy fingerwork maneuver, I picked one up at the restaurant that you can use to avoid being force-fed. When you think you have had enough, cover your plate with your right hand with all the fingers splayed out. It is an Indian custom to keep serving you more, and this gesture is the polite way to keep your plate from being refilled.

Natraj

Unfortunately, Maurice can no longer recall the name of the restaurant he went to that day, but meal quality is fairly standard in most *thaali* restaurants. To get started, head for Natraj, which serves some of the best *thaalis* in Udaipur. Not too many tourists come here, but the restaurant is famous among locals and easy to find. It is located in Udaipur's New Bapu Bazar area behind Ashoka Cinema.

GENERAL NORTH INDIA

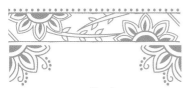

Small Bites around North India

With so many restaurants, cafés, and street stalls to choose from, our writers had a hard time narrowing down their favorites. Along with the essays in this chapter, they wanted to add a few nibbles to whet your appetite for your travels throughout North India.

DELHI

Choko La
New Delhi, Delhi

I am a bit of a chocolate snob, and when my sweet tooth kicks in and I begin to yearn for some good-quality dark chocolate and European pastries, I head for a place called Choko La, which is located in south Delhi's well-known Priya Cinema Complex in Vasant Vihar. Besides a killer selection of truffles, breads, and pastries, Choko La serves a very thick and authentic, French-style hot chocolate that you won't find elsewhere in the city. Choko La's entire fresh baked goods selection is sold at a 50 percent discount from 8:00 p.m. every day until closing time, and that's a good reason to go there a little late in the evening. (Lora Defries)

HIMACHAL PRADESH

Ogo's Café Italiano
Dharamshala, Himachal Pradesh

Unlike most travelers in Dharamshala, I did not use the town's many cafés as places to meet and network with fellow travelers. My café time was strictly my alone time, when I spent a few hours in my own company, eating a relaxed dinner and updating my travel journal. My favorite haunt, where I turned up most evenings, was Ogo's Café Italiano, a tiny little place on Jogiwara Road with maybe half a dozen tables. I always ordered the same meal—a piping hot tomato or minestrone soup, a thin-crust pizza, and iced tea. The menu had a good selection of pastas and chicken and lamb entrees, but I wanted something I could eat while I wrote, and the pizzas came topped with some really wonderful cheeses. The two cheerful waitresses at Ogo's didn't seem to care how long I lingered over the food, and in time, started to treat me as part of the furniture, which suited me very well. (Michael Roberts)

JAMMU & KASHMIR

Pumpernickel German Bakery
Leh, Jammu & Kashmir

Among the many German bakeries and restaurants that dot the town, this one was my favorite. Pumpernickel is located on the narrow lane that leads out of Leh's Main Bazar toward the taxi stand. The Sikh gentleman who runs the place sells some of the best yak cheese I have tasted in the Ladakh region. Made from thick and fragrant yak's milk, this strong artisanal cheese is dry-cured in Tibetan red salt and goes well with wine. I would often buy a portion and some rolls of bread and throw them into my backpack before heading off into the mountains for a daylong trek. Or I carried them over to the Peace Café next door and

enjoyed them with a cup of spicy hot tea. (Amiya Dasgupta)

Sultan Bakery
Srinagar, Jammu & Kashmir

Srinagar has the best breakfasts-on-the-move for early risers like me. After my morning yoga, I would walk a short distance from my hotel to the Dal Gate Chowk Bazar, where the old, traditional Kashmiri bakeries open their doors by 6:00 a.m. It was usually at Sultan Bakery that I'd buy some of Kashmir's unique breads for my morning meal—flaky *bakarkhani* pastry bread, golden rice-flour crepes fried in mustard oil, sweet *sheermal* milk bread, and *tsochvoru* buns sprinkled liberally with poppy seeds. I'd wash it all down with a cup of steaming *nun chai* (salted tea) like I had seen the locals do and rush off to begin my day's sightseeing. On the one free morning I had in the city, I treated myself to another Kashmiri breakfast special, the *nahari*. This is a stew of beef flavored with exotic ingredients like sandalwood powder and dried rose petals. *Sheermal* was served with the *nahari*, and I enjoyed every mouthful, knowing I was unlikely to get this dish anywhere outside the state of Jammu & Kashmir. (Deblina Sarkar)

PUNJAB

Surjit Chicken House
Amritsar, Punjab

Like all good eateries in Amritsar, this one too is a *dhaba*—a word that once indicated roadside eateries for truck drivers but now suggests any small place serving wholesome Punjabi-style food. You will forgive this restaurant in the Nehru Shopping Complex on Lawrence Road for its lack of ambience the moment you bite into a succulent piece of its signature dish: the tandoori chicken. The item is ubiquitous in North India, but nobody in my experience does it as well as Surjit. Yes, I make this claim after having tasted the dish at Moti Mahal, the mecca of tandoor-cooking in Delhi. Maybe the trick is in the marinade, or maybe it has something to do with the temperature of the charcoal-fired clay oven, but the spicing always seems thicker and the chicken more crisply roasted at Surjit. While you are there, try the butter chicken with rotis as well. (Frank Goodman)

RAJASTHAN

Chokhi Dhani
Jaipur, Rajasthan
www.chokhidhani.com

Chokhi Dhani has been designed to resemble a typical Rajasthani village with prettily painted mud huts and gaming grounds strewn over a large property. You can enjoy as much outdoor activity as you want (most of the games and shows are complimentary) before heading for the food hall, where a *thaali*-style meal is served. Diners sit on cushions on the floor, which can be a little difficult if you're not used to eating that way. A battery of servers brings piping hot food from the kitchen, and then—to

my great astonishment during my visit—they start forcing spoonfuls into everybody's mouth! Apparently, it's a Rajasthani custom to force guests to eat more, and this goes on amid much hilarity before the servers finally leave you alone to enjoy the marvelous many-course vegetarian feast. The environment at Chokhi Dhani is kid-friendly, and it's a great option for an evening out if you are traveling with children. My daughter quickly bonded with all the camels and bullocks there, and it was tough for me to detach her from her new-found playmates when it was finally time to leave. (Naomi Naam)

Indiana
Jaipur, Rajasthan

At this lively, no-fuss dinner venue at J 234 Mahavir Road, I enjoyed many satisfying plates of stroganoff, spaghetti, and roast chicken. The menu is multicuisine, but somewhat homesick after four months on the road, I couldn't resist all the familiar dishes among the Western selections. The restaurant is spread out on a lawn, with multicolored cane chairs and tables that quickly fill up by eight in the evening. There is live folk dancing, too, and guests are encouraged to join in. The one time I tried to match steps with the nimble Rajasthani girls, my two left feet got entangled in their whirling skirts, but if you're a more accomplished dancer than I, then you'll definitely enjoy this part of the night. (Jason Staring)

Rawat Misthan Bhandar
Jaipur, Rajasthan

I hesitate to describe this Jaipur snack for fear of scaring away readers who have a low tolerance for spices. But believe me, the *mirchi vadas* (fried chili peppers) are not the sort that have a lot of heat. The green chilies used to make *mirchi vadas* are long with thick, aromatic skins, which when fried, give off a uniquely piquant aroma. Split down the middle, these chilies are deseeded and stuffed with spiced potatoes before they are dropped in a *gram* flour batter and fried in enormous iron woks.

Hawkers cook *mirchi vadas* and sell them on the streets in Jaipur's marketplaces, but I didn't want to risk stomach problems and forced myself to ignore the inviting smells coming off the handcarts every time I passed them. Instead, I went to a shop called Rawat Misthan Bhandar, opposite Polo Victory Cinema on Station Road. Rawat is an old establishment that has survived from the days when its owners supplied sweets and savories to the royals of Jaipur. The passage of time has not reduced this shop's popularity, and the *mirchi vadas* they make are simply the best. Jodhpur, I'd been told, was the place to eat the finest *mirchi vadas* in Rajasthan, but after having tried them there, I still preferred Rawat's version. (Ananya Basu)

The Omlette Man
Jodhpur, Rajasthan

The Omlette Man is one of Jodhpur's culinary legends. He has one frying pan, on which he reputedly cooks an average of one thousand eggs per day. And there is only one item on his menu: omlette. He operates out of a shack near the Clock Tower in Sadar Bazar, where he has set up a few benches for his customers. You won't get much of an ambience—just the pleasure of sitting amid a pile of egg cartons and eating what is probably the best omlette in India. There is no precise address for the Omlette Man, but I was told that his shack isn't difficult to find. When I went to the Clock Tower, however, I was confused by several me-too omlette establishments that have come up after the success of the original. It was only by asking around that I found the real Omlette Man from among the imposters. (Asha Mallya)

Paratha Hut
Udaipur, Rajasthan

For a *paratha*-crazy person like me, Paratha Hut was a dream discovery. I love the fried breads with meat and vegetable stuffing, and this small restaurant on the Lake Palace Road opposite Rang Niwas taxi stand in Udaipur boasted thirty varieties! All vegetarian, of course, this being Udaipur, where there is hardly any nonvegetarian food to be found outside the five-star hotels. My favorite *parathe* were stuffed with lightly spiced radish and *paneer*, which went well with dal *baati* (baked wheat dumplings in a lentil broth), one of Rajasthan's signature dishes. The owners have strung up a "satisfaction bell" on the premises, and I rang it loudly every time I went there to convey my compliments to the chef. (Helene Shapiro)

UTTAR PRADESH

Railway station *pethas*
Agra, Uttar Pradesh

I so loved Agra's traditional sweet, the *petha*, that I was a little surprised to learn that these crunchy, juice-filled little tidbits were nothing but pieces of ordinary white pumpkin. The vegetable, after being cooked and flavored, turns into this translucent, firm, jellylike substance that crumbles delightfully in the mouth with each bite. *Pethas* are instantly recognizable in any sweet shop in Agra. The sellers pile them into colorful mountains, and you buy by weight after choosing your flavor. The *angoori petha* filled with coconut and the *gilori petha* with nuts were my personal favorites from among at least ten different kinds I found in the city. Since I was using Agra as my base to explore all the heritage sites in Uttar Pradesh, I was often at the railway station. In my opinion, the *pethas* sold in boxes there were the freshest and the best. The regular ones cost $1 for two pounds, though the price can go up to about $50 for the fancier versions. They keep well, so if you really like them, buy a box or two to take home. (Cynthia Chesterfield)

Dussheri mangoes
Lucknow, Uttar Pradesh

My trip to India coincided with the country's mango season (spring into early summer), and I was looking forward to gorging on my favorite fruit at the end of every meal. The only mango of Indian descent I knew of was the fat, orange-skinned Alphonso that is sold in American groceries, but when I was in Lucknow, I discovered a locally grown mango of an entirely different strain called the Dussheri. Its appearance was very different from the Alphonso: it was slimmer, longer, and had a thin, yellow skin. And compared to the more celebrated Alphonso, it had a stronger aroma. A local showed me how a Dussheri was commonly eaten in Lucknow: You press down firmly on the fruit while rolling it between your palms. This action turns the flesh into mush, and once the fruit begins to feel smooth and squishy inside, you make a small hole in the skin and suck the flesh out. Eating the Dussheri Lucknow-style means there are no messy leftovers, and I could carry some with me in my rucksack when I was on the move. The Dussheri mango is a much tastier fruit than the Alphonso, while costing half the price. In Lucknow during my visit, it was all the more delicious because it was freshly plucked from the tree and was at the peak of its juiciness. (Linda Saleh)

Babu Nandan
Varanasi, Uttar Pradesh

If you're into exotic epicurean adventures, try Varanasi's *paan* for an

GENERAL NORTH INDIA

adrenaline fix. The initiation is rough, but once the palate has acclimatized to the strong flavors and you have resisted the urge to spit it out, you might end up as an obsessive *paan*-chewer like me. The *paan* is a triangle of betel leaf, filled with lime paste and an assortment of herbs, seeds, and nuts. Upon chewing, unfamiliar flavors burst out of it in three swift stages. The first is the toe-curling sharpness of the betel leaf. Then comes the sweetness of thickened rosewater syrup and sugared areca nuts. And finally, an intoxicating aroma of herbs like saffron and aniseed that fills your mouth, nose, and throat with a complex, slightly mentholated thrill.

I tasted Varanasi's legendary *paan* for the first time at Babu Nandan's popular shop in Varanasi's Thatheri Bazar. I placed the moist triangle in my mouth and then held my breath, trying to deal with its complexities while Babu Nandan told me what sounded like tall tales of "bed-breaker" *paans* that miraculously made a man three times more potent. As I had no desire to put on a bed-breaking performance during my time in the religious city, I had Babu Nandan make me a takeaway packet of the ordinary stuff, and I ate all of them that very same evening. In the process, I became a *paan* junkie. I ate some *paan* later in Delhi, as well, but it wasn't as good as the Varanasi version. (Maurice Young)

Hayat's
Varanasi, Uttar Pradesh

The low, bed-style seating at the back of this Middle Eastern restaurant near Assi Ghat is perfect for relaxing with friends over a sampler platter of delicious baba ghanoush, hummus, *lebneh*, salad, falafel, and freshly baked pita bread. Hayat's has an outstanding lemon-and-mint drink on the menu that goes wonderfully with the food. The Jordanian owners of the establishment claim it as Hayat's own invention. (Linda Saleh)

A vendor offering coconut wedges to an autorickshaw rider

Fruit vendor in Delhi

GENERAL NORTH INDIA

SEEING THE SIGHTS

Fresh perspectives on exploring must-see attractions

Travelers usually come to North India with two kinds of holidays in mind. The first focuses on royal Rajasthan. They want to see grand palaces, explore ancient forts, ride majestically on liveried elephants, and perhaps even sit down to dinner with a true blue Maharaja. The second encompasses the mighty Himalayas, with its hiking, biking, and remote, high-altitude camping. Far from tourist attractions, visitors live in picturesque villages with local folks and revel in the incredible natural beauty of the world's most famous mountain range.

Thankfully, North India more than lives up to its reputation in these two areas and keeps travelers well supplied with an itinerary loaded with sightseeing options. There's no shortage of Himalayan experiences for nature lovers and thrill seekers, and there's no shortage of palaces and kings either, for those who want a taste of North India's royal heritage.

A number of essays in this chapter travel through princely Rajasthan. For those with limited time, William Potter offers a thorough tour of Jaipur's forts and palaces in a single day. And for those who want to linger, Paul and Melissa Yeung open the doors to their royal living quarters in the palace of Karauli, where a Maharaja is still in residence. Deepanjana Sarkar's essay about Chittor fort and its beautiful, doomed queen tells a story of valor and self-sacrifice that is the very essence of the history of this proud state. Finally, Vir Sanghvi ties the whole royal Rajasthan theme up with insider anecdotes about rulers and ruling families that won't be found in your typical guidebook.

As for the Himalayas, you will find many suggestions in the "Into the Wild" chapter. But we start you off here with A. Murray's adrenaline-pumping flight from Delhi to Leh, as he wonders if the pilot really can land a Boeing 737 safely on Leh's impossibly tiny airstrip. This chapter also introduces you to gems along some of North India's less-traveled routes. Mark Moxon takes you to the quiet hill town of Mt. Abu to

Visitors at Agra Fort, a UNESCO World Heritage site

see the Dilwara Temples, one of those sights that truly must be seen to be believed. Rinoti Amin stumbles upon exquisitely hand-painted mansions while chasing nomads around the Shekhawati region, and Jenni Wadams marvels at eccentric curiosities, like a miniature wine train chugging along on silver rail tracks to distribute alcohol and cigars, at a small palace museum in Gwalior.

If you loosen up your schedule just a little, you can enjoy royal tours and Himalayan treks and still have time for out-of-the-way excursions. You don't have to go far off your chosen course to take in a few of the region's lesser-known delights. Along whatever route you take, there will be something unique to see. Unless you have a plane to catch, stop and explore, for who knows when you will come this way again.

NEW DELHI

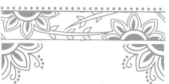

Indranil Gupta angles for the perfect shot of a Delhi landmark

During the years before digital cameras, I used up more film in my attempts to do justice to the many faces of the Qutab Minar than on any of New Delhi's countless other tourist sites. A sandstone-and-marble pillar monument, which loses diameter as it climbs to a height of over seventy meters, the Minar is, in my opinion, one of the most astounding examples of Indo-Islamic architecture in the country.

The Minar stands in the middle of a complex strewn with broken bits of walls, doorways, and arches, and some of my best photographs of it have been shot from a distance with these ancient ruins in the foreground. The structure is slightly tilted from all of the tremors it has withstood over the centuries, but the leaning effect takes nothing away from its magnificence. In fact, it makes for very interesting photography, especially in winter, when the Minar seems to be straining to catch scraps of the city's legendary fog and make them float like ragged white flags from its tip. I used to love climbing the 379 steps inside it to take aerial shots of Delhi from the highest viewing gallery, but several suicides later, the authorities don't allow visitors up there anymore.

The Qutab grounds are quite big and have other historical structures that are worth photographing, such as Quwwat-ul-Islam, the oldest surviving Mughal mosque in the country. But my favorite, after the Minar itself of course, is a fourth-century iron column—a most curious antique, because it bears no sign of rust or decomposition after all these years. Legend has it that your most fervent wish will come true if you wrap your arms all the way around the column. Easier said than done, though, since there is a small fence around it, and because if you do get close to it, you must stand with your back against the structure and then stretch backward and make the fingers of both hands meet.

It always amuses me to take pictures of tourists trying valiantly to embrace the pillar in full glare of the public eye. I've tried it myself a few times when no one was looking, to avoid all the good-natured whistles and catcalls, but only got a stiff shoulder and mild forearm tendonitis to show for my trouble. I do know, however, that it can be done, because a tall, big-boned Israeli acquaintance of mine was successful in the attempt. Afterward, he said he had wished for the love of a good Indian woman who would cook him elaborate vegetarian meals. I should look him up and find out if

the pillar did indeed keep its promise and he's waking up each morning to the hot breakfast of *idlis* and coconut chutney he dreamed of.

Qutab Minar complex

The complex is located in the Mehrauli neighborhood in southwest Delhi. As it is a major monument, taxi and autorickshaw drivers know where it is located.

Unfulfilled dreams

The building of the Qutab Minar was started at the end of the twelfth century by Delhi's first Muslim king, Qutbuddin Aibak, to mark the glory of his reign, but he died before the project progressed beyond the base. It was his successors who ultimately completed the monument. Besides the Qutab Minar, the complex also houses its rival, the Alai Minar. This monument was the dream project of the Khilji sultan Ala-ud-din, who wanted a victory tower of his own like the Qutab Minar, but twice as high. But the Alai Minar was destined to remain a dream. Ala-ud-din died when the structure had only reached one story. After his death, nobody was willing to continue with his overambitious project. The incomplete stump of the Alai Minar stands north of the Qutab Minar, showing visitors what it might have been.

NEW DELHI TO LEH

A. Murray flies high (and low) from Delhi to Leh

If you're heading for the Ladakh region, consider flying out of the capital instead of taking the land route. I doubt if there is a more exhilarating plane journey in a major-sized Boeing than the one from Delhi to Leh. Sure, you can get in a four-seater prop and land on some dirt track in the Congo, but it's an entirely different story when you are expecting a normal flight that takes you from one city to another without the sort of adrenaline rush that calls for the Indiana Jones theme music playing in the background.

My Jet Airways flight had taken off from Delhi, and I was comfortably settled in my seat, looking out the window at the flat plains below and wondering if the crew would do a full meal service on this short sector. Then, without any warning, they appeared—the mighty Himalayas. Peak after peak in an endless chain that seemed to have swallowed up the earth and was now threatening to crash into my window. The shock of that first encounter stopped my heart

for a few beats, and I could feel panic rise up in my stomach. Was everything all right in the cockpit? Had a big gust of wind pulled the plane off its course and dropped it into this dangerous territory?

I looked back at the galley for reassurance and watched a female crew member bring out a pocket mirror and fix a smudge in her lipstick. That made me feel immeasurably better. She'd hardly be thinking of makeup if we were in any sort of trouble. I sat back and drank some lime juice from the small bottle we had been given after takeoff and returned my attention to the scene playing out outside my window.

It seems a ridiculous thing to say about the world's highest mountain range, but my God, it was high! We were flying at a decent cruising altitude, I'm sure, and yet the mountains were so close that with each bump it felt like the belly of the aircraft had grazed one of their jagged peaks. Fortunately, my panic retreated, and I began to enjoy the brilliant sight of snow peaks stretching as far as the eye could see, like a giant sea of meringue with tips toasted golden brown by the afternoon sun.

The crew served a lovely food tray, and as I bit into my cucumber sandwich and drank a hot cup of tea, I watched the breathtaking view of melted snow moving between the mountains like streams in slow motion. The hour and fifteen minutes' flight passed all too quickly, and soon it was time to land.

The seat belt sign was switched on, and the plane dipped suddenly and commenced its descent. But descent to where? The snow peaks around us had been replaced by barren brown mountains, but there was still no sign of level ground. Except for one tiny little open space between two mountains and … oh no! … the plane was headed that way. It was sheer audacity to consider landing a commercial jetliner on a strip of land that looked too small for even a Cessna 150. A nervous hush fell over the passengers as each tried to peer out of the window to see how the plane could make such an impossible landing.

The Boeing 737 seemed to skid in the air, and then, with a nerve-racking whine, began to spiral as it lost altitude. Round and round it went in tight circles as the ground rushed up to meet us at an alarming speed. A short runway came into view. "Too small! Too small!" the man sitting next to me wailed to his wife. "Don't worry; it's okay," the woman said, patting her husband's hand, which was holding the seat handle in a death grip. "They do this every day. Don't look."

I too closed my eyes and waited for the moment of contact with the ground. The plane touched down abruptly, and I was shunted forward in my seat by a handful of major bumps. As the pilot slammed on the brakes and put the engine in reverse thrust, I ground my braking foot into the carpet reflexively. The aircraft jerked to a halt, with just inches of runway to spare, and the pilot shut down the engine. All in a day's work

for him. The same couldn't be said for the rest of us.

Down the stairs and onto the tarmac, I allowed myself to be directed by members of the Indian Armed Forces toward the small airport building. Although the surroundings were spectacular, they requested "No photos please," and I guessed we were in a military air base that allowed a limited number of commercial flights. I looked back at the Jet Airways plane, which was being unloaded, and said a silent goodbye. We'd probably meet again on the journey back to Delhi, and I was surprised to feel excited at the prospect. Now that I knew what to expect, I couldn't wait to do it all over again.

Flying between Delhi and Leh

Jet Airways

Jet Airways flies between Delhi and Leh up to seven times a week, depending on the season. www.jetairways.com

Air India

For another option, this popular airline also operates a flight on the Delhi-Leh route three times a week.

http://indian-airlines.nic.in

GWAILOR

*Jenni Wadams
marvels at royal
excess in Gwalior*

Not so far back in India's history, there were Rajas and Maharajas who played chess with human beings for rooks and bishops. They built expensive palaces and then changed their minds about moving into them. They spent fortunes to marry off their favorite cats to eligible monkeys, and then had tons of silver shards poured over the events' settings to create the illusion of a full moon night.

The whims of India's royalty went as far as imaginations could stretch, and I was amazed to see some instances of this at the Jai Vilas Palace in Gwalior. After marveling at the various objects that are displayed in the public areas of this current residence of the ruling Scindia family, I doubt I will pooh-pooh a "can you believe this" anecdote about royal excess ever again.

The Jai Vilas looked like an enormous white wedding cake placed in the middle of extensive lawns and gardens. The interiors, however, were somewhat shabby, and a layer of dust seemed to coat everything—clearly, no one wanted the job of dusting in this huge palace, which was built in 1875 and has more than two hundred rooms. Our guide, Madhav, led us in through a side entrance, and one of the first things I decided was that the Scindia family obviously had a hand in destroying the local tiger population. Snarling, moth-eaten stuffed tigers stared blankly out of glass cases everywhere. Not surprisingly, there are no longer any tigers in this pocket of the state of Madhya Pradesh. In this hall I was also impressed by a chandelier of red Venetian glass, little knowing what greater treasures were ahead of me.

As we wandered through a maze of opulent rooms, Madhav gave a brief commentary on each of the exhibits. A living room contained armchairs made from cut glass, while the children's nursery had miniature, drivable versions of expensive European cars. The main dining room had—besides a banquet table to seat a hundred people at a time—the strangest piece of engineering I've ever encountered in my life. On a table with miniature train tracks, a train of solid silver circled, carrying brandy, sherry, dried fruit, and cigars for the Maharaja and his guests to enjoy after dinner. When the guests felt like a drink, they removed a glass decanter from the train, which caused it to stop. When the decanter was replaced, the train tooted its horn and chugged off toward the next person.

While all this was notable, the best was yet to come: two massive chandeliers in the reception room that made the red bauble at the entranceway look like a flashlight with a low battery. These chandeliers, Madhav informed us, were the second largest in the world, each weighing 3.5 tons and rising to a height of 12.5 meters. The sockets could hold 248 candles at a time, although the candles have now been replaced with electric lights.

I was nervous about walking directly under the chandeliers, for fear of their crashing down at any moment like something out of *Phantom of the Opera*. Apparently, this had also concerned the Maharaja and his architects, and they decided to use elephants to make sure the ceiling could bear the weight of the mammoth light fittings. I guess if you have chandeliers that size and elephants are plentiful, such imaginative solutions may seem logical. By then, I was ready to believe anything, and I didn't raise an eyebrow when Madhav explained that the Maharaja ordered the elephants to be suspended from the ceiling for several days. Not surprisingly, there is no record of what the elephants thought of this treatment.

A hundred years on, the chandeliers are still hanging in there, and on our way out of Raj Vilas we had a fun time trying to out-imagine each other as to what reward the architects should have received for pulling off such a feat. By my reckoning, the Maharaja should have given them nothing less exciting than the choo-choo train drink service. But then, we were only choosing from the items the Scindia royal family allows the public to see. Who knows what

other incredible treasures they keep in their residence for the private viewing pleasure of their family and friends?

Getting to Gwalior

Gwalior is located near the northern tip of the state of Madhya Pradesh. It is well connected to many major cities in India by air, rail, and road.

Jai Vilas Palace Museum

The museum is officially known as the H. Maharaja Jiwaji Rao Scindia Museum, though few taxi drivers will recognize this name. Ask for it by Jai Vilas Palace.

Jayendraganj, Lashkar
Gwalior

Gwalior Fort

Inside the walls of this fifteenth-century sandstone fort, there are ancient temples and palaces that date as far back as the ninth and tenth centuries. Most impressive among them is the Man Singh Palace, embellished on the outside with stunning turquoise and yellow tiles. An appealing aspect of this fort complex is the sheer variety of architectural styles, which, because the buildings are set apart at considerable distances, can be appreciated in isolation from each other. The best time to visit is late in the afternoon around three, when Gwalior Fort turns golden in the light of the setting sun.

RAJASTHAN

CHITTOR

*Deblina Sarkar
is saddened by the fate
of India's Helen of Troy*

I had wanted to visit Chittorgarh since I was about thirteen. My favorite storybook told the tale of this fort and its queen, and I read it again and again, imagining how beautiful Padmini must have been. I admired the bravery of the soldiers of the town of Chittor, who died trying to defend her, and sighed at Padmini's decision to destroy her cursed beauty when the war against an enemy king who fought to possess her was lost. I can still vividly recall the illustration of Padmini on the cover of the book. She stood proudly at the edge of a roaring fire with a garland in her hand, ready to immolate herself in order to save her honor.

Many years later, when I was in Udaipur, I had the chance to visit Chittorgarh. With my cousin and her husband, I took a day off from sightseeing in the city and drove the 112 kilometers northeast to dusty little Chittor, dominated by the massive fort sitting on top of a hill. We dawdled in town for half an hour while my cousin selected a guide who she felt wouldn't tell us fibs, since in our

experience guides in smaller tourist spots like this can make up some preposterously tall tales. Then we took a slow, winding route up the hill to the fort's main entrance.

This led us directly into an empty stable, where the king's horses and elephants used to be tethered. We clattered through the dark, stone-paved building and stepped out on the other side. As our eyes readjusted to the brilliant light of the morning sun, we saw the remains of the Chittorgarh, gloriously laid out in front of us.

If you can conceive of such a thing as a "perfect ruin," then this had to be it. A monochromatic, yellow sandstone maze of heavily carved towers, turrets, courtyards, temples, and palaces spread out over seven hundred acres of undulating land. Of some structures, only the outer walls remained. Elsewhere, a staircase or a stretch of pillared pavilion stood incongruously, leading to nowhere. No tourist groups were in immediate view, noisily taking pictures. No sight of soda cans, ice cream wrappers, and other tourist-generated litter either, which often make historical monuments in India look like public playgrounds. Everything was so peaceful and undisturbed, we could well have been the first people to venture this way in a hundred years.

The first site our guide led us to was the long underground cellar inside which Padmini and three thousand women in her attendance had jumped into the fire. It was crumbling, and tourists were not allowed to go inside, but I could look down the sides of the plank that covered the roofless space and clearly see a portion of the wall blackened by the funeral pyre. A series of fires had been built down there to accommodate all the women living inside the fort, and it was unnerving to still be able to see tendrils of soot. The guide launched into his story about Padmini, and I listened with the eagerness of someone who was hearing the tale for the first time.

Ala-ud-din was the Sultan of Delhi when Padmini ruled over Chittorgarh with her husband Ratan Singh. When legends of the queen's incomparable beauty reached the ears of the avaricious sultan, he became obsessed with the idea of possessing her. He landed in Chittor, and after a glimpse of Padmini's reflection in a mirror, waged war against the fort and abducted Ratan Singh. The fort's Hindu soldiers fought bravely for the release of their king, but the Delhi army beat them in sheer numbers.

Word arrived to Padmini instructing her to prepare herself for the sultan, for the end was near. But the brave queen would sooner die and destroy the ill-fated beauty that had caused so much devastation than allow her honor to be compromised at the hands of the sultan. As the last battalion of Chittor's army was preparing to meet the enemy at the gates, huge fires were built in exactly the spot above which my cousin and I were now standing. When the fires were ready, Padmini and her attendants jumped into the flames.

I was amazed to find that Padmini's story, with all of its elements of high tragedy, still had the power to move me. My mature, twenty-seven-year-old mind was as much a victim of the mournful romance as it had been when it was thirteen. When the rest of my party moved on to other sites inside Chittorgarh, I stayed back to spend a few moments by myself near the ruins of the pyres.

In the quietness that fell after the others left, I imagined the scene that must have taken place right here on that fateful day in 1303. A scene bereft of men, all of whom were either killed or fighting their last battle outside the fort. I could hear the wail of women in the cellar, as they hurried about to raise the bonfires before the sultan's army broke in. The deafening roar of the flames that must have swallowed their cries as one by one, three thousand women ended their lives. And then ... smoke and silence.

The hot noon sun was right above my head, but a cold shiver ran up my spine. My flight of fancy seemed to have brought the site to life, and only at the sound of my cousin's voice calling out to her husband in the distance did I manage to get a grip on myself. I looked down at the blackened wall of the cellar one last time to bid Padmini a silent goodbye, and then walked quickly away to find the others.

Getting to Chittor

The town of Chittor is a comfortable two-and-a-half-hour drive from Udaipur. Once in Chittor, the fort is impossible not to find, as it makes up most of the town.

RAJASTHAN

RAJASTHAN

Staying in Chittor

Most visitors come to Chittor on day trips from Udaipur. If you would like to spend a night or two here, the best accommodation you'll find in this small town is at the Bassi Fort Palace.

www.bassifortpalace.com

The story of Padmini

To learn more about Padmini, read *Rani Padmini: The Heroine Of Chittor*, by B. K. Karkra, published by Rupa & Co.

JAIPUR

William Potter travels back in time in Jaipur

Here's an interesting bit of legend I heard about Sawai Jai Singh II, the founder of Jaipur. The king, I was told, was at least 25 percent more intelligent than anybody of his time, and in recognition of this honor, the mughuls awarded him the title of "Sawai," which means "one and a quarter." As well, during his reign, Jaipur flew two flags—a full-sized and a quarter-sized one.

These days Sawai's flags are no longer in evidence, but I found the

pink sandstone city standing as proud and tall as it must have done at the time of its founding in the early 1700s. As Rajasthan's capital city, Jaipur cannot help being overgrown and overpopulated, but in between the press of bullock carts, rickshaws, and pedestrians, I could see its history peeking back at me from every street corner. It was easy to mentally edit out the crowds and weave the palaces, forts, and monuments together to create an awe-inspiring picture of a princely past.

On my first day in town, I commandeered an autorickshaw and set out to see one of Jaipur's famous landmarks: the Hawa Mahal (Palace of Winds), which was constructed as a viewing station for the ladies of the royal court. To avoid the beggars and postcard merchants who throng the street outside the monument, I chose to admire it from the rooftop of the shops directly across the street. I had to feign an interest in the merchandise to merit the lookout, but the view was more than worth the five minutes of browsing through silver jewelry. For a fee, you can go inside the Hawa Mahal, but in my opinion, the structure is most impressive from outside.

From my perch, I could see the innumerable apertures built cleverly into the building's exterior, through which the women watched street processions and other celebratory events without being observed. The pyramidlike structure with its tiny lattice windows reminded me of a golden cage more than anything—a superb piece of architecture, devised to give womenfolk a peep at the outside world they weren't allowed to step into.

My next stop was the Amber Fort, which lay north of the city within a great wall that circled the crown of a rocky hill. An elephant ride took me up to it in the style of a Maharaja, before I set out to explore its various sites on foot. From the entranceway, Amber Fort looked like a massive set constructed to shoot a period film. There were enormous structures everywhere, facing onto open courtyards, and I felt like an insignificant extra, who had been hired along with all the other tourists to populate it.

My guide wanted to begin the tour with the meeting halls where the king attended to the businesses of state, but I preferred to start with the Sukh Niwas (Palace of Pleasures). Debauchery is always more interesting than political intrigue, and I was looking forward to seeing the royal version of a sixteenth-century bordello.

To my surprise, the Sukh Niwas turned out to be quite bare, except for a narrow channel that cut through its center. According to my guide, perfumed water once flowed through this channel to cool the hall. But it was up to my imagination to add the sumptuous carpets, glittering chandeliers, and all the other trappings that go into creating an ambience in which a king and his courtesans might comfortably enjoy one another's company.

Instead, the most memorable space I saw inside the Amber Fort was the Sheesh Mahal (Palace of Glass), which required no assistance from my imagination to re-create its luxurious past. It was a small room covered completely with small pieces of mirrors. Pretty though it was, I failed at first to see its point until my guide closed the doors and lit a matchstick.

Instantly, the darkness inside the room dissolved in the light of a million stars. The flame of the match reflected back and forth on the mirrors. The room no longer seemed tiny—twinkling stars spread as far as the eye could see, and what wouldn't I have given right then to lie down under this mesmerizing firmament for just a few uninterrupted moments? The king could keep his Palace of Pleasures, as far as I was concerned. The charms of a haremful of beautiful women couldn't compete with this magical starscape.

My last bit of sightseeing for the day was Gaitor, the royal crematorium, also on the outskirts of Jaipur. It contained the cenotaphs of various Maharajas of Jaipur, erected under shady banyan trees swarming with monkeys. I kept an eye out for these mischievous creatures while my guide reeled off what he knew about the interred rulers in an amusing commentary: "Seven feet tall, four feet wide, very fat, three hundred wives, no children, too fat"; "Brain hemorrhage, too much drinking"; "This one, 120 children in total, all die"; "Polo player, fall off horse, die …"

When I got back to my hotel, it was still early, and instead of watching TV in my room, I thought I'd catch a show at the Raj Mandir, India's most luxurious cinema. I was taken aback when my hotel manager offered to pull some strings to get me a ticket— I had no idea that I'd have to book well in advance to watch a film there.

The candy-colored building stood on busy Bhawandas Road looking like an incredibly large confection. The sugary white decorations on its pink exterior made my mouth water. I remembered I hadn't had any lunch that day. There was just enough time to buy a bag of popcorn before I entered to watch the latest Bollywood blockbuster playing to a packed house. The Hindi language stumped me, but the sequences were colorful, the music was great, and the reactions of the audience were infectious. Three hours later (Bollywood movies are incredibly long), I emerged from the hall feeling happy and charged and very, very hungry.

I considered grabbing a quick dinner at one of the many Rajasthani restaurants near the cinema, but finally settled for a room service sandwich. My first day in Jaipur had been reserved for sightseeing, and it had gone off incredibly well. Tomorrow, I would give the city's local food and shopping their turn to court my palate and my purse.

Hawa Mahal

This palace with its latticed "viewing" facade wall stands in the midst of Jaipur's busy Tripolia Bazar area. The five-story structure is peppered with tiny windows that allow cool winds to circulate through the palace. Hence the name Hawa Mahal, or Palace of Winds. Built in 1799, the pink sandstone structure is a fine example of the fusion of Rajput and Mughal architecture.

Amber Fort

The sixteenth-century fort is often referred to as "Amer" by locals. The ruggedness of the exterior of this defensive structure gives no clue as to the opulence that lies within. The fort complex is made up of palaces, meeting halls, pleasure quarters, and other royal accommodation, decorated lavishly with frescoes, mosaics, mirror work, and tile art. Amber Fort is perched on top of a hill, and visitors can hire elephants to ride up to the main entrance. It is located eleven kilometers away from Jaipur on the Delhi-Jaipur highway.

Gaitor

This peaceful royal cremation ground lies about fifteen kilometers from Jaipur, opposite Lake Man Sagar. It is an oasis of gleaming marble *chhatris* (cenotaphs), each built in the preferred style of the Jaipur ruler it immortalizes. The association with death gives Gaitor a somewhat eerie feel, especially in the evenings, when the dying sun bleaches the marble domes and pillars to a pearly bone-white color.

Raj Mandir

The cinema has some seats reserved for tourists. If you haven't

booked in advance, take your
passport with you and show it at
the ticket counter. There's a good
chance you'll get in.

JAISALMER

Adrian Murray heats up in the desert city of Jaisalmer

I had booked a ticket on a deluxe
bus without air-conditioning, to travel
three-hundred-odd kilometers from
Jodhpur to Jaisalmer. The weather
forecast for the next few days was
"fine, 43 C." I said a quick prayer to the
Lord Ganesha, Remover of Obstacles,
to keep the passenger load light, so I
didn't have to rub sweaty arms with
total strangers and breathe the hot
desert air bouncing off their necks.

I had no idea that buses in Rajasthan sell tickets for the seats and then
stop along the way to pick up extra
people, who stand for the duration
of the trip. There is also room on the
roof if needed, for luggage or even
more passengers. For an extra 10
rupees, the attendant placed my
belongings in the trunk under the bus.
I was thankful for this consideration.
I'd had visions of my underwear floating away one by one from the top of

the bus, and I had no desire to leave
such an intimate Hansel-and-Gretel-
style trail across the desert.

As our journey started, the skies
darkened ominously, and I could see
sand dunes, scrub, the occasional
camel, and herds of goats with their
shepherds ... all gradually fading
from view. Sure enough, we were
heading directly into a sandstorm.
The windows were quickly closed so
that the sand wouldn't fly in, but lack
of ventilation turned the interior into a
steaming sauna. Sand lashed loudly
against the bus, and visibility dropped
almost to zero, as we lurched through
the most inhospitable terrain I'd ever
encountered in my life. As the six-hour
ride went by like this, I couldn't imagine what it would have been like if I'd
gone for the so-called cheap bus.

Upon arrival at Jaisalmer, an
autorickshaw whisked me upward to
the more than eight-hundred-year-
old Jaisalmer Fort, standing high
on a hill like a sentinel guarding the
sprawl of new settlements below.
The whole city was once contained
within its golden sandstone walls,
and even today, more than a quarter
of the population still lives inside it.
My guesthouse was in the fort, too,
and I had a room that afforded a
splendid view of the plains.

After the heat I endured on the bus
ride, the weather was beginning to
worry me. I was told that I was brave
being here in May, but in June the
temperatures would rise even further.
To avoid the worst of the sun, I
scheduled my city tours for the morn-

RAJASTHAN

ings. But because I was in Jaisalmer, I couldn't miss the camel trekking.

The idea of a camel trek is to spend a couple of days exploring the desert, going to ghost town villages and temples, and listening to singing guides and flatulent camels. As I could not think of anything more horrendous than being on a camel for more than a day in the oven that is the Thar Desert at that time of year, I booked myself on the "junior tour." This would last seven hours and included a short camel ride.

The excursion started out in a jeep that stopped at several sites before taking a break in a small village in the middle of nowhere. Of course, visitors in these remote parts mean the local children come rushing out to see them, and after it was established that I was from "Australia ... Ricky Ponting!" (the Aussie cricket hero much revered in India), the call went up, a team of players magically materialized, and I was involved in an impromptu game of cricket.

The kids handed me a bat, and I took in the field placing that included a genuine cow standing at the cow corner, just backward of deep square leg. An early one through the defenses, and ... out! My batting inning was over embarrassingly fast. But luck intervened shortly after in the form of a drinks break, and my poor performance went without comment as out wandered a local woman holding up a bottle and asking me the all-important question: "Pepsi?"

When we arrived later at another village farther into the desert, the driver handed our small tour group over to a new guide, eleven-year-old Mr. Singh— "Three years' experience, no school for English"—and his nine-year-old trusty sidekick, Raju. In the age of child labor law litigation, somewhere a travel agent in Jaisalmer city thought it was wise to send four Westerners out into the Thar Desert with two children.

We were only on camels for about ninety minutes, on our way to the Khuri dunes. The desert is mostly sand, scrub, and rough dirt, but Khuri is postcard perfect with endless, undisturbed dune formations. I could see the ripples in the sand, with no footprints for miles, though I was soon distracted. With my legs dangling down the sides of the heaving camel, essentially all of the pressure was on my hamstrings at my groin. Hence, I now know what it feels like to be a giant wishbone. At Khuri we enjoyed a truly serene sunset, and by nine thirty the stars were out. The rest of my tour group planned to remain overnight, but I headed back to Jaisalmer.

At around eleven I arrived at the guesthouse, as dry and thirsty as I'll ever be, but thankful that I was safely indoors. My bastion window banged against the wall, as another sandstorm brewed. I thought of those in my group who were staying out in the elements, facing a dirt-blown night and another long day on the camels. They needed every ounce of luck that I could send their way. We were facing another scorcher. My guesthouse owner had informed me, "Hot tomorrow, 44 C, I think."

Camel treks

Treks on camels can be the most amazing experience of your India trip—provided your back can stand it! Travel agents in Jaisalmer offer rides to different destinations, lasting one to five days. If you're unsure about how well you'll stand up to the rigors of a camel-back ride, choose a short one. Travel agents are happy to take tourists out in jeeps to the really scenic spots where they have the camels waiting.

Jaisalmer Desert Festival

January and February are pleasant months to visit Jaisalmer, when the weather is cooler and the Desert Festival is on. Snake charmers, puppeteers, and acrobats all come together to entertain tourists, and several competitions—such as the turban-tying challenge in which foreigners are encouraged to participate—take place every day. Prizes are given for entertaining achievements. For example, possession of the longest mustache. As well, the handsomest men in the gathering might find themselves competing for the Mr. Desert title. In the evenings, there are camel races and great local food. You can find out more about the festival and other activities in Rajasthan at the region's official website.

www.rajasthantourism.gov.in

KARAULI

Paul and Melissa Yeung live like royalty in Karauli

While in Rajasthan, we were determined to spend a few nights at one of the state's many palace hotels. We looked at all the options available to us in the medium price range and finally settled on Bhanwar Vilas, the royal residence of the former "seventeen-gun-salute" Maharaja of Karauli.

The business of gun salutes—a charming tradition among India's royalty—requires some explaining. At the time of Independence in 1947, British-ruled India had within its borders hundreds of states, each with its own Raja (king). The Rajas who were more powerful than the others were elevated to the status of Maharaja (great king). The importance and prestige of a Maharaja could be estimated easily by the number of gun salutes he commanded. The maximum was twenty-one, and there were only five states whose Maharajas were accorded as many. Because the Maharaja of Karauli, a remote province in Rajasthan, was a seventeen-gun-salute leader, this probably meant he could dominate

RAJASTHAN

a nine-gun lightweight like the Maharaja of Sonepur, but would lose in a salute-off with a maximum-gun-salute big shot like the Maharaja of Mysore.

With the coming of Independence, the various Maharajas and Rajas of India lost their power, and they all had to scramble to find alternative sources of income to support their expensive lifestyles. While the royal purses were taken away by the government, the palaces were still their private property, and tourism was an obvious way to go to. So our Maharaja of Karauli, as with many others like him, gave rooms in his palace out on rent and became a hotelier. His royal Art Deco residence, built in the 1930s, became Bhanwar Vilas Palace hotel, and now any yahoo off the street can stay within its walls for a few thousand rupees a night.

As our taxi drove through the impressive palace gates, we had our first glimpse of Bhanwar Vilas, a citrine-colored jewel of a building with many arched doors and windows. It looked comfortable, compact, and cozy. It wasn't as grand as, say, the Rambagh Palace hotel in Jaipur or the Taj Lake Palace hotel in Udaipur, but with its landscaped gardens; wide, cool verandahs; and elegant rooms arrayed around a sheltered open courtyard, it had an Old World charm of its own.

The building had definitely seen better days, but the ghosts of grandeur still lingered, and we could easily imagine the Maharaja living there, hosting exalted guests of state,

organizing glittering banquets, and discharging his royal duties. At the front porch, we were met by a very old man dressed in royal livery and an oversize orange turban. He was a retainer of the palace, he said, and had served the Maharaja's family for many decades. With a pinch of red paste, he marked our foreheads with the traditional *tikaa* of welcome, and then escorted us into the palace.

The large reception area attested to the Maharaja's prowess in hunting. Stuffed tigers and heads of boars and other wild animals were mounted everywhere. Family portraits of generations past hung from the light blue walls. We quickly finished all the check-in formalities and were then led to our room—a luxuriously appointed, high-ceilinged living space with every amenity we could think of.

The forty-third and current Maharaja, Shri Krishan Chandra Pal, still lived with his family in one section of the property, which was off-limits, but the rest of the palace has been converted into luxury suites and rooms. Unlike the luxury suites, the rooms were not strictly "heritage"—they were added when the palace was being converted into a hotel—but we didn't let that bother us. After all, every top-rung palace hotel in Rajasthan had to construct new rooms to accommodate larger numbers of guests, and we had all the well-preserved public areas at our disposal to explore and enjoy.

In spite of our best intentions to wake up early the next day, we emerged from our room well past the breakfast hour. The palace was quiet, as most of the guests were out sightseeing. We decided to go out as well and find something to eat at a nearby restaurant, but the Bhanwar Vilas's staff was fully prepared for tardy guests like us and reopened the grand dining room. It was an amazing experience, sitting at the long banquet table by ourselves and being served an elaborate breakfast by a battery of staff, who bent low and filled our plates with so much ceremony, one would imagine we were royalty ourselves.

Mealtimes, in fact, were always memorable at the Bhanwar Vilas. The kitchen served up an array of dishes that came from the palace's own book of recipes, and at the end of a busy day of camel cart rides to the village or to the lake, it was fun to dress up and go to the dining room to taste the treats that had pleased many a royal palate. The Maharaja apparently dined often at the hotel when he was in residence, but during our short stay, he didn't put in an appearance.

Even without the royal company, we fully enjoyed the hotel and spent many happy hours relaxing with a cup of coffee in one of the public rooms and admiring all its treasures. The service was so gracious and personal, we felt thoroughly spoilt and wondered how we'd ever readjust to staying in ordinary hotels. The friendliness of the residents of Karauli, always ready to smile and wave when we passed by, added to the experience, and we even found

ourselves roped into an impromptu game of cricket outside the palace compound by a bunch of village kids who clapped and cheered as we took a swing at the bat.

When it was time to leave, it was like saying farewell to dear friends. The staff gathered on the porch to wish us a safe journey and gave us a small memento to remember them by. After Karauli, we continued with our tour of Rajasthan and visited many celebrated palaces and forts, but the brief stay at the home of our seventeen-gun-salute Maharaja remained our fondest memory.

Getting to Karauli

The village of Karauli lies southeast of Jaipur, and you can do the distance in less than four hours by car. Karauli does not have its own railway station, but is serviced by the railhead in Gangapur, thirty kilometers away. There are regular buses traveling from Gangapur to Karauli, and the bus stop is near the Bhanwar Vilas Palace.

Bhanwar Vilas Palace

http://bhanwarvilas.com
www.karauli.com

Living like kings

For more on royal accommodations in Rajasthan, continue on to the following essay and go to Helene Shapiro's essay on page 94.

RAJASTHAN

General Rajasthan

Vir Sanghvi reminisces about the palace hotels of Rajasthan

I was eight years old when I first stayed in a palace. My room was large and spacious and dominated by a four-poster bed. The staff wore white uniforms with flowing turbans and bowed deeply each time any member of my family passed by. It was a strange feeling for a child who was otherwise used to the more restricted environs of an apartment in Mumbai. But that was meant to be part of the charm. For a fairly substantial sum of money, anyone could pretend to be a Maharaja for a day. The staff would spoil and pamper you—until the moment you checked out, after which, of course, they wouldn't give you a second look.

This experience was at the Rambagh Palace hotel in Jaipur. Up to a few years before my stay, it had been the home of the Jaipur royal family. When I arrived, all the guest rooms were pretty much as they had been when the Maharaja and Maharani lived there. Even the staff were old family retainers who had now been retrained to perform such functions as housekeeping and room service.

The Rambagh is one of India's grandest palace hotels, but the property fades in comparison to the Lake Palace. The Taj Lake Palace was built as a pleasure parlor for the Maharaja of Udaipur and looks it—a gleaming white structure in the middle of the shimmering waters of the Pichola Lake. Guests reach it by boat, and if they are lucky, as we were, they get to stay in one of the historic suites, where the stained glass windows are hundreds of years old.

By the time I entered my teens, the palace hotel was a pretty standard fixture on the Indian tourist scene. As room rates edged up, the Maharajas decided to ask hotel chains to manage their properties. The Taj hotel group took over both the Rambagh and the Lake Palace. The advantage of professional management is that the food improved, the air-conditioning never failed, and TVs were installed in every room. But something about adding experienced hoteliers seemed to work against the ambience. The palaces were still beautiful, but somehow I felt they seemed slightly more theme-parkish than they had been in the days when the Maharajas ran them.

In Rajasthan, the Maharajas were the medieval equivalent of kings, but the state also had a flourishing aristocracy. Though Maharajas were thin on the ground among my fellow students at the school I went to in central Rajasthan, there was no shortage of the aristocrats. While the rest of us went on to find jobs, many of the nobles decided to go into the hotel business. They had the castles. They had the benefit of a good education. Why did they need to work for anybody else?

The consequence of all this is that the Rajasthan countryside is now dotted with small, successful, independently run palace hotels, most of which are managed by people I went to school with. Because the aristocrats are eager to distance themselves from the chain hotels with their $500-a-night room rates, they have chosen to run them on their own and prices are entirely reasonable. Few of these hotels have the grandeur of the Rambagh or the romance of the Lake Palace, but they are still pretty spectacular in their own right.

Take the Deogarh Mahal near Udaipur, rated by Britain's *Tatler* magazine as one of the world's best hotels. When I read about it, I wondered which of my old school friends was in charge of it. It wasn't till I got to Deogarh that I learned it was owned and managed by my former history teacher.

"Sir," I said with some surprise, "how did you end up managing a hotel?"

The answer was simple enough. Although he was an aristocrat, he could not afford to keep his palace afloat. Sensing an opportunity, he chucked his day job and turned the palace into a hotel. He's never looked back, and the Deogarh Mahal contin-

ues to be regarded as one of India's finest heritage hotels.

So, when people ask me if I know any of the Maharajas who own the new palace hotels, I always respond by saying that not only do I know them, there was a time when many of them used to mark my history exam papers. It's an exaggeration, I know. But it makes for a good story, just like staying in a palace hotel.

Taj palace hotels

Hotels run by this group include the Rambagh Palace in Jaipur and the Taj Lake Palace in Udaipur. To read more about the Lake Palace experience, go to Helene Shapiro's essay on page 94.

www.tajhotels.com

Deogarh Mahal
www.deogarhmahal.com

RAJASTHAN

MT. ABU

Mark Moxon gives in to "guidebookese" at the temples of Mt. Abu

According to my guidebook, there was precious little going on in the small town of Mt. Abu, the only hill station in Rajasthan and the summer resort of the state's erstwhile Rajput kings. I'd only stopped there to break up a long and tiring journey north and wasn't expecting any surprises, but after hanging round the place for a while, I realized that my guidebook's opinion of it was utterly false.

Sufficiently off the beaten path, the town surrounding picturesque Nakki Lake was instead a haven for Indian travelers. The general lack of Westerners was a major part of Mt. Abu's appeal—I could watch the locals at play without having to screen out the impact of foreign tourism. But what really made Mt. Abu such an unforgettable experience for me were the Delwara Jain temples. They were, without doubt, the most impressive pieces of architecture I had seen in India, and that includes the Taj Mahal and all the Mughal tombs I could muster the energy to explore.

As I wandered into the complex, I bought a slim, locally published guide and marveled at its overwrought prose: "The profundity of sculptured splendor is beyond fitting description. The marble has yielded itself with a loving docility to fastidious chiseling ... No description or drawing can convey an adequate expression of the great beauty and the delicately carved compositions of human beings and animal effigies." Reading this, I thought that if the temples were even a quarter of what was described so passionately, my trip wouldn't be wasted.

It wasn't.

If you can possibly imagine walking into a carved-ivory bubble, well, the interiors of the Delwara temples were something like that. The guidebook, effervescent though it was, had got it spot-on. The ceilings of the corridors surrounding the central shrines were thick with fine detailing. Every square inch was covered in geometric designs, many-armed gods and goddesses from the Hindu and Jain pantheons, scenes from everyday life, and excerpts from the lives of the *tirthankars*, those enlightened beings of the Jain religion. The range of artistry was beyond comprehension. To believe Delwara, you really do have to see it for yourself. My words would only sound like more of that guidebookese. What can I say except, "The profundity of sculptured splendor is beyond fitting description ..."

Interestingly, the Delwara Temples were the only ones I have visited where photography is totally forbidden. There was no camera charge because cameras were *not* allowed. Oddly enough, I was pleased. Not only did this save my reeling off rolls of film trying to capture the layers of intricacy, but it also saved my discovering the expensive way that it is impossible to capture effectively such an immense work of art. No doubt Britain's National Archives contain some old black-and-white pictures of the temples, but that possibility aside, images of Delwara's marble brilliance reside only in the minds of those who have been there.

Getting to Mt. Abu

The nearest airport is in Udaipur. By rail, the most convenient hub cities are New Delhi, Mumbai, Jaipur, and Ahmedabad. A good network of roadways also connects the hill station with the rest of Rajasthan and neighboring states.

The Delwara Temples

Of the two main temples at Delwara, the Vimal Vasahi dates from 1031 and took fifteen hundred artisans and twelve hundred laborers fourteen years to build. The Luna Vasahi, dating from 1230, is even more impressive than its neighbor. As for Delwara's three other temples, they are pleasant but have nothing on these two. The temples are located a few kilometers outside Mt. Abu.

More about tirthankars

Tirthankars are considered the "avatars" of the Jain religion—human beings who have attained a degree of enlightenment, like Lord Buddha. Jainism, like Buddhism, is an offshoot of the Hindu religion, but less celebrated because it did not cross the Indian border and go abroad.

Exploring Mt. Abu

Like all hill stations in India, Mt. Abu has a number of "points"—places in and around the town from where you catch the best views—in this case of the surrounding Aravalli mountain range. Horses are available on hire, and you can negotiate a trip that includes a certain number of these points for a fixed rate. In the evenings, take a boat out into Nakki Lake, a winding body of water that was supposedly scratched out by a Hindu god with his nails (*nakki*). The lake also has some lovely walkways along its shores.

SHEKHAWATI

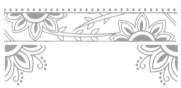

Rinoti Amin chases nomads around the Shekhawati countryside

"I want to meet the nomads!" Since coming to the Shekhawati region in north Rajasthan, this has

RAJASTHAN

been my constant refrain, and Rajesh, my guide, is happy to oblige. "Umm ... there is a camp of the Lohar people some distance away from here," he says, speaking of a nomadic tribe of blacksmiths. "We'll have to catch them early in the day before they leave to work."

Appeased, I settle down to enjoy my curry dinner. Rajesh, in my opinion, is the best kind of guide. If he finds it odd that I am so insistent about wanting to see nomads, he gives no sign of it. You see, usually it is the province's marvelous collection of painted *havelis* (historic mansions) that draws a handful of culturally inspired tourists here. Shekhawati's location on the ancient Silk Route made the locals rich, and in the 1800s and early 1900s they built mansions that testified to their wealth and artistic sensibilities. The *haveli* owners competed to have the biggest and finest murals painted on their ceilings and walls, and in the process, transformed Shekhawati into a massive art gallery.

The early murals had predictable mythological themes, but at the turn of the twentieth century, the mansions began to display a bizarre hybrid of motifs. The artists wanted to appear modern, and among the paintings of Hindu gods and goddesses, they added trains, planes, Englishmen and Englishwomen, and whatever else they thought was fashionably Occidental. Some even managed to merge the two, dispatching Lord Krishna and his consort Radha on a pleasure drive in their brand new automobile, for instance,

while Lord Vishnu took his ease and listened to music playing on the gramophone.

But a *haveli* tour will have to wait. At the crack of dawn the next day, I am off with Rajesh on his motorcycle, riding through the Shekhawati countryside in search of nomads. We pass quaint hamlets and millet fields. The *khejri* trees, whose fruits were part of our last night's dinner, are aplenty, but the Lohar nomads are nowhere to be found. As we come to a halt, a baffled Rajesh scratches his head and mumbles, "I promise you, they were right here a few days ago. They must have moved."

This is to be expected, since they are nomads, but I am still disappointed, and the expression on my face prompts Rajesh to say, "Okay, let's ride on to the village of Parsurampura. It's nearby, and somebody there is bound to know where the Lohars went."

Crossing a dry riverbed and maneuvering the motorcycle over sandy tracts, we finally reach the village at around eight in the morning. Rajesh zigzags through the narrow cobbled streets, telling me that we are going to meet a man named Maharaj.

Maharaj is the old caretaker of a *haveli* called Shamji Saraf, and after our introduction, he offers to show me around this typical Shekhawati mansion. He says nothing about nomads, and I wonder if my crafty guide hasn't brought me here under false pretext, to make sure I don't miss the main attraction of the area. But as Maharaj offers us tea, I find myself forgetting about the nomads for an hour or so.

We sit under the shade of a banyan tree and enjoy his hospitality while a flock of peacocks prances around us.

When our teacups are empty, the caretaker leads me inside the Shamji Saraf *haveli*. As I cross the courtyard, I find myself looking straight into the eyes of an old woman, who stares back at me from a detailed mural painted on the opposite wall. Next to her is a spinner, smiling as she works at her spinning wheel, and an English lady with a parasol and brightly colored shoes. This tableau is the most evocative piece of artwork I have seen in a while, and I stand in front of it, trying to comprehend the artistic passion from which the elderly woman and her company must have sprung forth.

Maharaj continues with his tour, pointing out other interesting aspects of the *haveli* with a stick, but it is the image of the old woman that my mind lingers over long after we have thanked him for his time and set off again on our motorcycle. After a good bit of riding, we come up to an ancient step-well, which sits dry and deserted, and decide to stop for a break. I flop down near the well, trying to ease the stiffness of my limbs and reconcile myself to the possibility that we might not find the nomads, when the sound of shuffling footsteps draws my attention toward a pair of scruffy young boys. They come nearer and sit down a little distance away, as if uncertain of their welcome. "What is your name?" I ask the taller of the two.

"Kaalu," he responds, "because I am so *kaala* [dark]."

I do not know how to respond to this simple acceptance of the color discrimination that is still prevalent in Indian society. "Why aren't you at school?" I ask instead.

"I don't go to school because my family is always moving to a different place," Kaalu says. "We go from village to village, singing songs and playing music. We came to this village to sing at a wedding. My mother will sing and my father will play the *dhol* [drum]. Everyone in my family sings."

His description sparks a memory of something I had read recently about a tribe of nomadic bards in Rajasthan, and when I mention this, Rajesh's vigorous nodding confirms my suspicion. Indeed, Kaalu must belong to a tribe of itinerant musicians who wander throughout the state, entertaining villagers with songs about kings and wars and Rajasthan's glorious past.

I have found my nomads after all, even if they are in the form of two little boys. For the next few moments, I don't know what to say. I am as much in awe of Kaalu as he is of me. Hesitantly, I ask, "Will you sing a song for us?"

At first he shakes his head, reluctant, but after some cajoling, he takes two small pieces of glass out of his pocket and starts clicking them together in a desert beat. His companion finds an empty can of Coke to use as a makeshift drum. Rajesh joins them, clapping enthusiastically.

Lying back against a rock, I let Kaalu's full-throated voice wash over me. I have a million questions to ask him about his nomadic life. Perhaps, he'll even take me to meet his family.

But all that will come later. Right now, I am happy to just listen to him sing.

Getting to Shekhawati

From the nearest airport in Jaipur, you can take a taxi or bus for the 185-kilometer journey to Shekhawati. The railway line connecting Delhi, Jaipur, and Bikaner passes through the Shekhawati region as well, and that gives travelers many convenient locations for starting their Shekhawati trips. Once you are in Shekhawati, you will have to depend on the local transport network of buses, shared jeeps, and autorickshaws that connects the small villages in the region. Distances are not significant, and walking or bicycling is sometimes the quickest way to explore.

The nomads of Rajasthan

Camel and horse tours in Shekhawati province often give travelers an opportunity to interact with Rajasthan's great many tribes of nomads, who travel long distances in this desert terrain to graze their cattle or ply their trades. The most visible among them are the Gaduliya Lohar, who take their blacksmithing skills from village to village in their colorfully decorated carts. The itinerant lifestyle, unique attire, and customs of these elusive people make them worth seeking out.

Eco-friendly lodging

Apani Dhani in Shekhawati's Nawalgarh village offers "rural" accommodation in quaint, hand-painted huts built with mud and straw. The hotel runs a farm on the property, which supplies the kitchen with organic ingredients. In the arid, water-starved Shekhawati region, Apani Dhani functions as an inspiring example of sustainable living. For example, guests are encouraged to bathe in the traditional Indian style with buckets and mugs to reduce the wasting of water. Food is served on plates made of leaves, which can later be composted. Apani Dhani offers excursions on horseback and activities with locals such as cooking classes and traditional craft making. It is located near the Nawalgarh bus stand (five hundred meters) and the railway station (one kilometer). Autorickshaws are available, but if you are traveling light, you can do the distance by foot.

www.apanidhani.com

Jan Polatschek learns to "Look up!" in Shekhawati province

"Jan, why India? Why now?"

The answers are that India is close to Thailand, where I live, and there's no time like the present. Both are true. Very true. But the real reason is that my friends in Mumbai, Paawan and Sushma, invited me to an auspicious family celebration.

I met Paawan and Sushma Seksaria in Hanoi four years ago when they were on their honeymoon. Now they have a one-and-a-half-year-old son, Agastya. And when a Hindu boy reaches that age, he must endure a traditional hair-cutting—the hair sacrifice ceremony known as Mundan Sanskar.

Paawan and Sushma and I meet in Jaipur, and the next morning we rendezvous with Paawan's parents. In a two-car caravan we drive north to the Shekhawati region to the town of Nawalgarh and the family *haveli*. *Haveli* is translated as a "traditional, often ornately decorated residence." This particular two-story *haveli* is the largest and most prominent building in Nawalgarh. It was built about sixty years ago by Paawan's great-grandfather who was a successful cotton speculator and trader. A plaque in his honor is installed at the Chicago Rice and Cotton Exchange.

The approach to the one-hundred-room Seksaria *haveli* is impressive. The exterior is a series of archways of different widths. The carved stonework above the arches is intricate and artistic. The full complement of household staff greets us at the top of the driveway. The chief housekeeper escorts us through the grassy central courtyard to one of the four smaller inner courtyards. The tile walkways and floors have elegant geometric designs. The surrounding upper walkways and bedroom doors look down onto this family area.

For two days I accompany the family as we visit several temples and shrines in the area. These religious sites are significant for my hosts, their extended family, and their ancestors. At our very first temple visit, we mount the stairs to the crowded main sanctuary. Paawan and Sushma present their small son to the priest, who proceeds to clip large swatches of the boy's hair. The hair is left behind as an offering in the temple. The parents are happy; the grandparents are beaming and proud; and Agastya, well, he is feeling around his shaved head, and I must say he is not happy at all. Perhaps that is part of the meaning of the ceremony. The boy is learning to face surprises, disappointment, and sacrifice.

Paawan and his parents are the most generous hosts. We eat lunch in restaurants on the road, but breakfast and dinner are served at the *haveli*. Since the family are strict vegetarians, the cooks provide an unending array of salads; savory, crunchy desert beans; corn or peas and cottage cheese in a rich butter-and-tomato sauce; chutneys; mango pickles; yogurt soups; and the ubiquitous dal, prepared each day with different ingredients—sometimes a bit spicy. My favorite dish is a slightly sweet wheat germ pudding. Several types of bread—wheat or rice, baked or fried—are always available from the constantly circling servants.

Because the Seksarias understand my needs as an independent traveler, one day they just turn me loose in Nawalgarh. I wend my way through the narrow streets, past the shops and markets. My destination is the area's famous painted *havelis*.

Just like my "home" here in Nawalgarh, the large *havelis* in the Shekhawati region were built by wealthy industrial merchants and traders from the late eighteenth to the early twentieth century. Two of the *havelis* are now museums. The Morarka Haveli Museum focuses on conservation. The Podar Haveli Museum restores its paintings using the ancient system of dyes from ground minerals and vegetables. Vividly colorful frescoes cover the outer walls, eaves, and inner walls of these splendid ancestral homes. In Nawalgarh and in surrounding towns, I also find several abandoned and sadly decaying *havelis* where the images on the walls are fading.

One of my secrets of traveling is to look up, straight up. In the old buildings of Shekhawati I see decorated ceilings and carved brackets, gargoyles, lintels, and pillars. I stretch just a little

bit to spot elephants and snakes, flowers and birds, and the most ingenious, fanciful designs. Beneath the eaves I find the deserted *havelis'* treasures—bright paintings forever protected from the sun and the rain. Look up! There is so much to discover.

Getting to Shekhawati
Go to the fact file in the previous essay.

Morarka Haveli Museum
http://morarkahavelimuseum.com

Podar Haveli Museum
www.podarhavelimuseum.org

AGRA

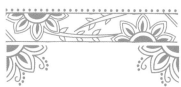

A. Murray
seeks out unusual
views of the Taj Mahal

I remember a Russian tour guide once telling me something quite interesting. "There are two man-made structures in the world whose beauty has never been fully captured in photographs. One is the Saint Basil's Cathedral in Moscow's Red Square. The other is Agra's Taj Mahal."

Standing in Agra, at the entrance to the Taj complex from where the "classic" shot of the structure is usually taken, I had to concede that there was truth to her claim. The long ornamental lake was directly in front of me, and beyond it stood the marble wonder with its four towers and onion-shaped dome in dead center. I was so familiar with this angle that the Taj appeared somewhat spiritless and one-dimensional, like a caricature of its own photographs.

There had to be other perspectives from which to view the Taj Mahal. Unusual angles that captured its different moods. Perhaps, distance was one element that could be used to introduce some exciting new variations. With this thought in mind, I began to explore the area around the Taj, and I was delighted to discover some excellent vantage points from the rooftop terraces of the budget hotels in the Tajganj neighborhood.

My first look at the Taj from one such terrace was in the minutes preceding sunset. The end of the day was still stiflingly hot, as are all summer days in Agra, but from the top of this four-story building, I could catch the slightest of breezes as I gazed. And it was simply that—an exercise in gazing. Looking over the blue roofs with a heat haze shimmering off the buildings, past the rusty red and white marble Taj Mahal gate, through to the dome and minarets. Just taking it in. While the sky gradually lost color and the dome turned many shades of purple before finally disappearing into the night.

The search for more long-range viewing spots took me to the Musamman Burj in Agra Fort next, where I found the tower's balcony, another great perspective from a distance of a few kilometers. But the spectacular view from this location depends on the day being bright and clear. I happened to be there once when a thick smog was settling on the horizon, and I could only look on in horror as a veil of smoke and sulfur dioxide gradually wrapped the Taj Mahal in its folds and made it disappear entirely from view.

My newfound interest in long-distance compositions kept me busy jumping on and off any elevated ground I could find around the Taj, and it was two full days before I could concentrate on something else that the classic Taj Mahal photograph cannot capture: the beauty of the inlay designs that embellish the structure's surfaces. Turquoise from Tibet, sapphire from Sri Lanka, carnelian from Baghdad, and jade from China, all combined with an unbelievably fine hand to create stunning floral and arabesque motifs in the signature Mughal style. The gradations of color and the play of light and shade achieved by mixing and matching bits of precious stones were so magnificent that I was momentarily stunned by the sheer scale of the work in front of me.

I must hasten to add here that the different viewing options I have put down are mere suggestions. It isn't my place to comment on how someone chooses to admire such an object of near perfection, but I

UTTAR PRADESH

must confess that it pains me to see people spend all their time organizing a customary photo-op with their spouses on the "lover's bench," with the monument tidily in the background. Or queuing up in front of the entrance to take the classic snapshot. It seems a pity to waste this great opportunity to find a new vista and take home your very own memory of the Taj Mahal.

Day trip to Agra

There's much to see in the city of Agra besides the Taj Mahal—Akbar's tomb, for example, and the Agra Fort. If you're going all the way there just for the Taj, it is possible to make a day trip out of it. Convenient trains from Delhi leave early in the morning and return to the capital in the evening. Otherwise, you can hire a taxi for this two-hundred-kilometer journey. Another option is to make the Keoladeo Ghana National Park (see page 181) your base for your Agra visit.

The Qutab Minar in Delhi has the world's tallest brick minaret

Rickshaws and autorickshaws await passengers

General North India

Secret Gardens

Where to hide away from the touring masses

Quiet corners are a precious commodity in a country as crowded as India. After a couple of years of living in Delhi, the only place I have discovered where I can truly be alone is my apartment in the Defence Colony. And that too just at night. Most of the work that has gone into this book has happened between one and four in the morning, when the city, like an overactive toddler, has worn itself out and finally gone to sleep, and the ambient noises of automobiles, animals, hawkers, and pedestrians have ceased for a short space of time.

During the day, it is almost impossible to walk twenty paces without running into people, and even if you happen to find a perfect spot to be alone with your thoughts, a couple of inquisitive kids and at least one stray dog will follow faithfully at your heels. Aside from hiding away in my apartment, the only other way that I can step back from the frenetic activity going on around me and enjoy a few private moments is by converting these intrusions into scenic background props and constructing secret gardens on my own terms.

Visit Delhi's busy PVR Saket cinema complex after midnight and you'll understand what I mean. These are my favorite time and place to just sit with coffee and a friend and feel a strange sense of privacy among the cheerful, late-night moviegoers, who let down their guard in the anonymity of the dark and amuse everybody around with their good-natured jokes and tomfoolery. Scores of upscale restaurants, bookstores, cafés, and juice stalls are laid out in this small area that houses one of Delhi's best movie theaters, and it's fun to just *be* in those unlikely hours of the morning, among the young adults as they snack and smoke and get into impromptu popcorn fights and seem in no hurry to go home either.

While working on the essays included in this chapter, I realized that like me, many of the writers had also abandoned any hope of genuine seclusion and built their own secret gardens by

detaching their minds from the busyness of their surroundings. Naomi Naam, for instance, writes about a magical world he created in the company of injured birds inside a busy temple precinct in Delhi. And Beverley Millar used a burst of rain to cut herself off from other visitors in a popular park in the capital, arriving at a plane of consciousness where nothing existed but herself and the turbulence of an Indian monsoon.

Outside urban areas, it is easier to come across oases of solitude, and they seem all the more attractive for the remoteness of their locations. Kate Wiseman's discovery of the sleepy village of Vashisht, hidden in the wilderness of the Kullu Valley, is a great example of such a precious find. The natural hot springs of Vashisht have attracted semiresident bands of musicians and hashish smokers who live like the flower children of the sixties, and Kate enjoyed a few days in the laid-back little hippie world they have created.

Overall, secret gardens haven't as much to do with geography as they have with feelings. The beauty of these encounters is in their randomness. You cannot plan them. You cannot always seek out your secret garden. At an odd time, at an odd place, and invariably in a crowd if you are in India, it will simply creep up on you and welcome you into its tranquility.

NEW DELHI

Beverley Millar savors a monsoon moment in Delhi

The interesting thing about most public gardens in Delhi is that they all seem to contain a bit of history. Not only do they show up as manicured bits of green on the city map, they also give visitors the pleasure of exploring some beautiful old ruins.

While I was in the capital, I went to the Lodi Garden almost every other day. I'd carry a picnic with me and join the lovers and small family groups who came in the evening to get away from the intrusions of city life. Built in the fifteenth and sixteenth centuries, the park serves as a graveyard for the Lodi and Sayyid dynasties, and there are several tombs still standing—all eerie, crumbly, and overgrown with ancient-looking creepers. I was often tempted to examine the ruins more closely, but others warned me of snakes, so I kept my distance.

Locals who came to this garden mostly stayed around the periphery or used a jogging track that was lit up at night for runners to make use of. Not too many people explored the vast green space at the center or even knew what it had to offer besides the old tombs and rolling grassland. A bonsai park, for example, was a hidden away feature. It was a little tricky to find (and to get out of), and I treated this patch as my private domain whenever I visited.

There was also an ancient, arched bridge that cut through a portion of the gardens and was believed to have been built during the reign of Mughal emperor Akbar. I came upon it quite by chance one day when I was seeking shelter from a heavy downpour. I was soaked through by the time I reached it, so I just ran to the middle and let the cool rain wash over me. It was one of the most freeing moments of my life, standing alone with my arms and face raised up to a heavy gray sky as it broke open with deep rolls of thunder.

It was a typical Indian monsoon rain—on and on it went, cutting me off from the rest of the world. Like an unsupervised child, I took off my shoes and splashed around in the puddles, feeling the mud squish pleasurably between my toes. My soul felt cleansed in the relentless downpour, and I laughed out loud in the sheer joy of the moment, knowing nobody could hear me. Finally, out of breath, I sat hugging my knees on the bridge for almost an hour, listening to the frogs croaking from the nearby pond.

I waited until the rain let off completely to find an autorickshaw to take me back to my hotel. In the twenty minutes or so it took to reach my lodgings in the Paharganj neighborhood, I dried out completely, and there was no cold or cough afterward—thank God!—to mar the beauty of that once-in-a-lifetime experience.

Lodi Garden

The garden adjoins the India International Center on Lodi Road. Inside it, the massive tomb of Mohammad Shah, built in 1450, is clearly visible from the road.

Naomi Naam retreats among the injured birds of Delhi

The first time I visited the Digambar Jain temple in Delhi, it was only to admire the interesting architecture of its many sandstone crests and crowns. I had no idea that the followers of the Jain religion ran a humane institution for birds in the yard of this seventeenth-century structure until I stumbled upon it.

During all my research on Delhi, I had not noticed any mention of the Jain Bird Hospital. Yet here it was, treating at least sixty newly injured birds every day and giving them a temporary home until they were well enough to fly away. Judging by the number of birds perched around the yard, it looked as if many had returned, perhaps to acknowledge

the gift of rebirth they had found here. Born wild, they had lost their fear of humans while being tended at the hospital, and they pecked happily at the grains of wheat that I held out in my hand. The deep silence of the temple was enlivened by their constant chirping, and I felt so at peace that first day that I went back to spend many twilight hours in the company of these little feathered creatures.

Over time, I became acquainted with some of the hospital staff and learnt how they came to gather wounded birds in such numbers. During summer, the birds collapsed in the intense Delhi heat, and in winter the dense fog that hung over the city caused them to fly into electric poles and moving vehicles. The number of patients increased sharply during kite-flying season in Delhi. The poor birds got tangled in the kite strings and were often brought to the hospital with serious wounds. The kite strings were coated with powdered glass (to make them sharp enough to cut off other kites during competitions), and this further exacerbated the injuries.

Since the hospital was guided by the Jain philosophy of not harming even the smallest living creature, the recuperating birds were fed a vegetarian diet of vegetables, nuts, and grains. And—this bit of information I found very interesting—the hospital never treated nonvegetarian birds. The thought that wounded carrion eaters like vultures would be turned away because they fed on flesh was a little disturbing, but the Jain religion had strict rules about vegetarianism, and there was little to be done about it.

I made it a point to visit the hospital every Saturday, when hundreds of healthy birds were released from the roof. Though I had made no contribution in giving them back their health, I felt an immense sense of pleasure in witnessing their return to freedom.

A particular feathered friend I had in the crowd was one very friendly pigeon who seemed to have taken up permanent residence in the yard. I recognized him every time because the feathers on his wing had broken off in a peculiar way. The pigeon knew I always carried some goodies on me, and as soon as I arrived he would fly up and stick his head into my pockets. I felt sad when I heard later from one of the doctors that the pigeon had had a hard time of it since his recovery. For some reason, the flock to which he had belonged refused to accept him back, and after many attempts to reintegrate, the bird finally gave up and made the hospital his home.

When it was time for me to leave Delhi, I felt I was abandoning the pigeon the same way his flock had done. I brought him a pack of Maries, a brand of cookies he favored, and explained why I had to go back home. Cocking his head, the bird stared at me. Then he rubbed his neck in my palm for a few moments, accepting my explanation and letting me know that it was okay, before he flew away.

Jain Bird Hospital

The hospital runs on donations, and even small monetary contributions of a rupee or two are accepted with gratitude.

Digambar Jain Temple
Netaji Subhas Marg
Chandni Chowk
New Delhi

KURUKSHETRA

Robin Searle guides you to the ancient town of Kurukshetra

After a grueling week of cycling through the foothills of Himachal Pradesh, we were glad to get back to the plains for the final leg of our overland ride to Delhi. We planned to cover the distance quickly, but the traffic was busy and a couple of punctures slowed us down further. Having missed lunch, we were hungry and thirsty, and when yet another flat tire forced us to stop, we gave up any hope of reaching Delhi that day and turned off into Kurukshetra, the nearest town, to look for a hotel.

Our guidebook barely mentioned Kurukshetra. It only said that the place had the largest water tank in

India. We had no idea that the tank, known as the Brahma Sarovar, was one of the holiest bodies of water in India—the exact point from which Lord Brahma created the earth, according to Hindu beliefs. Nor did we know that the famous eighteen-day climax battle in the epic *Mahabharata* was fought in Kurukshetra, and on this very site, Lord Krishna sang the *Bhagavad Gita* to epic hero Arjuna.

Having checked into the Hotel Krishna, we went to see the Brahma Sarovar, since we had some time to spare before dark. The words *water tank* were misleading. It was like a man-made sea. Apparently, Lord Brahma had laid down the plans for this tank as part of the original creation, though he had left the hard work of excavating it to a much later Aryan king. Sadhus and other holy men were congregated on its banks, and many appeared to have set up semipermanent homes under the alcoves and archways built along the edges of the water.

After walking only part of the way around the tank in the glow of sunset, we headed back to the hotel in the company of some local students. They were amusing, describing themselves as "true Indians, strict vegetarians," and they told us we were the first foreigners they had ever met, which should tell you how many travelers stop in Kurukshetra. We ate cheaply that night, being charged local prices. Everyone in the restaurant was keen to know about our journey. It was like when we had traveled in Pakistan—people are so happy and excited to see a foreigner they just want to talk to you rather than try to rip you off or overcharge you, as often happens in touristed places.

Next morning we went back to the Brahma Sarovar for a final look before setting off for Delhi. The tank was so quiet and peaceful, we simply couldn't leave and decided to stay another day and look around the rest of the town. We checked out of the Hotel Krishna, as it was too pricey for the quality, and tried to find a place that might have cheap camping facilities. We were instead directed to a temple complex where there was a pilgrim's hostel, and we got a large, clean room with two *charpoys* to sleep on for about $1. The hostel was mostly full of schoolgirls who had come from other parts of India to compete in a sports event. They excitedly questioned my partner, Erika, about all sorts of things before running away giggling when she told them I was her husband and we had a "love marriage."

We spent most of the day back at the Brahma Sarovar resting and relaxing in the sun and watching the daily rituals of the holy men living there. The atmosphere was timeless, and hours passed in what seemed like minutes as we gazed out across the water.

While we watched the sunset, as water birds and kingfishers swooped all around us, we made a mental note to check out any potentially interesting place that got only a one-line mention in the guidebooks. Here we were at one of the most sacred places in India, and there were no tourists, no tourist touts, no tourist bazar, or tourist anything.

Well before dawn the next day, we were woken by the sound of pilgrims performing morning *puja* in the temple. This gave us a good early start for the last leg of the journey back to Delhi. We left happy to have discovered a hidden treasure such as Kurukshetra, so close and yet so far from the usual travelers' trails.

Getting to Kurukshetra

The village is located 160 kilometers north of Delhi on the NH 1 national highway. Regular bus services run to Kurukshetra from Delhi and Chandigarh. Kurukshetra has a railway junction, and the village is well connected to neighboring large towns and cities by train as well. More information on Kurukshetra can be found at the region's official government website.

http://haryanatourism.gov.in

Staying in Kurukshetra

There are several *dharamshalas* (rest houses) near the Brahma Sarovar where you will find decent rooms at cheap rates. You can also stay free of charge at the ashram at the Modi Mandir for up to two days.

KASAULI

Amiya Dasgupta is charmed by Kasauli's lack of action

"Nah, you won't enjoy Kasauli," a retired brigadier from the Indian army told me when he heard I was planning a trip there. "There's absolutely nothing to do. Go to Shimla instead, and you'll have a much better time."

I'm glad I didn't pay heed to the brigadier's advice. I was looking for a quiet, scenic break from the stress of living in Delhi, and Kasauli turned out to be just the kind of place I needed at the time.

Perched at an altitude of about eighteen hundred meters, the small hill town offered breathtaking views of the Shimla hills, and the many walks I enjoyed down its rocky trails lined with Himalayan oak, apricot, and plum trees were some of the best I've known. The air was heavy with the scent of pine and wild rose, and there were flowers, fruit, and solitude everywhere.

Most of the old Raj-style houses in Kasauli have been owned by princely Punjab families and retired staff of the Indian army since the time of Independence. With individual garden patches and signature red roofs overlaid with wisteria, they reiterated the Old World atmosphere that hung over the town. It wasn't difficult to understand why artists loved to come here and paint, and I wondered if Kasauli wasn't on the tourist map simply because locals, such as the brigadier, didn't want travelers to arrive in great numbers and spoil the peace. Holidaymakers would mean more hotels, more shops, more restaurants, and in no time at all the quiet cantonment town would metamorphose into another overgrown concrete jungle like the nearby tourist city of Shimla.

While I was in Kasauli, I didn't have much use for company. I made a few friends though in the bazar, where I'd drop in every afternoon for tea and buns. I enjoyed hearing tidbits about the town's history at the famous Guptaji's shop, where everybody is always welcome for chocolates and a chat. A couple of regulars at Guptaji's advised me to stay away from the haunted house in Khetarpal Marg, as its resident ghost follows people who pass by after eight at night. They pointed out an old black-and-white photograph of this abandoned house hanging on the wall. I had a mind to go and check out the house in broad daylight, but visions of the ghost noticing which way I had come from and paying me a night visit kept me from venturing in that direction. The mournful silence that fell after dark was enough to give me the creeps as I walked down Kasauli's lonely, cobbled lanes.

Since there wasn't anything that could be described as "tourist entertainment" in town, I did what the residents of Kasauli do in the evenings: go to the Kasauli Club. Temporary memberships were available, and I spent many cozy hours in the ancient wood-paneled bar in front of a roaring fire, nursing a drink and listening to snatches of conversation that floated my way.

I heard about Kasauli's brewery and distillery from a retired army officer who played rummy with his cronies at the bar every evening. Apparently, this was the highest brewery in the world and was started by the Englishman Edward Dyer in the early 1800s to produce Scottish-grade whiskey. The brewery's single malt—Solan No. 1, named after a nearby town—was very popular in days past. The brewery also had the distinction of producing Lion, Asia's first beer. The next evening, the same gentleman arrived at the club with the news that the upstart girls from the posh Sanawar boarding school were giving Kasauli a bad name, parading up and down Mall Road in ridiculously small clothing. Given the range of his interests, I could see why his friends called him PTI (Press Trust of India).

I was staying at the Alasia Hotel, which was as old as everything else in Kasauli, and after I had concluded my day with a drink and PTI's latest news bulletin at the club, I looked forward to returning to its genteel shabbiness and the British-style dinners the chefs still served up in many courses. After a hearty meal, I'd take a short walk to admire the Kasauli night sky before I turned in.

Having spent most of my life in smoggy, polluted cities, I had no idea that a sky could hold so many stars. Looking up at them, I'd always feel an irresistible urge to swipe my hand and take the brilliant debris back with me to bed. I'd put it in a small pile next to my pillow and fall into a deep sleep, unconscious as the sun crept in and inevitably stole my treasure in the early hours of the morning.

Getting to Kasauli

Travelers can reach Kasauli by bus or taxi from other nearby tourist towns such as Shimla and Chandigarh in about three hours. Kalka is the nearest major railway station that travelers can use to reach Kasauli from other parts of the country.

Kasauli Club

Sadly, since Amiya visited Kasauli, the Kasauli Club burned to the ground. The club has been rebuilt, and although it is no longer the Old World bastion it once was, it is still a place of great camaraderie and local socializing.

www.kasauliclub.in

Alasia Hotel

Information about this historic hotel can be found on the Heritage Hotels of India website in the section on Himachal Pradesh.

www.heritagehotelsofindia.com

VASHISHT

*Kate Wiseman
soaks up the laid-back
vibe of Vashisht*

The monsoon hit Ladakh unexpectedly, and no one was getting in or out. I had escaped just in time, but the heavy rains caught up with me in the Kullu Valley. Thoughts of moving on were quickly dismissed by a fear of death by landslide; this is not an uncommon occurrence once the rain comes, so I decided to maroon myself in the tiny village of Vashisht, a few kilometers north of Manali.

Vashisht is an attractive, quaint, and ultrarelaxed place. Charmed by its convivial atmosphere, many travelers find it agreeable to stay here on a long-term basis. Or, perhaps, seduced by the ready supply of *charas*, the hashish that grows profusely in the Himalayas, they simply find it impossible to move on. Vashisht is small, so within a couple of days I ended up meeting all the usual suspects in all the usual tea shops—the oddballs, music lovers, and potheads of the less-transient traveling population.

In England, we talk about it raining cats and dogs. Here, I figured, it must have rained cows at night when I was asleep. In the narrow and steep paths of this little paradise, there seemed to be more cows per square foot than anywhere else in India. Even my guesthouse at the end of the village came with its own cow.

Vashisht is all about water even without the monsoon. The area has natural hot springs, and two bathing platforms have been custom built in the village's tiny temple: one for men and one for women. The guesthouses and hotels have no need of showers with this facility provided by the village. Daily, I made the pilgrimage to the temple baths. Not daring to face the extreme heat of the pools directly, I waited in line for a tap to become available. It was communal, fun, and extremely hot. There we would be, a motley crowd of locals and tourists, stripped down to our underwear and united in our cleansing rituals. This collective near-nakedness was a strangely leveling experience.

During a break in the rain, a short twenty-minute walk through wooded slopes would take me to another of Vashisht's water features—a waterfall. It wasn't exactly Victoria Falls, but the music of the rushing water tumbling down the mountainside provided the perfect accompaniment to a ginger-lemon-honey tea at the little café nearby.

With living as simple as this, time passed in relaxed, easy strides. The monsoon remained consistent, filling hour after hour with unrelenting rain. I forgot that the mountains had tops, not having seen them for days due to the heavy cloud cover. But it didn't matter as I watched shreds of low-flying clouds floating like candy floss down the valley. The views were good, the food eclectic, the company easy, and the music from regular village jam sessions inspiring. Even in the turbulent throes of a monsoon, Vashisht was a laid-back, hippie-India-in-the-sixties sort of a break, and I'm glad the weather pushed me in that direction.

Hanging out in Vashisht

Vashisht is one of those places that feels made for just hanging out. Guesthouses and hotels are plentiful, and many have open courtyards and/or terraces on rooftops, set up with tables and chairs so that guests can take in a breathtaking 360-degree view of the Himalayas. There is decent food in the numerous restaurants and cafés. Entertainment is also available for the rain-soaked days and nights. Most notably, a semiresident bunch of talented musicians means regular jam sessions all over the village.

SRINAGAR

Mahalakshmi Gupta savors dawn on Srinagar's Dal Lake

At five thirty in the morning, Kashmir's summer capital, Srinagar, hasn't woken up, and it's a perfect time to have Dal Lake to myself. A light mist hangs over the quiet water, but in a few hours, it will look different. It will play out its role as the most celebrated tourist spot in Kashmir and gleam prettily as holidaymakers row across it, enjoying the spectacular scenery surrounding it on all sides. It will serve as the nerve center of Srinagar and provide livelihood to thousands of locals who make money off it in one way or another. In short, the day will begin, and this peace will be disturbed.

But for now, the Dal is at my service alone. I wake a sleeping *shikara* man and hire his boat, a charming piece of confectionary with a gaily painted yellow body, curtains, and frills. Unlike the gondoliers in Venice, the *shikara* men do not sing and make cheerful conversation if you don't want them to. They do not charge 60 Euros for half an hour either. Perfect.

Once the man has untied his boat, I lie back on plush cushions and stare up at the sky, waiting for the veil of mist to roll up and the show to begin. The rhythm of the boatman's oars emphasizes the silence around me, and a hundred pleasurable thoughts chase each other through my head. It's a feeling similar to one I get when I enjoy a good massage. The sensation of pleasure is heightened by the knowledge that soon it will be over ... and it is.

Long, narrow boats laden with fresh flowers, fruits, and vegetables have begun to gather in one corner of the lake. From a distance they look like colorful butterflies, moving toward each other and forming a cluster, which will become the floating market for the next hour or so. Local farmers will sell their produce to market stall owners, who in turn will sell it to the people of Srinagar. I urge my boatman to steer his *shikara* in that direction and watch the goings-on from afar.

The floating market is similar to the more celebrated one in Bangkok, but here on the Dal, the scene does not seem so frenetic. Perhaps this is because the clamor of voices dissipates by the time it reaches me over the vast green waters. My view of the market is always from a distance, so I cannot say for sure. Once the buyers come in their boats to haggle over prices and load and unload goods, I know a new day in Srinagar has officially begun. But the floating market does not disturb my peace. The buyers and sellers are all actors in my little scenario, playing their parts while my *shikara* floats by. We move on and the backdrop changes.

I can see the terraced lawns and cascading fountains of the Mughal Gardens—the vision of paradise of three emperors. The grounds comprise three separate gardens, but I've never actually visited any of them. I only view them from my *shikara*, so they are a vague, beautiful impression of knot gardens and vibrant flowerbeds. Some distance ahead, I also see the white structure of the Hazratbal Mosque, holding up its pearly dome to the early morning sun. The mosque is said to be the repository of one sacred strand of Prophet Mohammed's hair, brought to Kashmir from Medina, and Muslims come to pray here from all over the Kashmir Valley.

The *shikara* travels on, past hovels bending into the water on rotten stilts, past quaint blocks of ancient buildings painted bright orange and yellow, past banks of sparkling green *chinar* trees. Each scene is reflected clearly in the Dal, like a big wet canvas an artist has left out to dry. My boatman indicates that the two hours I paid for are almost up. I tell him to start rowing toward the shore. I collect a handful of willow leaves floating by. When I go back to my lodgings I will soak my feet in willow leaf water, which is excellent therapy for the head and eyes.

Before I get off the *shikara* and bid my boatman goodbye, I look around the lake one last time. The mist has thinned, and the sun is reflecting

off the icy Pir Panjal peaks. People living in the houseboats tied to the shore are going about their morning routines. A few early tourists are out, hiring *shikaras* to enjoy a morning's excursion on the Dal. The peace has traveled on for yet another day.

A houseboat holiday

The houseboats on Dal Lake were built by British officers in the nineteenth century, when the Maharaja of Kashmir denied them the right to buy land in the Kashmir Valley. Today, many of these houseboats are rented out to tourists looking for an unusual accommodation or some peace and quiet. They generally come with an attendant who acts as a valet, keeping the rooms in order, arranging meals, and running little errands. *Shikara* men selling carpets, shawls, woodcarvings, etc. will often cruise by the houseboat to show you their wares, and even masseurs, tailors, and barbers will make a visit if you require their services. Because there have been cases of tourists being cheated, it is advisable to rent your houseboat through a reputable company such as WelcomHeritage. Srinagar houseboat rentals can be found by searching the following website under the state heading of Jammu and Kashmir.

www.welcomheritagehotels.com

Bhedaghat

Maurice Young takes a moonlight trip along the Narmada River

It was a clear, full moon night in Bhedaghat village. I had arranged a rendezvous with Bhanu the boatman, and his canoe was waiting for me when I arrived at the riverside. Clumsily, I stumbled onto the old, patched-up little vessel and settled myself down on a rough wooden bench, and we were off—to see the marble rock formations on the Narmada River by moonlight. The water was calm, and the boat slid noiselessly over its smooth, silvery surface. If it wasn't for Bhanu's thin, shadowy frame leaning back and forth as he worked the oars, I could imagine the canoe moving of its own accord.

We sailed for a few minutes, and then the shore suddenly began to close in on us. It squeezed the river from both sides, making it twist and turn with the effort of pushing forward. I watched Bhanu's back tense and straighten up as he negotiated the curves. How much farther before the marble rocks came into view? I asked.

"Just round the corner, sir," Bhanu replied without taking his eyes off the oars.

The boat took another turn, and yes, there they were: hundred-meter tall cliffs of pure marble, stretching as far as the eye could see. Rising and sloping on both sides of the river, the craggy heads and sharp inclines shining like polished platinum in the light of the full moon.

My first response to this spectacular sight was one of disbelief. The feeling that comes when you encounter something so beautiful you cannot rationalize its existence. Bhanu and I seemed to be floating in a river of molten white metal, the edges of which had dried and hardened into humongous masses. No other color to distract from the lunar vignette of white, silver, and gray. I had heard tales of the Taj Mahal glowing like a pearl on full moon nights. The scene around me was certainly no less captivating—perhaps more so because of the organic nature of its existence.

Bhanu pointed out different shapes in the marble rocks and ascribed them names: a sage in a yoga pose of prayer, a deer, the head of a cow. I sighed with impatience at Bhanu's chatter. I didn't care what resemblances the rocks bore to any human or animal. I wished he would just be quiet and row.

After a spell, Bhanu sensed my mood and cut off the commentary. We sailed maybe a kilometer more in silence, until we hit a turbulent patch of water. A current pulled at our

MADHYA PRADESH

canoe, and I had to hold firmly on to the sides to keep my balance.

"Look ahead, the Narmada River is turning into a waterfall," Bhanu shouted, the exertion of keeping the boat on its course clearly showing in his voice. "It drops a good fifty meters from there, and it won't be safe to get any closer."

We were twenty meters or so from the head of the waterfall, and I could hear the roar of the drop. The fall wasn't a big one, but in the darkness of night it had the power to arouse fear in my nonswimmer's heart.

After watching the rising clouds of spray for a few moments, I motioned to the boatman to turn back. Bhanu rowed hard for a while, and then loosened his grip on the oars once we reentered the calm waters. I asked him to take the boat closer to the water's edge, so I could study more closely the dark, volcanic seams spreading like lace on some parts of its surface. In daylight, they would have appeared green, but the night had turned them into shadowy webs, like imperfections on the surface of the moon.

"You can take some of this marble back with you if you want, sir," Bhanu told me. "The locals of Bhedaghat village quarry it and make decorative items."

Bhanu, of course, knew a dealer in the village who would offer me a very special price. I grinned at this bald attempt at commission-based marketing and said I wasn't interested. Marble bowls and figurines would not be the right mementos of this trip.

The vivid images of the marble rocks I had stored in my memory would serve better than that.

The return journey passed all too quickly. In no time at all we had left the marble rocks behind us and rowed up to the landing platform. The boat collided against the wooden poles and bobbed up and down. Bhanu rushed about to secure it with ropes and then helped me out. I paid him his fare, and he thanked me for the generous tip before turning away to attend to his boat. I headed back to my waiting taxi, walking close to the edge of the water.

It was on an impulse that I had peeled away from my group and come to Bhedaghat to see the rocks. My guidebook had given only a boring description of them, and had I depended on its opinion, I would have never been here. I pulled out the slim *Madhya Pradesh Calls* guide from my backpack and swore at its uselessness. Then I sent it spinning across the water. It landed about ten feet away with a dull plop and gradually disappeared from view.

Bhedaghat marble rocks

Bhedaghat is a small village, just over twenty kilometers from the city of Jabalpur in Madhya Pradesh. Boats can be hired in town on the Narmada River from November to May. If you arrive at any other time, you can enjoy splendid views of the marble rocks from Bhedaghat's Chausat Yogini Temple.

Cultural differences

In editing this piece, there was great debate on whether or not throwing the guidebook into the river was polluting. To the series editor, an American, it definitely was. But to the volume editor, an Indian, the ending made perfect sense. She writes: "Why? Because we make a wish on a candle and float it in the river. Certain parts of the human body that don't burn are 'given' to the river after cremation. After a marriage or religious ceremony we give the wedding garlands to the river. In Hinduism, we give the river our good things and bad."

SHIVPURI FOREST

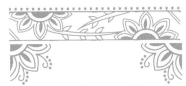

Deepanjana Sarkar befriends a lonely castle in Shivpuri

I knew how I would feel if an invited dinner guest failed to show up and a carefully prepared meal had to be thrown in the trash. Disappointed. Perhaps even a little angry. But I couldn't begin to imagine how I would react—especially if I were a king—if I built a whole new castle to entertain a special guest for a *single* day and the guest didn't bother to come.

That's exactly what happened in 1911 to Maharaja Jiyaji Rao Scindia, who constructed the George Castle to host King George V. The British monarch was traveling in India, and he expressed a desire to go hunting in the Shivpuri forests that belonged to the Scindia royal family. Jiyaji Rao wanted to entertain his guest in great style, and putting him up in one of the royal hunting lodges simply didn't cut it. So he ordered the new castle, where George V could stay for one night.

George Castle went up well before the scheduled date of the British king's visit. But while making his way through the forests, George V managed to shoot so many tigers that he quickly lost interest in the sport and turned back before he reached his destination. In the end, George Castle did not welcome its royal guest, and it has been standing empty ever since.

I stumbled upon this abandoned folly quite by accident. I had stopped at a tea shop near the Shivpuri forests looking for something to drink, when a local told me all about the castle's fascinating history. He was related to the caretaker couple who had looked after it for more than fifty years, and when he was young, they used to unlock it and allow him to play inside. He described huge bathrooms and marble bathtubs and colored tiles on the floors. Alas, that was all he could remember. During the monsoon season, the castle

MADHYA PRADESH

grounds were infested with snakes, and he stopped going there after his brother was almost bitten. The man had no idea if people were allowed to go inside anymore. He hadn't been that way in twenty-five years.

I made enquiries in the area and found a young lad who showed me the way to George Castle for a few coins. It was a fantastic, turreted, British-style structure standing incongruously in the middle of the thick jungle. The building was crumbling in places, and some of the Belgian glass windows were cracked and broken. I thought I could see some signs of restoration work, but that too seemed to have been abandoned long ago. Now the forest was reclaiming the land at its own pace, to wipe out this reminder of the Scindia royal family's humiliation forever.

An atmosphere of defeat seemed to hang over the castle. Or maybe it was just my overactive imagination endowing the old building with feelings. But the George Castle looked so alone and unwanted that I felt impelled to visit it again and again.

I would fill a thermos with tea, collect my book and radio, and spend the last hours of daylight on its front staircase. I don't think I ever opened the book or listened too long to the radio. The gusty premonsoon wind would constantly make the castle moan and creak, and I felt as if the building were trying to tell me the sad story of its life. About how it was born out of a whim and then was cast aside in a fit of pique. My heart went out to the crumbling ruin, but

there was little I could do to alleviate its pain. Except perhaps keep it company for a while. Together, we would watch the sun set over the lake nearby, and I hoped the castle felt happier in those moments.

When it was time for me to return to Gwalior after a week of animal spotting in the Shivpuri forests, I took a lot of photographs of the castle. Every time I look at those pictures now, I wonder why I had felt such a strong emotional connection with a pile of bricks and mortar. Perhaps the George Castle's extraordinary history had made me fanciful. Or could it be that the castle, in its misery, really had spoken to me?

Shivpuri District

With luxuriant forests and undulating hills, Shivpuri was the summer resort of the Scindia royal family. Over centuries, the area's large population of tigers and elephants became prey to the royal passion for *shikaar* (hunting), until the thickly wooded land was declared the Madhav National Park and tigers began to be bred in captivity. Today, besides tigers, the park is also home to leopards, jackals, crocodiles, antelopes, and a variety of birds. George Castle is located in its center at its highest point. For more on Shivpuri, including information on how to get there, go to the region's official government website.

http://shivpuri.mp.gov.in

BUNDI

Jeroen van Marle follows Kipling to the hill town of Bundi

Following Rudyard Kipling's footsteps, I arrived in Bundi in southern Rajasthan. Kipling came here in the early 1900s, and the picturesque little hill town inspired him to write one of my favorite books, *Kim*. A century had passed between his trip and mine, so I wasn't expecting Bundi to be preserved exactly as Kipling had captured it. But I still hoped to retrace his path.

My first pleasant surprise was the complete absence of busloads of travelers. The town is not a great distance away from hubs like Udaipur and Jaipur, but by some miracle it managed to slip under the tourist radar. This meant that I had the Sukh Mahal summer palace, where Kipling stayed, entirely to myself. The tranquil Sukh Sagar Lake was just outside, and as I toured the grounds, I saw the writer's beloved kingfishers and langur monkeys playing near the water. Even the laundrymen were still in place, beating clothes on stone slabs along the shore and spreading them out to dry in colorful patches on the grass.

Dragging myself away from this idyllic scene, I set off to visit the Bundi Palace, an architectural marvel that Kipling described in amazement as an "avalanche of masonry." Indeed, the sixteenth-century structure seemed to roll off the side of a hill in wave after wave of elegant domes and balconies. I thought of Kipling's words that "the Palace of Boondi, even in broad daylight, is such a Palace as men build for themselves in uneasy dreams—the work of goblins more than of men."

The exterior was an awe-inspiring example of Bundi architecture, while the interior held the most glorious collection of Bundi's unique art. The Chitra Shala (Hall of Arts) was literally awash with murals done in a style known as the Bundi School of painting—painstakingly detailed miniatures in grades of green, blue, and maroon, somewhat reminiscent of Mughal motifs. The palace caretaker, after much cajoling, agreed to unlock some doors to the protected areas, where tourists are not allowed entry. I found more Bundi paintings there, but they were all in desperate need of restoration. The precious murals were peeling right off the walls, and large scraps had already gone missing, and I wondered if this had been their condition in Kipling's time, or if he had seen them in a better state. Graciously, the caretaker allowed me to take a few pictures, so long as I didn't use a flash.

Pleased by how much of Kipling's world I had found remaining so far, I left the Bundi Palace to climb farther up to another of his favorite spots: the fourteenth-century Taragarh Fort, set within a horseshoe-shaped fold at the tip of the hill. Where thousands of soldiers once guarded this fort, the job has now passed on to a colony of monkeys, who eyed me from the ramparts. The afternoon went by enjoyably in exploring all the crenellations and remnants of other defense structures, and by the time I took a break near a window on the outside wall, the sun was setting. I had a splendid view of the sleepy little town below as it soaked in the last of the daylight. The lakes, hills, and blue-painted houses seemed to float in a swirl of a light fog. From this height, Bundi looked like one of the miniature paintings it is so famous for.

In a matter of minutes, however, the scene changed, and Bundi was plunged into the gray of late dusk. As dimples of lanterns and electric lights began to spread over the town, I returned to my hotel, a centuries-old *haveli* called Braj Bhushanjee. I visited the onsite handicraft shop and made a few small purchases before thinking about dinner. I had planned to eat at Darikhana, the hotel's beautiful little Rajasthani restaurant, but suddenly I wasn't in the mood to be among people. So I went back to my room and ordered room service, before settling down in the cozy little alcove opposite my bed.

I opened the stained glass windows to let in the gentle, balmy breeze that was blowing over the town. And there I sat, rereading my favorite passages in *Kim*, while I enjoyed a predinner glass of *kesar kasturi*—an alcoholic concoction the Bundi kings had loved to drink. Despite the century that had passed, I was certain I could feel the spirit of Rudyard Kipling in the darkness of that quiet Bundi night.

Getting to Bundi

Departing from Jaipur, Udaipur, or Agra, you can take the bus or train to Bundi. Because Bundi does not have its own railway station, you will have to get off the train in Kota, which is an hour's drive away by taxi or car hire.

Haveli Braj Bhushanjee

www.kiplingsbundi.com

UDAIPUR

Helene Shapiro experiences a suite moment in Udaipur

Instead of the typical single-occupancy room I usually booked while traveling, I decided to splurge and check into one of the prestigious suites at Udaipur's Taj Lake Palace. For two days, I would live like a queen in true royal style, before returning to a rented apartment, a nursing job, and a commoner's life in New York.

Choosing the hotel had been easy. Having watched James Bond's *Octopussy*, I wanted to stay on the property where much of the movie was shot. The Taj Lake Palace, sitting in the middle of a placid lake in Udaipur, had looked extraordinarily beautiful in the film. In reality, it was even more so.

The suite I chose for my indulgent escape was called Khush Mahal, and it was a grand collection of rooms once used by the ruling family of Udaipur. As far as luxury went, Khush Mahal was well worth the royal tariff I was paying for the use of it. The living area extended into a covered verandah space with arched, stained glass windows. Through them, I could see the emerald green waters of Lake Pichola, in the middle of which floated my hotel like a creamy white pearl.

Equally mesmerizing, the open-plan bedroom-cum-drawing room boasted an intricately crafted brass swing, which was suspended from the ceiling right at its center. I loved sitting cross-legged on its bolstered seat, all warm and cozy, admiring the mosaics and marble curlicues picked out on the butterscotch-colored walls while I sipped endless cups of Darjeeling's famous Makaibari tea.

The Khush Mahal changed moods with the position of the sun—from noon's feisty yellow to the calm salmon pink of dusk. At night, the soft, soothing sounds of lake water lapping against the outside walls lulled me into a deep, relaxed sleep. As for the unique enchantment of Khush Mahal, I experienced it on my second day there, when I woke up in the morning in the massive four-poster bed. As I emerged from sleep, the rays of the sun were glancing off the lake at a mysterious angle, and the walls caught the reflection of the rippling waters through the stained glass in a dancing medley of colors. Bursts of red, yellow, blue, and green rose and fell in misty waves throughout the room, transforming the Khush Mahal into a magical underwater world. Lying back on the bed, I felt as if I were floating, my body light as air as the swirling colors tossed me playfully around in a sea that seemed to have swallowed up a rainbow.

The startling play of lights kept me hypnotized for almost half an hour. Then, suddenly, it was gone. At some point on its journey westward across the sky, the sun lost its bewitching connection with the lake, and the light inside the suite settled back into a smooth, solid yellow. I railed at myself for not having woken up sooner, so that I could have seen the entirety of the sun's performance, and for having to leave the Lake Palace that very same evening and not getting another chance to experience this beauty again. So entranced, I hadn't even had the presence of mind to jump out of bed and capture Khush Mahal's glorious morning performance with my camera. But the spectacle lives on in my mind, as bright and alive as it had been when playing across the walls of my suite.

Taj Lake Palace

The Khush Mahal suite was once the living quarters of one of the two queens of the ruler of Udaipur. At $4,000 per night at the time of publication, it is a splurge—but well worth it, as Helene attests. To read more about staying in palace hotels, go to page 64.

www.tajhotels.com
lakepalace.udaipur@tajhotels.com

RISHIKESH

Jorden Leighton takes a magical mystery tour in Rishikesh

I arrived in Rishikesh with numerous goals in mind. Principal among them was to explore a significant piece of rock 'n' roll history: the once-famous ashram of the Maharishi Mahesh Yogi.

In 1968, the Beatles arrived here seeking peace, enlightenment, and respite from their legions of fans.

The band had become enchanted with the acclaimed Maharishi Mahesh, a guru whose message of transcendental meditation was taking hold across the world. Initially, they swore by his teachings, but later the relationship rapidly went downhill as rumors of his sexual improprieties came to light. Reported scandals notwithstanding, the Beatles are said to have composed as many as forty-eight songs at the ashram, many of which surfaced in the chart-busting *White Album*. Being an infatuated fan, I felt that a visit to this spot was key to understanding their musical evolution.

To locate the ashram, my friends and I wandered south along the Ganga River. As the path veered slowly toward the riverbank, we occasionally saw holy men inhabiting tiny natural caves and wondered at how little space a human being actually requires in order to survive. We continued on, until we reached a flight of broken steps. At the top was a worn-out fence that we easily scaled.

When setting out to find the ashram, I knew that it had been vacant for at least a decade, but I'd not expected that the years of neglect had turned it into a ruin. Poor villagers from nearby areas had stolen most of the wooden fixtures and anything else that could be sold or recycled. The walls had cracked under the onslaught of weeds, and there were gaping holes everywhere, covered with green moss. Rainwater had left puddles all over the floor, and judging by the mounds of leavings, an army of rats had taken up residence.

We ventured into what used to be the vegetarian food hall, and I had a fleeting picture in my mind of John, Paul, George, and Ringo eating rice and roti with their hands in the company of other Maharishi Mahesh Yogi devotees.

Aside from the two main buildings, there were scores of abandoned beehivelike structures made of gray stone bricks. These were the meditation huts, slowly being reclaimed by the surrounding forest. One of these huts had a swastika painted on its back side, and I was surprised until a friend reminded me that this ancient symbol was one of peace, good luck, and well-being thousands of years before the Nazis co-opted it.

As we stood out in the open and watched a group of monkeys play a game of tag on the low-hanging branches of the trees, an odd silence fell over our party. Although I could not define it, there was something about this place, an intense energy that hovered in the air like an invisible fog. Maharishi Mahesh Yogi may have been long gone, but the promise of spiritual rejuvenation that had drawn the Beatles had somehow been preserved through the decades. The Beatles fan inside me was responding to the vibe that had inspired them to create some of their most memorable music. My traveling companions were also affected, and we found ourselves content to just sit there and take in the atmosphere.

It was when somebody mentioned being hungry that a rumor I had heard in town the day before came back to me. The owner of the tea shop where we usually ate our breakfast had been talking about a proposal to restore the ashram. Apparently, the former actress Maggie O'Hara was seeking permission from the government to convert it into a shelter for street children. Her plans also included a small eco-friendly hotel on the premises to provide accommodation for volunteers and visitors.

As we made our way back along the Ganga River, I prayed for the plans to work out. Fans from all over the world would come to visit, and the money generated from tourism would go toward a good cause. I couldn't think of a better way to preserve the spirit of peace and understanding that is so much a part of the Beatles' music.

Getting to Rishikesh

A bus ride from Delhi to Rishikesh usually takes about six hours, depending on road conditions. Hardwar, another religious town just over twenty kilometers away, is the nearest railhead. Forty kilometers away, Dehradun is the nearest airport.

Visiting the ashram

While in Rishikesh, Jorden learnt that the government had shut down the ashram because of tax issues, but Beatles fans, crazy creatures that they are, were always going in and out of the property. As long as the establishment was not operational, the authorities, quite sportingly, turned a blind eye. To get to the ashram, just ask around. Rishikesh is a small town, and finding it will be easy.

The Beatles in Rishikesh

Professional photographers were not allowed in the ashram while the Beatles were staying there, so Paul Saltzman is probably the only person in the world to have quality photographs of the band during this time period. At twenty-three, he just happened to be in Rishikesh "in search of himself," certainly a case of being in the right place at the right time. Featuring seventy-five original, previously unpublished photographs as well as personal anecdotes of encounters with the hip and beautiful personalities of the 1960s who came to the ashram with the Beatles (Mia Farrow, Donovan, and Mike Love of the Beach Boys), Saltzman's book, *The Beatles in Rishikesh*, is an intimate look at the world's most influential band.

www.thebeatlesinindia.com

A man walks in the Qutab Minar complex in Delhi

GENERAL NORTH INDIA

On the grounds of Delhi's India Gate

RETAIL THERAPY

An insiders' primer to boutiques and markets

As the tagline on this book's cover clearly states, this is a guide for connoisseurs. For people who travel with a passion and not with a checklist. Were it not so, I would send you to Delhi's Dilli Haat. You can buy all the souvenirs you want at this permanent exhibition ground and be done with your shopping in one afternoon.

But you're not the sort of traveler who is short on either time or curiosity. So I'm taking you instead on a leisurely shopping tour, knowing full well that you will treasure the experiences as much as the goods. In this chapter, a number of writers have shared the little adventures they had while shopping in North India: the personal contacts, the brief glimpses of history, or the discovery of an unusual item that made each of their purchases a memorable one.

Jenni Wadams, for example, visits an Agra carpet factory, where the exquisite rugs come alive when she weaves into them the memory of a roomful of illiterate carpet makers singing out the pattern to each other. Or take the pair of puppets Cynthia Chesterfield purchased in Jaipur. They would merely be pretty wall hangings if she hadn't discovered that they were Rajasthan's version of Romeo and Juliet, who moved women to tears with their tale of doomed love during village puppet shows. Such details are important when you shop for exotic goods in a foreign country. They give a context and enable you to establish greater intimacy with the culture.

The same spirit of curiosity and adventure guides the essays from the modern capital of Delhi, as well. As Naomi Naam digs into baskets of antiques at the Tibetan Market, we can smell the dust and rust and envision the starkly beautiful pieces being made by hardworking Tibetans in a remote Himalayan village lost in the clouds. And when Carol Koster wonders if she should spend three weeks of her travel budget on a pair of gold bracelets, we too are caught up in her quandary. Can

the purchase really be worth it? Will she end up regretting her decision later? Whether meeting a local clothing dyer, posing for your own Bollywood poster, or searching for silver on the lyrically named Street of the Incomparable Pearl, these aren't everyday experiences.

When I am enjoying myself so much, it is sometimes difficult to remember boring things like word count and space restrictions. As editor, it was my job to exercise some control over the amount of material that went into this chapter. So I devised a simple Suitcase Rule: essays on any product that didn't comfortably fit into a suitcase had to be counted out. I know you will wonder how Jenni Wadams's carpet got in then, but she does explain that the Agra carpet sellers are experts at folding their wares into small, travel-friendly packages. Anyway, by suitcase I mean one of those maximum-size monsters that airline baggage handlers dislike so much.

It breaks my heart to think of all the exciting essays that fell foul of the Suitcase Rule, but you're a shopping connoisseur, and I am certain that the recommendations here will prove to be useful tools when you're deciding on where to go and what to buy. The region has a wealth of arts and crafts just waiting to be discovered. The treasure hunt, I promise you, has only just begun.

New Delhi

Mahalakshmi Gupta dyes for new fabric in Delhi

The first time I went to Glamour Prints in Shankar Market, I was looking for suitable fabrics for an elaborate outfit I wanted to have custom-made. The attendants at the shop pulled out bolt after bolt of cloth for me, and when I still wanted to see more, they showed no signs of fatigue as they escorted me up a dark, dingy staircase that led into an enormous warehouse filled with some of the loveliest silks, chiffons, brocades, and cottons I had ever seen.

I had come with a particular color in mind, something approaching an eggplant purple, and the design of the outfit was such that it required that same color in three different fabrics. After trying to mix and match for over an hour with no success, I was ready to abandon my favorite shade and choose something else. But the shop assistant had another idea. He said, "Find the fabrics you want from the unbleached bolts, and I will take you to a dyer who will dye them in the exact color." I quickly chose two lengths in chiffon and one in silk and followed the man to a dyer who

worked out of a parking lot behind the market.

The dyer's establishment—a sheet of blue plastic strung up next to a smelly dumpster—did not inspire confidence. Neither did Bijoy the dyer, a short, sparely built man who was stirring a pot of boiling colored water with a bamboo stick. Near the pot, he had arranged small tins of pigment on a tray, and on a long clothesline scraps of deep pink cloth were drying out. I was certain that the pretty chiffons and silk I had just purchased would be quite ruined here. How in the world could Bijoy ever produce my precious eggplant color from those few bottles of pigment?

Before I could cut my losses and walk away, Bijoy thrust several dog-eared color charts at me and pointed a blue-stained finger at the purple and violet sections. I resigned myself to the outcome of this adventure and showed my color to him. He nodded approvingly and turned away to light a candle. Picking up the fabrics I had brought, he held a corner of each to the flame and then sniffed at the burnt patches. I asked the shop attendant what he was doing.

When Bijoy, clearly a man of few words, did not volunteer any explanation, the attendant said, "You can tell if a cloth can be dyed in this way."

"Come back in thirty minutes," Bijoy told me and returned to his boiling pot. This was the first time he had spoken during the whole exchange. I wanted to hang around and watch him do the job, but I wasn't sure I was welcome. Besides, it was muggy out, and the smell from the dumpster was particularly strong at this time of the afternoon. I escaped back inside the market, said goodbye to the shop attendant, and browsed through lace and appliqués in a nearby embroidery goods store.

When I returned to Bijoy's place half an hour later, I couldn't believe what he had managed to do in that short space of time. My fabrics were hanging on his clothesline—slightly damp, but in the exact eggplant purple color I had been dreaming of. Bijoy grinned at my surprise and waved his hand dismissively to indicate that it was no big deal. He took very little money for the job.

Since then, I have developed a fondness for quiet old Bijoy and returned to his ramshackle dyeing shop from time to time with other orders. His manner toward me has become warmer since our first encounter, and he has even suggested a couple of excellent tailors nearby who stitch outfits for about $6.

Though Shankar Market is located very close to Connaught Place, I have never seen tourists there. I doubt the market, with its niche merchandise, often finds mention in guidebooks either. But if you love Indian fabrics and want to design your own outfit from scratch, this should be the first place you visit.

Glamour Prints

Shankar Market is a wonderful destination with more than a hundred little shops, most of them selling fabrics at reasonable prices. When I go, though, I visit only this store. Their stock is so vast, and the owner and his assistants are so charming, I have never felt like trying out any of the other places around it. If you want to dye material, ask for Mr. Bijoy at this shop. One of the attendants will be happy to take you to him. Overall, afternoons are the best time to go to Shankar Market as the shops are not very crowded at that time.

24, Shankar Market
Connaught Place
New Delhi

Washing newly dyed clothes

If you purchase a hand-dyed garment, it might bleed in the first washing. It is safest not to put anything hand-dyed in the washing machine with other clothes until you are sure the dye has set. Soak the piece in a bucket of water with a bit of detergent for one day. If the water remains clear, it's okay to wash with other items. If the color runs, then we recommend you hand-wash it every time.

Dave Prager poses Bollywood-style with his wife in Delhi

There was once a time in Delhi when shining malls and Café Coffee

Days didn't exist as refuges from heat and stench. In this land before liberalization, sanctuary was found in the local cinema halls that dotted the Indian urban landscape. But multiplexes are driving these places out, and as collateral damage, taking with them the Bollywood poster painters who relied on their business.

Every year, my wife, Jenny, and I send out a Photoshopped holiday card to our friends and family. When we found out that some Bollywood poster painters are still eking out a living near Old Delhi, we knew that this year's card would be handmade. We dissected a bunch of old Bollywood posters for composition and style, took pictures of ourselves in our desired poses, and set out to a neighborhood near the Red Fort armed with vague contact instructions: "Find the Darya Ganj fire station. Make a right. Walk a hundred yards, and ask the *paan wallah* for Vijay."

The *paan wallah* sent us to a bicycle rickshaw stand, where sleeping rickshaw pullers competed for space with myriad parts strewn about. We sat at the stand and chatted with Manesh, who seemed to manage the rickshaw syndicate, until Vijay pulled up on a rickshaw of his own. Vijay and Manesh then took us up the dirt road across the street to Vijay's open-air studio. Fading starlets tossed us sultry glances from dusty wooden walls as we sat on a wooden *charpoy* to talk.

With Manesh translating, we told Vijay exactly what we wanted—the composition, the elements, the style, the poses, the title, the tagline. Happy for the business, Vijay was nonetheless confused about how we'd found him. Not sure how to explain our relationship with the woman on the expat Listserv who recommended him, we just said that he was "very famous." His smile told us that was what he was hoping to hear.

I came back the next weekend with my father and the money for the deposit. Manesh wasn't there. This time, we sat at the rickshaw stand with a drunk mechanic who kept telling us, "I speak English tutti-frutti," and "Vijay is my brother," and "You want some whiskey?" Finally Vijay and Ranjeet, his English-speaking partner, pulled up. We discussed again the poster while the drunken mechanic danced around, sent a peon for soda, and interrupted us with "Vijay famous artist!" and "My cousin-brother!" and yet more "You want whiskey?"

Jenny and I had anticipated a small poster, perhaps two feet in length—after all, our main goal was to reprint it on a postcard. Vijay, however, insisted that his work could be no less than five feet tall. We agreed, the peon returned, and we celebrated with Pepsi and whiskey. As we were walking out, the mechanic turned to me to whisper conspiratorially, "I speak English tutti-frutti."

A week later, we returned to examine the work in progress. Five feet had become six. Then, two weeks after we had commissioned it, Jenny and I came to Darya Ganj to behold our first starring role, captured in perfect 1970s Bollywood style. This poster accurately re-created the most exciting experiences we've had in Delhi so far: our spontaneous dances in various grand ballrooms, the time we fought criminals as special investigators in the Delhi police force, and that awful incident when our love of diamonds and danger forced us to turn our commandeered autorickshaws against each other.

And you thought we were working office jobs!

Life imitates art

As Vijay and his team presented their work with pride, Ranjeet reminded Dave that poster painting is a dying art, and that he should tell his friends. So we encourage you to seek out Vijay to capture your likeness in archaic Bollywood style. It's best to take photos of your face, check the artist's samples, and discuss the kinds of poses you want. You can find Vijay near the *paan wallah*, across from the rickshaw stand, down from the Darya Ganj fire station. Better yet, just email Ranjeet, and he'll make sure you find the way.

ranjeet_2870@rediffmail.com

Bollywood posters

Until a decade or so ago, Bollywood movies used to announce their release with a unique style of hand-painted publicity posters. Colorful, exaggerated, and completely over-the-top, they displayed crude representations of the hero valiantly fighting villains, the heroine dancing dramatically, and other such exciting sequences from a film. These unique pieces of art invited people to throng the cinemas, where they would stand around the posters and goggle at their favorite stars. If a movie became a hit at the box office, viewers and movie hall owners would place garlands of marigolds on the posters, just so everyone knew this film was a success and doing great business. Now that everything is high-tech, the art of painting Bollywood posters is pretty much dead. You might find some in small towns, but in cities it's all modern publicity. The painters are without jobs, and the art is dying out. By having your own Bollywood poster made, not only are you acquiring a unique souvenir, you are helping to keep a dying tradition alive.

Carol Koster breaks the bank for two gold bangles in Delhi

After cricket and Bollywood, the third thing Indians are obviously obsessive about is gold. I couldn't help but notice how every single woman wore at least a few bits of it somewhere on her person. The jewelry looked nothing like the machine-produced stuff you see in department stores in the West. It was all handmade and thick with exquisite filigree and stonework. After all the gold-watching I did during my travels through the country, I figured some bangles would look good on my wrists too. As soon as we returned to Delhi, I dragged my husband, Jarrod, out on a bangle-shopping spree.

Being savvy, we first looked up the market price of gold on the Internet, and armed with this knowledge, we stopped at countless gold shops, asking naive questions to test the waters. This initial foray threw up an unknown element that the Internet hadn't revealed: workmanship. Apparently, it greatly affected prices. Gauging the level of work that had gone into making a piece of jewelry required an expert eye.

Eventually, Jarrod was of the opinion that we should go back to our hotel and do some more research, but I did not want to return without my bangles. I did a quick study of the women browsing through jewelry in the shop we were in and zeroed in on a mother and daughter duo looking at a tray of earrings. Ignoring Jarrod's discomfort, I walked up to them and asked how much they would pay for the workmanship that had gone into a pair of bangles I had chosen. The design was fairly intricate, consisting of little circles piled into mini pyramids and joined together by a wavy line.

Besides wearing jewelry, Indians, I discovered, love handling and assessing it, and soon the two

were happily trying my bangles on, holding them up to the light, closely inspecting the surface details, and animatedly exchanging opinions. It reminded me of the excitement involved in choosing the perfect wedding dress. Finally, they reached a verdict: the asking price was fair.

We thanked the ladies profusely for their help, and then took ourselves off on a coffee break. We needed to talk this over and be absolutely certain we weren't making an impulse purchase. After all, we were parting with close to three weeks' worth of travel money. But the bangles were so pretty, I knew I wouldn't regret buying them afterward. I would treasure them always as a perfect memento of our happy times in India. Jarrod understood I had set my heart on the bangles, and finally we decided to go for it.

Returning to the gold shop, I watched nervously as our Visa card was approved. The bangles were packed into a red velvet box, and we received a certificate that guaranteed the purity and weight of the gold. With the certificate, I could sell back or exchange my bracelets for new pieces if I wanted. When we left the shop, I was in a bit of a daze, thrilled to possess a piece of authentic Indian jewelry.

Now, in true Indian style, I wanted some colored glass bangles to accent the gold ones. I needed a lot of them, as we had skimped on the gold by buying only two—normally, they are worn in sets of four. We made our way by cycle rickshaw to a nearby local market, where, among shops selling twine, fabric, and cooking pots, we found two brothers exclusively in the glass bangle business. I tried on every color and design in their stock and wore my pinky knuckle raw from squeezing pieces on and off. It took as long to choose the glass bangles as it did to buy my gold ones, but in the end I left with more than six dozen fragile pieces. I was anxious about getting them safely home without breaking any, but they had been packed so well, I didn't lose a single one.

The glass bangles are deep red, royal blue, a light leafy green, and solid black. Paired with my gold bracelets, they look as great with casual attire as they do with my little black cocktail dress. I adore the tinkling sound they make whenever I move my arm, and I find that my hand gestures increase whenever I happen to be wearing them.

Shopping for gold in Delhi

The largest congregations of jewelry shops in the city are located in the Karol Bagh and Dariba Kalan areas. Karol Bagh is a huge and famous neighborhood in west Delhi, crammed with lanes, by-lanes, and little shops. Dariba Kalan is a street in the Chandni Chowk area in Old Delhi. Buying jewelry in a big gold store is considered a safe thing to do, as the store will provide proof of quality with the purchase. On the upscale side, Tanishq is a trusted

brand name in jewelry. The company has branches in all major cities in North India. In Delhi, you can visit their flagship showroom.

A-7, Inner Circle
Connaught Place
New Delhi

www.tanishq.co.in

Naomi Naam sifts through Tibetan goods in Delhi

New Delhi's Tibetan Market was a wonderful introduction to Tibetan handicrafts and jewelry, something I'd get to see a lot of later during my travels through the Himalayan districts of North India. Heavy, cold, and stark in their lack of refinement and detail, they reflect the hard life and history of the displaced people who make them.

The market comprises no more than fifteen shops, crammed so full of dusty, ancient-looking metalwork, woodwork, and jewelry that baskets and benches have been set up outside to create extra display space. There's no logic to the presentation—Tibetan shop owners all over North India have this curious way of piling their goods in careless, unsorted jumbles and then hiding somewhere within, seemingly unconcerned about making a sale. The onus is entirely on the customer to select, consider, and then pay, without any prodding from the salesman.

Tibetan jewelry and handicrafts can be confusing. Often, I would pick up an attractive-looking item from a pile, but I simply had no idea what to do with it. During one visit I came across a heavy metal bit of something that looked like an impressive door handle—two door handles, actually, welded together at the tail and set off with large pieces of turquoise. What was it?

"*Dorje*," was all my Tibetan shopkeeper cared to offer by way of explanation.

Ah, *dorje*. Of course.

I put the *dorje* back in the pile and went off in search of something more recognizable. I found baskets full of bead, metal, and animal bone jewelry, all rough and tribal, like the stuff in African jungle movies. Many of the pieces were inscribed with the eight sacred symbols of Buddhism. I even unearthed a crown with cones of gold and silver stitched onto a moth-eaten, black velvet base. It was fascinating, and I could easily imagine it sitting on the head of some ancient Tibetan chief. The price underscored the crown's authenticity: $1,800. It was so attractive, I wished I had the money to buy it. It would have been worth the splurge.

Easier on the budget were quaint, four-edged Tibetan hats, trimmed with ribbon and sewn with fur. Designs of golden stitches apparently identified the caste and status of the wearer in Tibetan society. The asking price for the one I chose was 450 rupees (about $9). I offered two 50-rupee notes as an opening gambit, but they were accepted without fuss. No doubt I had picked something seriously low-caste.

If I had space in my suitcase I would have certainly bought some wooden bowls, which were hewn roughly out of mulberry and birch. They would have made excellent vases or salad bowls. They came in sets of three and were priced reasonably at about $4. Tibetans, I learnt later, set great store by these bowls. They take them along during their travels and even refer to them as their "lovers" in folk songs.

As I traveled through India, I was on the lookout for some unusual metal craftwork, and the Tibetan Market had it in plenty: masks, musical instruments, bells on long chains, snuff bottles set in coral, statuettes, carved boxes, bags, and weapons. Prices, on the whole, weren't as high as I had been led to believe they would be. After a few visits, I came to the conclusion that the seller's mood dictated the prices. On a good day, I could score a bargain. Other times I had to pay five times more, and no question about it.

A treasure hunt through the Tibetan Market invariably meant that I had to return to my hotel afterward to wash away the thin film of dust that covered my hands, face, and clothes. A long soak in the tub took care of the grime and eased the soreness in my back from bending over basket after basket of artifacts. But by the next day, all the minor aches and pains were gone, and I was ready for another visit, hoping to find something unique that I had overlooked the visit before.

Tibetan Market

This market is just a few hundred yards away from The Imperial Hotel in New Delhi's Janpath area. After you've finished there, cross the street and continue walking on Janpath Road toward Palika Bazar until you see a string of street-side hawkers selling heavily embroidered table and bed linens, which make nice gifts to take back home. The hawkers also have long, ornate silk skirts called *ghagra*. These are ideal for evening wear if you team them up with a matching silk blouse and perhaps a silk scarf. *Ghagras*, however, are not on display, and you have to request that they be brought out from a seller's hidden stock.

Adrianne Bourassa shops around at a historic Delhi mall

I arrived in India with a backpack filled only with necessities and weighing a carefully thought out fourteen pounds: a weight I could comfortably carry. A week and a half into my trip, I had to buy an extra duffel, and by the time I was ready to head for home, I was forced to upgrade to a bag large enough to accommodate a golden retriever. I am explaining this, just so you have some understanding of how easy it is to shop in Delhi.

If you happen to be staying at one of the hotels in Delhi's touristy Paharganj area, the local marketplace there would be the obvious and convenient choice, but if you want a slightly less chaotic experience, take a walk or short autorickshaw ride to Connaught Place and give yourself an entire afternoon to explore.

I love browsing in local bookstores, and Connaught Place has many stocked with both popular and hard-to-find books. You can buy all the absorbing novels you will need for long train rides, as well as some good works by Indian writers. India is a great place for traveling book lovers because people here write as often in English as they do in their vernacular. As a result, you can read about India and its concerns from an Indian point of view.

I loved Arundhati Roy's Booker Prize-winning semiautobiographical novel, *The God of Small Things*, but my admiration for her grew tenfold after I came to India and read about her relentless campaign on behalf of the poor farmer families who would lose their land and livelihood if a dam was built on the Narmada River in Southern India. Rohinton Mistry is another of my favorite Indian authors. His third book, *A Fine Balance*, paints a beautiful and heartbreaking picture of India from Independence through the 1970s.

Along with bookstores, there are scores of upscale clothing and leather shops in Connaught Place that carry sizes for Western bodies. If you have spent much time traveling in Asia, you must already have discovered that XL here can mean anything between size 12 and 16 by American standards. Same problem with footwear. I was delighted to find a gorgeous pair of shoes in the first leather outlet I walked into, when no shopkeeper in the Paharganj market had been able to find anything that accommodated my giant clown feet.

Handicrafts are another thing you'll see in plenty here—not so much the cheap, street-side stuff that's produced in volume almost exclusively for the tourist market, but the kind of items you'll be proud to display on your mantelpiece. Sifting through the stores, I fell in love with the Rajasthani hand-printed fabrics and bought several sets of pillowcases and cushion covers. I also admired ornate bedspreads that were simply adorable, with patches of bright fabrics stitched together with braids and covered with decorative stitches and mirrorwork. I picked out a full-size bedspread with embroidered squares in red, orange, and pink, but chose not to buy it in the end, as I simply didn't have the space to bring it back. It was a decision I still regret.

Darting in and out of all the stores lining Connaught Place can be quite tiring, and if you are in need of a snack break, then head for Wenger's bakery—an institution that has been serving wonderful pastries and savories for eighty years now. For a more substantial meal, though, my favorite is Banana Leaf. The restaurant specializes in authentic South Indian dishes like *vadas*—fried rings made of lentils and rice. It's fun to sample all the chutneys served with the food.

I read somewhere that the British designed Connaught Place like a horseshoe, believing that the shape would prove lucky for both shoppers and shopkeepers. There may be something in that superstition, because CP (as Connaught Place is locally called) continues to be the capital's premier shopping destination, in spite of all the glitzy malls and superstores that have come up since. As for my own good fortune, I've had terrific luck here finding mementos that remind me of my travels throughout India.

Connaught Place
www.connaughtplacemall.com
www.wengerspastry.com

Melly Goodman indulges in Delhi's designer clothing

As an expat who has lived in Delhi off and on for many years, I love the wonderful way designers in India have of combining traditional textiles and embellishments with Western cuts and styles. The result is smart, edgy fusion-wear that wouldn't be a bit out of place in fashion capitals like New York and Paris. The fine fabrics and subtle embroidery add so much elegance to my wardrobe that I feel confident whenever I wear them to social events. They don't come cheap, but I wouldn't go quibbling with Giorgio Armani about his price tags, and I am happy to pay Indian designers their due as well.

Among my favorites is Ritu Kumar. I discovered this designer the same way most people do—on the telly, during a Miss World beauty pageant. The costumes Miss India wore were the most exquisite I had ever seen: long flowing skirts teamed with strappy blouses that afforded tantalizing glimpses of a bare midriff. The designer's name was Ritu Kumar, and on asking around, I discovered that she was considered the doyen of Indian haute couture. Every outfit she designed was a sumptuous showcase of India's incredible heritage in traditional embroidery.

None of my friends owned one of Ritu Kumar's superexpensive outfits. They knew of her as I did, from seeing the clothes she designed for Indian beauty queens on television. Intrigued, I decided to visit Ritu Kumar's Vasant Kunj store in Delhi. At first, I was slightly disappointed because there weren't many of the Miss India-style outfits that I was hoping to see up close. The bulk of the collection here was a scaled-down version of what I had admired on television. The pieces were more "wearable," suitable for all sorts of

evening occasions. Not as spectacular and showy, but no less beautiful.

On the other hand, having come to just window shop, I was thrilled at the realization that I could actually afford some of the ready-to-wear outfits the store carried, with prices ranging between $100 and $300. *Kurtis*, for example. These Indian tunics had been elevated to couture status with smart, body-hugging cuts and Ritu Kumar's trademark hand-stitched garnishes. The color palette was also my favorite combination of earthy Indian hues.

My deliberation was long and difficult, but after an hour spent admiring and desiring every single *kurti* hanging on the racks, I finally managed to choose two that I loved a little bit more than all the others. Both were richly embroidered with the Indian "mango" paisley motif, but while one was a glittering rendition in golden threadwork, the other was subtle and monochromatic with a bluish green silk thread embroidery that perfectly matched the delicate silk fabric.

While chatting with a store associate at the checkout counter, I discovered that the Ritu Kumar clothes I had seen on television were in fact her bridal collection. The outfits were worn by not just brides but other women as well who were part of the wedding party. They weren't merely special occasion outfits—they were very, very special occasion outfits, which was why there weren't too many of them on display at this store.

When I left Ritu Kumar's boutique, my initial disappointment at not being able to see a wide variety of ultraelaborate costumes had evaporated with the pleasure of owning outfits designed by this legendary lady. At the time, my wardrobe held a lovely collection of casual and semiformal *kurtis*, but none of them had the antique look and feel that was Ritu Kumar's specialty. I felt that I had done more than bought myself two designer garments. I had purchased two precious pieces of India's art-and-craft heritage.

Ritu Kumar

Shop No. 282, DLF Promenade
Vasant Kunj
New Delhi

www.ritukumar.com

Ritu Kumar's bridal collection

The Miss India-style outfits Melly describes are known as *lehenga*. Unlike with *saris* and *kurtas*, the wearing of these skirt-and-blouse ensembles has become restricted to weddings and religious celebrations. To see more of Ritu Kumar's *lehenga* collection, visit the Label Archana bridal boutique at the Archana Shopping Complex.

34/42 Archana Shopping Complex
Greater Kailash I
New Delhi

Kurta versus Kurti

Kurtas and *kurtis* are essentially the same thing: long tunics that Indian women wear over loose trousers called *salwar* or skinny cotton/silk leggings called *churidaar*. The difference is in the length. While a *kurta* can be long enough to reach the ankles, a *kurti* does not go below the hip.

More of Melly's favorites

Abraham & Thakore

At a boutique run by designer duo Abraham and Thakore at the DLF Emporio Mall, there's plenty of that artisanal spirit that so attracts me to Indian fashions. Abraham & Thakore's lines are mostly Western, but they make good use of handloom materials and exquisite Indian appliqué. I bought a skirt and jacket in cerise silk with black floral appliqué, and whenever I wear it, the ensemble draws admiring comments from my friends. Whimsical scarves and silk occasional bags are two other things I often pick up from the Abraham & Thakore store. The designers do wonderful things with *kantha*—a running-stitch style of embroidery from the eastern state of Bengal. Instead of the traditional *kantha* patterns of flowers, creepers, and curlicues, they embellish with stark geometric designs that look extremely contemporary. The accessories from Abraham & Thakore are not too expensive, and I often buy them as gifts for my fashionista buddies back home.

DLF Emporio Mall
Nelson Mandela Marg
Vasant Kunj
New Delhi

www.abrahamandthakore.com

Tulsi

For India high fashion, another place I often suggest to friends who are visiting is the Santushti Shopping Complex near the Ashok Hotel. I love it as much for the location as for the shopping. It is a leafy enclave, a stone's throw from the prime minister's house, with stores located in self-contained cottages all over the property. Among all the Santushti shops, I most often visit Tulsi, which has a great collection of shawls and traditional Indian *kurtas*. The first time I went there, I picked up a handwoven lime green *kurta* on a hunch that it would combine well with straight-legged trousers. I went home and tried it on, and sure enough, they went brilliantly together. Since then, I have bought *kurtas* from Tulsi in bold oranges and pinks and accessorized them with matching scarves. The boutique is not for bargain hunters, but it is less expensive than many other designer stores. It does very well with Delhi's arty elite, and even Sonia Gandhi, India's uncrowned empress, has often been spotted there.

19, Santushti Shopping Complex
Race Course Road
New Wellington Camp
Chanakyapuri
New Delhi

Shopping and dining

The Santushti complex is a favorite with Delhi's expatriate and diplomatic crowd. It is home to a restaurant called Basil & Thyme—*the* place for lunch. The setting is bright and airy with enormous windows and lots of natural light. The contemporary, European menu puts emphasis on fresh ingredients. Be forewarned: lunch here does not come cheap.

Suparna Sharma still gets a thrill out of shopping in Delhi

I am the type of shopper who browses and takes a very long time to decide, and I make shopkeepers go to their storerooms for more stock—or better still, take me there so I can poke around for myself. I open dusty drawers and rusty cupboards looking for hidden treasures. When I tell you not to be a make-a-list-and-get-it-over-with shopper in Delhi, I speak from years of experience in tramping the markets in the city. Check out a few places first, and come back the next day if necessary.

That way, you won't feel cheated or disappointed if you see something better and cheaper elsewhere.

Chandni Chowk

I adore silver jewelry, and I believe Delhi has some of the best silver shops in India. For real bargains, I go to Dariba Kalan in the Chandni Chowk area. Dariba Kalan, or the Street of the Incomparable Pearl, has been popular for precious stones and metals since the seventeenth century. Today, countless small stores sell silver and costume jewelry, as well as *itra*, a strong Indian perfume. Items carry no price tags, and I love the fact that I can bargain prices down by at least 20 to 30 percent.

My favorite shop in Dariba Kalan is called Jewel Mine. It looks like a mini stock exchange. The owner sits in the middle of the shop floor, protected from haggling customers by a troupe of attendants as he negotiates prices with designers and boutique owners from around the world. Only a small percentage of Jewel Mine's stock is on display. Due to lack of space, the rest is stashed away in drawers and metal boxes.

If I'm in the mood to browse through old, interesting pieces, I ask one of the Jewel Mine attendants to show me a collection of earrings, necklaces, or bracelets. One by one, steel boxes full of silver goods are dragged in for me to sift through. I remember one occasion when I had to delve into seven of these intimidating boxes before I found a pair of earrings I simply could not resist.

Jewel Mine is a smoker-friendly establishment, but on the plus side, it has a fairly hygienic washroom. Use it while you have the chance, as there aren't too many clean toilet facilities in Dariba Kalan.

Khan Market

South Delhi's posh Khan Market is another place I like to frequent as it has three great stores that are always worth a visit. The first is Amrapali, a jewelry boutique. Arty, aesthetic, and air-conditioned, Amrapali is definitely comfort shopping. It has an exquisite collection of silver and gold jewelry, and even if the goods are quite pricey, the pieces are limited edition, and you won't find these designs elsewhere.

My next stop in Khan Market is Fabindia. Ethnic Indian block prints never go out of fashion in Delhi, and for years Fabindia has more or less defined how the city's upper class dresses through the summer. Every year, I put together a small new wardrobe of summer clothes here, consisting of stylish *kurtas*, pajamas, blouses, and skirts. I spend many happy hours in the garment section, mixing and matching different pieces in similar or contrasting design schemes to create my own ensembles in light, airy cotton and silk.

One word of caution: Beware of garments in a single, solid color, especially the plain reds, blues, and maroons. Vegetable dye, though beautiful, is quirky and might bleed in the first wash. Also, make sure to check out Fabindia's huge home furnishings wing, where you will find India's vibrant color palette combined with a contemporary touch to create refined, sophisticated products that appeal immensely to foreign tastes. The third Khan Market store I always make time for is Anokhi. The collection here is more expensive than Fabindia's, and not as vast, but the sensibility is the same. I'm fond of their silks, as I've bought some really smart quilted jackets in raw silk that I've not found elsewhere. The cost is about $120, but they are worth the splurge.

Sarojini Nagar Market

On days when I am feeling particularly energetic and more budget-minded, I head for Sarojini Nagar Market and rummage through piles of surplus made-for-export garments. After hitting four or five stalls, I almost always come back with samples from Gap, Next, Miss Selfridge, Monsoon, Zara, and other fashionable midmarket labels. Prices are so ridiculously low, I cannot even bring myself to bargain. For about $50, I stock up on more clothing than I can comfortably carry back to my car.

Janpath

Janpath, which was once the nucleus of alternative hang-loose clothing shops, has for over a decade now been caught in chaotic karmic cycles. While it earlier catered to Delhi's arty crowd and backpackers en route to Varanasi or Rishikesh, it now tries to please everybody from foreign visitors to local travelers on their Big Delhi Trip from smaller towns in India. Nonetheless, I go there every now and then to look for imitation jewelry, canvas bags, Rajasthani mirror-work skirts, and very good handmade camel-hide footwear.

As a local, I may have grown somewhat immune to all the sights and smells of Delhi's quaint, old shopping districts, but the diehard shopaholic in me never ceases to marvel at the variety of typically India-made goods available in the city's traditional marketplaces. After many years of living in Delhi, I still get excited at the prospect of spending an afternoon shopping in my own city. With fancy new stores opening up everywhere and old-style bazars remaining as colorful as ever, I cannot say that the novelty is anywhere close to wearing off.

Amrapali
39, Khan Market
New Delhi

www.amrapalijewels.com

Anokhi
32, Khan Market
New Delhi

www.anokhi.com

Fabindia
Central Hall
Khan Market
New Delhi

www.fabindia.com

Janpath Market
Janpath
Connaught Place
New Delhi

Jewel Mine
18, Babar Lane
Dariba Kalan
New Delhi

Sarojini Nagar Market
Sarojini Nagar
Southwest New Delhi

McLeodganj

Cassandra Brill elicits envy with toe socks from McLeodganj

In McLeodganj tourists often pick up small Tibetan souvenirs such as bags, statuettes, and painted scrolls from the little stalls that line the streets. The items are pretty, but not particularly unique, as most merchandise typically carried by handicraft shops in these parts is similar. Still, I managed to find a few special treasures that bring a smile to my face.

I preferred buying from the Tibetan shopkeepers, because I wanted to give them my business, as well as take away something that would remind me of this group of people living in exile here. Facing the bank and ATM counter on Temple Road, I discovered a stall run by a pleasant Tibetan woman who only sells antique Tibetan relics and some beautifully crafted jewelry. I bought a traditional silver-and-turquoise pendant with coral inlay that was one of my nicest purchases in India. I didn't want to spend extra on the beaded chain it came with, so she sold me just the pendant at a very fair (but not cheap) price. Upon learning how much I had fallen in love with the items I had seen at this store, a friend surprised me with a turquoise-encrusted Buddhist prayer wheel also from here. The original prayer was still inside, handwritten on a yellowing piece of parchment.

Another shop I must recommend is on the road to Dharamkot, a kilometer or so above McLeodganj. In one of the last stalls on your left, you will find a Tibetan seamstress who specializes in wool hats. When I was there she just had a few in stock, but I was able to choose some wool and have three custom-made. I selected two styles from her design book—one looked like a Mongolian helmet (attractive, I know), and the other was a floppy train driver's hat. Both are incredibly unique, and they're warm too.

While my hats are great, my most beloved purchase was a pair of the woman's hand-knit socks, in bright stripes of blue, green, and orange. Because the big toe was separate— like the thumb on a mitten—I could wear them with flip-flops. This genius little design feature added a surprising degree of functionality to the socks' warmth and comfort.

My socks have caused a fair amount of envy among travelers all over the world, and I have even had offers from a couple of people who wanted to buy them. I'm happy to say that I resisted their offers. I am actually wearing these precious socks right now as I write. One big toe is wriggling contentedly inside a stripe of blue wool, and I'm wishing I had bought more when I had the chance.

Getting to Dharamshala/ McLeodganj

Only a few flights land every week at the nearby Gaggal Airport from Delhi. You can also rent a taxi from Delhi, Chandigarh, or Shimla and drive down to Dharamshala. The nearest railhead is in Pathankot, which is connected to major cities in North India by regular train services.

Shopping in Dharamshala and McLeodganj

Keep in mind that small street-side shops and stalls come and go in tourist towns like these—a place that existed at the time of publication may not be around by the time you take your trip. But items such as the Tibetan jewelry and toe socks recommended by Cassandra are staples in this area, so you can count on finding similar items as you hunt through the shops.

Chuba

This sleeveless wraparound dress is worn by Tibetan women. Stitches of Tibet on Temple Road sells beautiful *chubas* made by refugee women newly arrived from Tibet. You can also choose the material and have one custom-made for you in one of the area's many tailor shops.

www.tibetanwomen.org/projects/sot/

Tibetan music

Buddhist meditation chants and melodies make ideal background music. Check out the CDs at Charitable Trust Bookstore, which also stocks books on Tibetan history and culture.

KASHMIR

Nabanita Dutt defends the overrated pashmina in Kashmir

Thanks to my mother's Nepalese childhood, pashminas—those gauzy, open-weave shawls made from the inner coat of a high-altitude Himalayan goat—have long been treasured in our family. While other women showed off their expensive *shahtoosh* and *jamevaar* shawls, my mother continued to collect her pashminas.

Kashmir, where she later came to live, produced pashminas of the same high quality as Nepal, but she always bought hers on her annual trips home to Kathmandu. The wool there was precious, since it came only from the inner coat of the goat's neck and belly. Gathering it was difficult, as the weavers had to wait for spring, when the goat shed its winter coat and left little balls of fleece caught in the bushes at an altitude of fourteen thousand feet.

The purest pashmina shawls were soft enough to pass through a ring, and while these were extremely rare, the weavers made their living from excellent second-grade pashminas that had a small, niche market among those in the know in Nepal and India. People were willing to pay upward of $1,000 for even this second grade's incredible softness and warmth.

Then came a time in the late 1990s when the arbiters of the Western fashion world decided to drag the pashmina out of its quiet, dignified existence and flaunt it on the catwalks of New York and Paris as the new wonder accessory. In the space of a season or two, the woolen wraps, shawls, and scarves became the au courant mink. *Newsweek* described it as the "fiber equivalent of meringue," and every fashionable woman worth her Birkin bag dreamed of possessing one.

The romance, however, proved short-lived. Synthetic blends purport-ing to be the real thing flooded the world market, making pashminas seem common, cheap, and tacky. Haute couture no longer had a place for the fine wool, whose imitations were selling for $10 in roadside souvenir shops. Finally, British *Vogue* ended the phenomenon by regretfully announcing the "death of the pashmina" in its August 1999 issue.

But my mother, innocent of the fact that fashion trends had stripped her precious pashmina of all its prestige, continued to lovingly add to her collection. Its image didn't suffer in the eyes of other Indians either, and the shawls are still revered in the Subcontinent as a part of our heritage that fashion pundits from the West cannot tarnish or undervalue.

So, if you want to buy a good-quality pashmina while you're in Kashmir, don't let the wool's fifteen minutes of fame deter you. You won't be investing in a trend, but in a centuries-old fabric legacy that will feel like gossamer against your skin and keep you warm and toasty in the severest winter weather.

Purchasing pashminas in Srinagar

Because pashminas in India are primarily made in Kashmir, travelers will find the best selection in Srinagar. We recommend buying only from a government emporium, since it is too easy to be cheated. Touts roam the streets of Srinagar looking for tourists to sell their fake pashminas to. As we have all

I accepted his apology gracefully, fingering the *parandis* I had pushed into the side pocket of my handbag. Later, I'd have to pass them off as something I picked up in Delhi. Of course, it was only a matter of time before Ali learned the truth.

Shopping for parandis

The souvenir shops running along the outside wall of the Golden Temple complex sell *parandis*. You can also buy them at Amritsar's Hall Bazar (next to the city's landmark Gandhi Gate) or in the Lawrence Road market (a five-minute walk from the Amritsar railway station).

JAIPUR

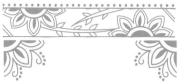

Cynthia Chesterfield gives her family the gift of Jaipur

A few years back, Christmas was "Made in India" for me. Or "Made in Jaipur" to be precise, since all the packages I put under the tree contained treasures from this city. For once, choosing presents for my rather large family had turned out to be quite painless. Jaipur was like a huge exhibition ground, and wherever

I went, I was always stumbling upon some indigenous product or another—colorful and handmade, and at unbeatable prices. I even wrapped the gifts in Jaipur's vibrant, block-printed rice paper to tie up the whole theme.

Traditional puppets

In a shop opposite Jaipur's Hawa Mahal, I bought a pair of the sweetest puppets. The place was tiny, more a shack than a store, with hundreds of colorfully clad puppets hanging from the ceiling or lying heaped in bamboo baskets on the floor. Each of these dolls had a painted wooden face with the typically sharp North Indian nose and wide-open eyes.

The seller drew my attention to two of the puppets, a mustachioed male and a coy female with a large nose ring. "Moomal and Mahendra," he said, the Romeo and Juliet of Rajasthani folklore. Through a misunderstanding their love is thwarted, but the story of their doomed relationship lives on in the *kathputli* (puppet) shows that are a traditional form of entertainment in the villages of Rajasthan. He had several pairs of Moomal-and-Mahendras, with prices as low as $6, but I splurged on a better-quality set for the intricately designed silk costumes. My sister Macy is an enthusiastic doll collector, and they were just the kind of thing she would love. One gift down, only four more to go.

Leheriya skirts

One day I found myself rooting through piles of Jaipur's typical tie-and-dye garments in a small shop in

Kishanpol Market. Every piece was coiled into a tight rope, to put crinkles in the fabric, and I had no idea what each one looked like until the shopkeeper untied the strings and pulled it open. The crinkles reminded me of Japanese designer Issey Miyake's signature Pleats Please collection, except that these were not permanent, and if desired, they could be smoothed out with an iron.

Among all the different tie-and-dye clothes I saw, the ones that most appealed to me were called *leheriya*. The word *leheriya* means "waves" in the local dialect, a fitting name for a process that puts undulating diagonal lines on very soft fabric. I decided to buy some gathered *leheriya* skirts for my two nieces, and the shopkeeper was amused with my choice, since I had unwittingly selected the very style that the royalty of Jaipur also favored. His claim was proved true a couple of days later when I was fortunate enough to catch a glimpse of Gayatri Devi, the erstwhile Maharani of Jaipur, at my hotel.

Curious about this woman, who is commonly regarded as the most beautiful in India, I had bought a copy of her biography, which contained many pictures of her in her youth. Here she was in real life, walking into the Rambagh Palace hotel that once used to be her home. Dressed in a sea green *leheriya* sari and a string of pearls, she was without doubt the most elegant person I had ever seen. I couldn't believe my luck at having such a close brush with royalty,

and about finding a gift with such a romantic story behind it.

Bagru block prints

On an impulse I took myself off to a small artisan village called Bagru, on the outskirts of Jaipur. Strolling through the Chippa Mohalla (Printer's Quarters), I watched Bagru families working on an eco-friendly method of block printing using natural sources. The result was a feast of earthy colors that came from turmeric, madder root, and pomegranate.

The fabrics that stood out from the others were a distinctive shade of indigo. I had seen a similar sort of blue on African mudcloths many years before and had been searching for it ever since. My best Bagru purchase featured this color: a reversible jacket with high collars and several roomy pockets. The indigo and white fabric had different designs on each side, and I knew my dad would love both the color and the quilted thickness. For $25, it was a steal and brought me yet one more step closer to filling out the family Christmas tree.

Blue pottery

I cannot be the first traveler to Jaipur who has left with regret about not being able to buy a few pieces of the city's famous blue pottery. Made of elements that include powdered quartz, the floral-patterned pottery is delicate and likely to break on the journey home. I considered myself lucky as I wandered around Kripal Kumbh, a gallery in Jaipur, admiring the bowls, vases, and tea sets, when

RAJASTHAN

I found a mismatched collection of door knobs tossed into a box that lay half-hidden in a corner. It was as if the shopkeeper expected nobody to buy them. They hadn't counted on me.

My parents were redoing their home, and these knobs would look great on the doors. There were smaller ones, too, that would work on my mother's kitchen drawers. Most were in turquoise blue, but I rummaged through the box until I made up a set of eight knobs with various designs on a bright yellow ochre base. They cost only about $6 each, but looked more expensive. Better yet, they were solid pieces and unlikely to get damaged in my suitcase.

One of the most enjoyable aspects of this experience was that my gifts from Jaipur came with a story. After dinner on Christmas day, I told each one as my family members excitedly unwrapped their presents. I talked about the city the items had come from, and about the people who had made them. Needless to say, they loved it all, except for my poor little nephew Austin, who had sincerely been expecting the elephant from India that I had foolishly promised him.

Shopping for puppets

One of the best areas in Jaipur for browsing puppets is Kathputli Nagar. The shops offer a large selection and excellent prices.

Kishanpol Market

This market is located within Jaipur's old walled city area. All locals know where it is, so once you reach the old city, simply ask around for directions.

Bagru village

The village is located about thirty-five kilometers from Jaipur on the Jaipur-Ajmer road.

Kripal Kumbh

The workshop, gallery, and sales floor for a master artisan, this venue is highly regarded for its blue pottery.

B-18A Shiv Marg
Bani Park

Gayatri Devi

As this book was preparing to go to press, Gayatri Devi passed away at the age of ninety. To learn more about her fascinating life, pick up a copy of *A Princess Remembers: The Memoirs of the Maharani of Jaipur*, which is recommended on page 252.

Helene Shapiro adorns herself with lac bracelets from Jaipur

I discovered lac bracelets one afternoon as I was making my way back from a Bollywood movie at Jaipur's gorgeous Rang Mahal cinema—fun, even without English subtitles. My autorickshaw broke down in an area called Maniharon Ka Raasta, and knowing that my friends would return late from their sightseeing trip (everybody had politely declined my kind offer to treat them to the film), I decided to wait out the traffic rush hour at the Jaipur Bangle Emporium, a costume jewelry shop. The narrow, potholed road was lined with scores of similar-looking shops, but Hamid, the owner of this particular establishment, wanted me to look at his wares. Since he spoke pretty good English I took him up on his offer.

The inside of Hamid's little emporium would make a striking backdrop for a fashion shoot, I thought, as I looked at the thousands of bracelets that washed the space in color. Some were spiked with tiny flashing mirrors, while others had dots of colored stones or complicated golden filigree. Indian women, I had noticed, loved to wear a collection of thin bracelets that ran halfway up their arms and tinkled charmingly when they moved. The store had stacks of these, but the style was too ethnic for my Western sensibilities. While I admired all of the embellishments, I wasn't sure they would look good on me.

Hamid, smart guy that he was, understood the situation and declared he had just the thing for American tastes. "I do not display them," he said. "They only sell with foreign customers." From behind a grubby curtain that hid a section of the showroom, he brought out several boxes full of the most gorgeous

bracelets I had ever seen. Unlike those on the shop's shelves, these lac bracelets were thick, ranging from an inch up to three wide, and they had not a hint of glitter. Made with a resinous substance that is produced by a kind of insect, they were quite muted in fact, with geometric and floral designs hand-painted with a glassy sort of finish.

Hamid pressed my fingers together and expertly slipped a few on, one after another. I noted with interest that he showed no hesitation in grabbing hold of my hand. Bracelet sellers, I decided, are the only men who can break the taboo of publicly touching a woman in India. The bracelets were cheap—ranging from $6 to $14—and with a mind to give away a few as gifts, I chose twelve thick ones in different colors. (Back home, though, I couldn't bear to part with any of them.)

Hamid threw in a free bracelet because he said I was such a good customer. He offered me a glass of tea and introduced me to his son, who was working behind the curtain, sticking beads onto newly made bracelets. Apparently, most of the goods in Hamid's emporium were made by members of his own family. In this back room I saw the lac-melting equipment, a small charcoal burner with an iron plate on top, and dozens of unfinished bracelets scattered on the floor.

Hamid's son, a timid-looking young man with a shy smile, handed me a bracelet he had just finished. It wasn't round and smooth like all the others, but bunched up with pleats and folds like a scrunchie hair band. According to Hamid, it was a new style his son was experimenting with. When I tried to return it, the boy shook his head and refused to take it. "I think he means to give this to you as a present. Keep it," said Hamid. I had already received a free bracelet from them and insisted on paying for this one. I was touched by their generosity.

When I left the shop, I took back not only some singular pieces of jewelry, but the warmth of Hamid and his son, and the memory of their genuine pleasure at my appreciation of their goods. Often, these small, personal interactions are lost in the flurry of sightseeing and hopping from city to city. But when I am back home, it is the hospitality and easy friendships of people like Hamid that come first to mind and make me want to return to India.

Maniharon Ka Raasta

Helene adds: Jaipur's lac bracelets blend beautifully with my Western clothes and add a subtle ethnic touch that complements rather than overloads an outfit. I'm glad I bought them in many colors while I had the chance, for I've got into the habit of slipping one on whenever I'm dressing for a special occasion. According to my friends, they are a quirk I picked up on my trip to India, but I love wearing these inexpensive beauties and enjoy the compliments I always receive for them. To purchase your own, go to Hamid's shop or any of the others in the lac artisan colony on Maniharon Ka Raasta lane next to Jaipur's Tripolia Bazar.

AGRA

Jenni Wadams sings the praises of the Agra carpet weavers

At the Kanu Carpet Factory showroom in Agra, an English-speaking salesman was going to give me a short tour of the factory. Before I made a purchase, I had told him, I wanted to know something about the making of the beautiful floral carpets all around me. You see, whenever I buy an expensive, ethnic product during my travels, I like to learn a little about its history. If nothing else, the knowledge makes me appreciate it more.

To my inexpert eye, the famous Agra carpets didn't look very different from the Persian or Turkish varieties. When I mentioned this, the salesman agreed that there was some superficial resemblance because the carpet-making craft had been imported by the Mughal emperor Akbar in the sixteenth century from Persia. Over time, the artisans of Agra integrated the same artistic character that makes the Taj

Mahal so unique. A later Mughal king's fascination with floral motifs further impacted the patterns, making flowers the central theme and giving rise to a school of carpet design that is known today as the "Agra style."

As we walked toward the factory's main hall, the salesman explained how a single carpet required many months of painstaking manual labor before it was ready for sale. He was about to say something more about the process, but was stopped mid-sentence by a loud humming noise that suddenly came from somewhere within the factory. It sounded like the rhythmic rise and fall of voices, as if a poetry class were in progress.

When we stepped into the work area, I saw the carpet weavers singing. One man was giving the lead from a corner of the room, and the workers picked up his refrain, repeating the same lyrics over and over. They were weaving on about ten upright wooden looms, and I could see portions of carpets taking shape on the stringed frames. Three weavers were assigned to each carpet, and they tied knots and cut the thread so fast that their hands were a blur of motion.

The singing, I imagined, was to entertain the weavers and make their work seem less monotonous, but the salesman explained it was part of Agra's carpet-making tradition. The song, translated into English, went something like this: "Queen's pink two, then royal blue two, then peacock blue one, then mango green two …"

In fact, it wasn't actually a song, but a method of keeping track of which color of wool was to be knotted next. The leader gave the cue, and the weavers chanted it back to him, making sure they weren't making a mistake with the order of the colors. A single knot tied out of turn would ruin the design of the whole carpet and diminish its value. The custom was so delightful, I couldn't hold back a smile.

"Notice the red base color of the design," the salesman said, drawing my attention back to the scraps of carpet hanging on the looms. "This red is a dye created by an insect called lac, and it's a specialty of our carpets. Notice also, the blue hue that is emerging." I looked closely, and sure enough, I could detect a subtle blue shadow mixed in with the red. The pinks and yellows of the flowers were so intensified against this background that the motifs almost looked enameled.

Once the laborious job of knotting was completed, what then? The salesman explained, "In the next stage, buckets of water will be poured over the carpets, and they will be raked over and over to make them durable. It will be a long while before the collection you see in front of you makes it to the showroom."

Talk of showrooms reminded me that I had come to buy a carpet to take home. The salesman led me back to the displays of finished carpets and handed me a chilled soda while a shop assistant rolled out selections in different sizes for my inspection. He invited me to walk on them, so I took off my dusty shoes and marched up and down, digging my toes into

UTTAR PRADESH

the deep pile. Indeed, the carpets were soft, as well as being beautiful. I would have loved to buy one of the larger ones, but my apartment in Tokyo was the size of a matchbox.

When the salesman heard that I lived in Tokyo, he proudly told me that the shop had carpets made especially for Japanese apartments. The assistant brought out a selection of tiny rugs measuring thirty by forty centimeters. These small versions were made by trainee weavers as practice pieces, but they appeared to be perfect miniatures of the larger carpets. I was drawn to one in a pretty shade of sandy yellow with lac red flowers, and leaves and creepers picked out in many hues of blue. I bought it to put in front of my bedside table.

I wondered how I would find space for it in my luggage, but the attendant folded it up so expertly, the package was no bigger than a large coffee table book. When I shook the carpet open in my apartment in Tokyo, I was alarmed to see deep grooves left by the tight folding, but a few days of walking on it smoothed them out easily enough. My miniature carpet looks lovely by the side of my bed, and whenever somebody asks me where I bought it, I tell them the story of the singing carpet weavers of Agra.

Kanu Carpet Factory

18/166/E Purani Mandi
Fatehabad Road
Agra

kanucarpet@yahoo.com

Responsible shopping

When buying rugs in India, look for the Rugmark certification, which guarantees fair trade practices and that child labor was not used in the making of the rug.

www.rugmarkindia.org

Alexandra Nassau-Brownstone price checks Agra's marble goods

I was in Agra and had done all the sightseeing my guidebook had suggested. I had marveled at the Taj Mahal, visited the fort, and driven down to the abandoned city of Fatehpur Sikri. Having discharged all my tourist duties, I was now free to engage in some serious shopping.

The thing to buy in Agra, in my opinion, is marble. Marble that is exquisitely inlaid with precious and semiprecious stones. The best example of Agra's expertise with marble is of course the Taj, but artisans did not stop practicing their trade after the grand structure was built. They continued to use the same inlay techniques on lesser objects, and the tradition passed on from generation to generation.

The few samples of Agra's marble products I had seen had intrigued me, but they were not cheap, so I set out with my friends to look into a few shops and do some price checking.

In the first big store we visited, the man at the counter was hell-bent on making a sale, and he did the dance around us, offering tea, soda, or anything else that would make us more comfortable. In his enthusiasm he even claimed to have a bottle of champagne cooling somewhere at the back. I was tempted to call him out on it, but my friends held me back. There was nothing to be gained by upsetting the guy, especially as he was giving us a lot of information about Agra's marble craft.

The local marble, he told us, was of superb quality. It was nonporous and did not absorb any particle matter. Had it not been so, the Taj would have turned black by now from centuries of exposure to environmental pollution. The other interesting feature was its translucence. Even a thick slab of marble, such as a tabletop, allowed light to pass through, giving it its signature luster.

What about the inlay work? The colored stones seemed to have been set in intricate designs all over the marble without a nick or a scratch. I wondered if precision machinery of some sort was used to achieve such perfection. At the mention of this, the man slapped his forehead a couple of times to let us know how horrified he was at the idea. "No, no, no, madam, no machine! Everything is hand-made!" he spluttered. "Every single item in this shop has been created by Agra's very best *parchin kari* artists."

Ignoring his tall claim about the quality of his stock, I asked, "*Parchin kari*?"

"Yes, that is the name of this kind of inlay work. Each design is the vision of a single master craftsman."

Master craftsmen, we learnt, were hugely respected in the *parchin kari* circuit, and referred to as *ustaads*. It was their job to plan the design, decide the color scheme, and select the marble and semiprecious stones that would be used. Sometimes, the designs were so elaborate that a single flower motif could contain more than one hundred individual pieces of colored stone and take over a week to complete.

The next step was cutting the stones into various shapes according to requirements of the design. The pieces then passed on to the inlay specialists, who made precise grooves in the marble so that the stones fit perfectly into them. The final stage involved hours of polishing, using a muslin cloth and a mix of natural powders. No wonder they cost so much.

We roamed around the shop, looking at the products with new respect and surveying prices. The shopkeeper quoted a sum for each and then announced he would discount anything we bought by 15 percent. One friend gave in and purchased a set of trivets for about $60 as a present for her parents. But as this was only our first shop, I felt that we should check out a few other places.

After visiting several marble shops, we had a feeling that the sellers were deliberately trying to confuse us into paying more for inferior quality. For example, the price of a photo frame in one shop couldn't be lowered because the semiprecious stones used were large. In another shop, the stones on a snuffbox I chose were quite small, but there were so many of them in the design, the price couldn't go down any further. At a third shop, the asking price for a pair of candlesticks, which had fewer and smaller stones, was somehow more than the other two.

After this happened a few times, we worked out that the salesmen were cleverly switching the variables to inflate prices.

It turned out that there were several aspects to consider: the quality of marble, the quality of the semiprecious stones, the size and number of the stones, and then the craftsmanship itself. Without knowledge of these variables, we would simply get taken in. So we changed tactic. We chose one particular product and then asked around for the price of that same item or similar items in different shops. Once we found a seller offering a better deal than the others, we went ahead and made our purchases at that outlet.

In my experience, the shopkeepers are aware when you appear informed about the different features of a piece and end up bringing the asking price down by half. Expect an opening offer of at least a 10 percent discount if you are confident, slightly disinterested, and—always—polite. And remember, if you are serious about bargaining, you must be ready to walk away, no matter how much you want that vase, snuffbox, or candlestick.

Agra Marble Shoppy

Agra's marble markets and shops are often located close to each other, so in an hour or so you can do a quick appraisal and make your purchases. The marble merchandize in this particular store is definitely more impressive than its name. It is located conveniently near the East Gate of the Taj Mahal.

LUCKNOW

Deepanjana Sarkar embroiders a tale of shopping in Lucknow

Unlike most nonresident Indians, I never felt the urge to hit the shops the moment I set foot on home soil. A jeans-and-T-shirt sort of girl who still hadn't outgrown her college wardrobe, I was happy to admire ornate Indian clothes from a distance, and it was a rare wedding or other social occasion when my mother could browbeat me into wearing anything with even a hint of embroidery.

It needed a Bollywood film to change my dismissive attitude toward India's embroidery tradition. One of its many traditions of embroidery, at least: the *chikankari*.

The film was called *Mohabbatein*, and in it, the female lead, Aishwarya Rai, looked amazing in clothes covered with a fine web of *chikankari* threadwork.

Of course, I had seen *chikankari* before, in garment stores in Delhi and Mumbai. But it had never looked so wispy, lightweight, and irresistibly beautiful. The fabric seemed to melt away on Aishwarya's skin, and all one could see was the superb *chikankari* needlework that floated around her. My mother, who knew more about these things than I, said it was definitely the work of the embroiderers of Lucknow. *Chikankari* is an ancient tradition of this historical city, and no *kaarigar* (craftsman) from elsewhere in India can match the skills of the *kaarigar* here.

By some stroke of luck, two years later, I made it to a *chikankari* shop in Lucknow. I was touring North India with a group of architecture students from Kuwait. I had a free afternoon in the city, and my hotel manager sent me to Chowk Market, where he said I would find scores of *chikankari* shops. I wasn't looking for bargains. What I wanted was a chance to see samples of high-grade *chikankari* work with my own eyes.

The portly, middle-aged woman who was serving me pulled her veil over her mouth and giggled when I mentioned the film *Mohabbatein*. "Aiyaa! That movie has been a blessing to our business," she said. "All the young girls now come looking for *chikankari* like Aishwarya Rai wore."

It was just after the lunch hour. Chewing on her after-meal betel leaf, the woman was mellow and in a chatty mood. Enjoying my curiosity, she spoke about the craft in a heavily accented Hindi that I had to strain my ears to understand. Basically, she told me, *chikankari* is a kind of "shadow stitch." The actual work is done on the back side of the material, and what I saw on the surface was just its shadow. With very small stitches, the shadows are outlined so the designs stand out. The more transparent the fabric, the better *chikankari* looks. Muslin is the material of choice for high-quality work, but these days, even modern synthetics like georgette and chiffon are being used.

The woman bent under the counter and pulled out a hefty package covered in plastic. "This lot has only just arrived from the *kaarigars*," she said. "I think it is what you are looking for." Inside were blouses in soft pastel shades. At the woman's urging, I slipped my arms into a pair of long sleeves. Sure enough, the material seemed to fade against my skin while the embroidery showed up prominently. I was enchanted.

All the blouses in the package had white embroidery, as did every other *chikankari* garment in the shop. I asked the woman why that was so. "It is the tradition," she said. "The thread is always white. It makes the embroidery look more elegant." In the choice of background color, however, the Lucknow *kaarigars* were moving with the times. *Chikankari* used to be done only on fabrics in five shades: lemon yellow, sky blue, pink, white, and mint green. Judging from what I saw around me, the palette had been extended to include every color under the sun.

Despite so much variety, I still favored white-on-white and bought a blouse and a scarf in this classic combination. For my sister, I tried to buy a shirt in her favorite color, maroon, but the woman stopped me. "*Chikankari* does not look quite so pretty on dark colors," she cautioned. "Take something lighter instead." To please her, I chose a delicate dove gray.

Before I left the shop, she insisted on showing me some new items being made with *chikankari* embroidery: cushion covers, pillowcases, blankets, and other home furnishings. I spied a primrose pink set in the pile of table mats and bought it as a gift for my mother, certain it would look lovely on our lacquered Japanese dining table.

I bid the woman goodbye and thanked her for all her help. She held my hands in hers and made me promise to come back. Maybe I would, if I was ever in Lucknow and if I could find her shop again in the crowded Chowk marketplace.

Back home in Kuwait, I was in the antiquity section of the local library one day, when my eyes fell upon a thick picture book on India's textile heritage. I leafed through the pages until I found a short entry on *chikankari*. This style of embroidery has been in vogue in India since 655 AD, according to the first paragraph. During the reign of the Mughals, it flourished under the patronage of Noor Jehan, the famous wife of Emperor Jehangir. Just as I once never imagined myself wearing embroidered clothing, I would never have imagined that something so innocuous as embroidery could have such rich history behind it. Standing in the steel-and-chrome library on the sixteenth floor of an ultramodern building in Kuwait, I thought about the importance of tradition and felt very proud to be an Indian.

Chowk Market

Primarily a wholesale market in the old Lucknow area, Chowk is the best place to buy *chikankari* clothing in Lucknow.

GENERAL NORTH INDIA

Colorful fabrics are one of the best gifts to bring home from India

A boy sells peacock feathers

Mystical India

Hinduism and beyond

Growing up in a land of 330 million gods is not easy—especially when they inveigle themselves into every aspect of your life. And that's talking only of the Hindu pantheon. In India, there's Buddhism, Jainism, and Islam to contend with as well. So how do Indians learn to cope with all of these religions?

Usually, mythology comes to the rescue. We take the delightful recourse of learning about our religion, culture, and heritage through mythological stories. When I was young, a series of comic books was introduced called Amar Chitra Katha, which tore an entire generation of kids away from Archie's romances and Tarzan's jungle adventures and fed their imaginations instead with tales of Hindu gods and the country's religious past.

Foreign travelers visiting India, obviously, don't have this advantage. They marvel at the country's antiquity, enjoy the monuments and temples, and then look totally confused when a guide tries to explain their significance. It is impossible to understand the complexities of India's religious beliefs and traditions without doing some serious homework, which most travelers don't have time to do. That is unfortunate, because much of what's beautiful about India lies therein.

The words *tantra* and *karma*, which turn up so often in any discussion about spirituality and India, are good examples of complex, barely understood concepts that are fundamental parts of Indian life. These words are tossed around because they are mysterious and somewhat magical—and surely they are appropriate if Hinduism or yoga is involved. I have discovered that people love certain words simply because they seem excitingly spiritual *and* Indian. My brother-in-law, for example, a German-American, suddenly developed a fondness for the word *kundalini*. It sounded rather tantric, something to do with power emerging from an individual's navel, and he adored that. For a period of three months, a time when his wife was seriously ill and he needed all the hope he could get

to see him through long hours of hospital duty, he even called himself Mr. Kundalini.

Neither he nor I ever had a very good idea about what kundalini is. If you ask an average Indian on the street, chances are that he won't be able to tell you either. The country's spiritual canvas is too vast, too complicated, and understanding it can be a lifelong process. Perhaps that is why we Indians can at times be as amazed by our country as a foreign visitor is. While compiling this book, I learnt so much from the contributors that on many occasions I felt they were describing a country not entirely my own. I read about experiences that made them seem more Hindu than I.

This chapter was a bit of a struggle to put together precisely for this reason. There were so many religions to include, so many regional beliefs to accommodate, so many rituals to explore. So I chose a middle ground and attempted to find a balance of offerings. Some are spectacles, like the temple of rats in Deshnok. A few are religious practices, including the death rituals in Varanasi. Tibetan philosophy finds a place via a surprisingly aggressive arguing session among monks, as do a touch of religious pornography, superstition, ayurveda, and even yoga. Because spirituality is woven so deeply into the culture, you will find traces of it in many of the essays in other chapters in this book, as well.

This is a tasting menu, if you will, of the spiritualism and mysticism this country has to offer. There are no spinning dervishes here to pump up the excitement, nor any mention of the Great Indian Rope Trick. As you are about to discover, the magic of India's genuine spiritual customs well surpasses these tired old clichés.

New Delhi

Jeannine Hohmann submits to ayurvedic healing in Delhi

I thought I knew something about ayurveda, but when my friend Stacy launched into an enthusiastic discussion about *kaphas*, *vittas*, and *doshas*, my arsenal of ayurvedic terms like herbs, yoga, and diet were shown up for what they were: an oversimplified summing up of this ancient system of healing that I remembered from a *Good Housekeeping* article I read several years ago.

Stacy had reason to be excited. She'd heard of a wonderful ayurvedic doctor whose clinic was very near our hotel in Delhi's Paharganj area. She had only just fixed an appointment to see him, and she suddenly had another idea. Why didn't I come along as well? I had been down with yet another bout of cough and cold, and all the over-the-counter capsules I was swallowing three times a day weren't doing me much good. What was the harm in letting this doctor have a shot at me?

The next afternoon, Stacy and I found ourselves at Dr. Jaggi's clinic. It certainly wasn't posh. In fact, it consisted of nothing much more than a long table. Dr. Jaggi sat behind it, a big, jolly old man in a gray undershirt. He motioned us to settle ourselves down on the narrow bench in front of him that functioned as a waiting room. An English lady went before us, and we listened interestedly to the symptoms she narrated to the good doctor. Her consultation didn't take long, but this was her second visit, we learned, so Dr. Jaggi was perhaps already familiar with her case.

Then it was our turn. I went first and started to explain my problem: congestion in the lungs, constant coughing, and some difficulty in breathing. It sounded tame after the English lady's colorful description of digestive issues, but Dr. Jaggi didn't seem to miss the drama. Instead, he asked a series of questions and quoted his fee: 500 rupees. For approximately $10, he could guarantee great relief.

I was led into a tiny massage room, which had been created by hanging a bedsheet as a makeshift wall next to Dr. Jaggi's office area. A helpful lady was in attendance, and she indicated that I should remove my outer clothes and lie down on the massage table, which was an extremely hard plank of raised wood. It wasn't as if Dr. Jaggi were scrimping, though. All Indian massage centers seem to favor this uncomfortable bit of furniture.

First came the sesame treatment. For forty minutes, hot sesame oil was dripped onto my forehead from a clay vessel suspended from the ceiling. The sensation was peculiar. Think about how often you may have been touched at the precise midpoint between your eyebrows: hardly ever. Until this experience, I had no idea that this part of my body was so sensitive.

It took some getting used to, but after the initial shock, I began to enjoy the heightened feeling. My body loosened, my mind seemed to swell, and I almost went to sleep. For a long time afterward, thin currents of sensation continued to shoot out from that precise spot on my forehead. The oil has many medicinal benefits, Dr. Jaggi came in to explain to me, and the drip helped to align the *nadas*, the channels that *prana* and energy flow through. *Nadas*? *Pranas*? I may have been lost, but the clearing out of previously blocked passages certainly felt good.

While I was lying under the sesame drip, the assistant mixed up a concoction of herbs, which I now inhaled using a steamer. Dr. Jaggi returned to the massage room holding a cup of oily orange fluid in his hand, and the assistant had me snort it up my nose. This orange substance would later reach my digestive system. Once the oil ceased to trickle back out of my nose, Dr. Jaggi declared that the treatment was over. I put on my clothes and returned to the front office to wait for Stacy to have her turn.

I cannot pretend I understood what happened in the clinic that day, but then, what do I know of the medicines I so trustfully take upon doctor's advice in the West? As for the result, the next morning I was taken

aback to discover that my chronic cough of weeks had disappeared. Usually, when I woke up it was at its worst. This day, however, there was no familiar itch inside my chest.

I've left India a long time since that treatment, and the cough—on the rare occasion that it does show up—is never as bad as it used to be. I could credit all that good Indian sunshine, or the healthy food I ate while I was there. But I know the truth. Dr. Jaggi's forehead drips and nose baths healed me.

Dr Jaggi's Body & Soul Clinic

If you have a health problem that's been with you for a while, you may want to consider an ayurvedic consultation. Dr. Jaggi's was a humble operation, but you will also find upscale clinics in almost all the cities and towns in North India. The practitioners have a habit of talking in "ayurvedese" when they explain what they are doing, so you may not fully understand the principles of the treatment, just as Jeannine didn't. But the experience is worthwhile, not only for your health but for an introduction into this unique Indian tradition.

47-49, Chandiwali Street
Paharganj
New Delhi

More about ayurveda

For basic information about ayurveda, including the nasal treatment that Jeannine experienced, go to the following website.

www.holisticonline.com/ayurveda/ayv_home.htm

Suzie Chiodo
learns a lesson in tolerance
at a Delhi mosque

The mosque was one of those old architectural marvels I came across so often in Delhi, standing incongruously and somewhat out of context in the midst of modern high-rises and shanty colonies. There was nothing extraordinary to mark it out, except perhaps a strange, heavy silence that seemed at odds with the busyness of its surroundings. It was a blisteringly hot Delhi afternoon, and nobody seemed to be about.

My friend Nadia and I were not sure if we would be welcome, but we decided on an impulse to step inside anyway. Having worked in the Muslim world, I was aware of the customs that had to be followed in a place of worship, and we made sure our heads and legs were fully covered before we tiptoed through the passageway that led off the entrance. The silence followed us, confirming our suspicion that the mosque was deserted. So when the passage opened sud-denly into a large courtyard, we were startled to find ourselves standing in the middle of an open-air classroom for Koranic studies.

The class had just given over, and little kids were milling about, collecting their books and preparing to leave. We spotted their teacher in the crowd, an old, white-haired mullah, wearing a kufi (Islamic prayer cap) and a long beard. Nadia clutched hold of my hand in fear, and we stood transfixed. We had been caught trespassing in a mosque, and the mullah looked so grim, we were certain we had landed ourselves in serious trouble.

Controlling the impulse to run away, Nadia and I waited for the wrath of the mullah to break upon us. To our surprise and immense relief, he smiled instead, displaying a row of gleaming gold and yellow teeth, and indicated that we should follow him. Contrary to our expectations, the mullah wanted to give us a tour of the mosque.

Timidly, we trailed behind him, and as we passed under the shade of the stone colonnades surrounding the courtyard, the mullah pointed out various architectural points of interest. His English wasn't good, and we had to follow his gestures to understand what he was telling us. When we reached an elongated sink, our host turned on a tap and mimed washing his face—his ears, nose, and mouth—as well as his hands, arms, neck, and feet. He was showing us how Muslims perform *wudu*, I realized, the act of washing themselves before prayer.

He then escorted us into the heart of the mosque, which was a massive prayer hall, laid down with richly hued carpets and decorated with what looked like Arabic calligraphy on the walls. It could easily accommodate a couple of hundred people, and the mullah told us that devout Muslims congregated here from the surrounding neighborhoods when the muezzin sounded his call.

Opposite the entrance to the prayer hall was the *qibla*, the wall facing toward Mecca. An ornately carved niche was cut into the center of the wall, and the mullah stopped in front of it, slowly raising his hands to his ears. He kept encouraging us to do the same until it finally dawned on us that the mullah was trying to teach us how to pray. Although we struggled to understand what he was saying, we learned how to bow, kneel, and prostrate ourselves. When we had finished, he waved away our thanks and invited us to return whenever we wanted.

The incident, though a minor one, remained in my mind long after I left Delhi. Everything that transpired in the mosque that afternoon ran counter to the militant image some fundamentalist elements have given Islam in today's political climate. The religion isn't as intolerant as many non-Muslims in the Western world have been led to believe, and an experience like this went a long way in clearing up that notion. Mosques in India make no distinctions of race, sex, and religion, and I would strongly recommend that every traveler visit one. If you're lucky and arrive at a quiet time of day, and you happen to meet a mullah, he might even introduce you to the basics of Muslim prayer.

Observing Muslim ceremonies

Delhi's Jama Masjid mosque receives only passing mention in this book because it is so celebrated and "obvious" as a tourist attraction. That said, it really is a treat for travelers. Another good place to visit is Nizamuddin Dargah. Along with observing all Muslim prayer ceremonies, this sixteenth-century Delhi mausoleum on Mathura Road holds a *qawali*—song-and-dance recital by mystics of the Sufi sect—every Thursday. The *qawali* attracts a huge audience, and the fervor with which it is performed makes it an unforgettable experience.

KULLU

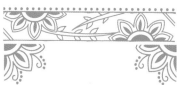

Rinoti Amin encounters "living gods" in the Kullu Valley

The mountain air of Himachal Pradesh kept me in a constant state of happy light-headedness, and my spirit, emboldened by the sudden freedom from the constraints of city life, ached for unusual experiences. So when I heard about "living gods" at the Dussehra Festival in Himachal's Kullu Valley, I knew I had my adventure right there.

I did some quick reading on the culture of Kullu and found that the people of this region infused the idols of their gods with human emotions and feelings. Their gods were as prone to being kind and benevolent as they were to being moody, jealous, and quarrelsome. But they were much wiser than their subjects, and therefore, to be honored at the festival, a weeklong celebration held in the valley's main town of Kullu. The idols presiding over different villages were carried here to meet, greet, and catch up with each other. As luck would have it, the festival was due to begin in just a few days' time, and I quickly packed my bags and set off in a high state of excitement. No way was I going to miss this opportunity to be part of the annual reunion of the Kullu gods.

I also had another goal: to encounter Jhamlu Devta. My research had thrown up some intriguing stories about this particular god, who was considered the most temperamental and opinionated in Kullu Valley's pantheon. The capricious and willful nature of Jhamlu Devta piqued my curiosity, and I had a burning desire to see him. Since all the village deities attended the festival, I was sure he would be present as well.

Although Jhamlu Devta stood out for me personally, the star of this weeklong affair was yet another god called Raghunathji. It was in Raghunathji's honor that the Dussehra Festival was organized, and once I got into Kullu, I followed the crowds until I saw his elaborately adorned chariot being pulled by ropes toward an open field. Too many hands were tugging at the ropes, causing much confusion, but somehow Raghunathji's chariot managed to lurch to the center of a field, where it would stand for the next six days. Idols of innumerable village gods and goddesses, all wearing gold masks and shimmering robes, were then carried up to the chariot in palanquins, so they could pay their respects to Raghunathji. Each idol had its own entourage of musicians, who beat on *dhols* (drums) and blew into long, rustic flutes to announce their approach.

After meeting with Raghunathji, the village gods retreated to their own designated places in the field, and their human subjects ensured they were comfortable before camping out next to them. *Gaddis* (mattresses), *chaddars* (sheets), and pots and pans were thrown down, and the visibly tired villagers lolled on the ground, puffing on pipes packed with strong-smelling hashish, taking toke after toke until their eyes turned glassy. The atmosphere was so pagan, so unlike any reality I had known, that at times I thought I was dreaming.

As I wandered, I encountered a wizened old man sitting on a stoop, rubbing a piece of tobacco. When he saw the look of tourist's awe on my face, he explained in halting

Hindi that the villagers could have been walking for as many as twenty days over the mountains to bring their local deities here. "These days, though, the young generation of rogues has started hopping onto the bus instead," he grumbled. "The gods don't approve of this new trend." He crumpled his eyebrows to illustrate the gods' displeasure.

The mention of disapproving gods brought my newly discovered favorite, Jhamlu Devta, to mind. Surely, he should have been here by now, presiding over a large coterie and trying to hog the limelight? "Sir, can you tell me where Jhamlu is?" I asked, cringing even as the words slipped out of my mouth. I was casually referring to one of the leading gods of the region by his first name, as if he were a naughty eight-year-old temporarily missing from home.

"Who?" the old man asked, scratching his jaw.

"Jhamlu Devta." I wondered if I was mispronouncing the name. I added, "The local god of the village of Malana. The most important god of the Kullu region."

"Oh, that one," the old man snorted. "He doesn't come here. He thinks the Dussehra Festival is beneath him. That one has too much arrogance. He stands on the other side and watches from a distance." His tobacco-stained forefinger pointed carelessly across the Beas River. I stared hard, half-expecting to catch a glimpse of a gold mask watching us from behind the thick bushes. But I saw nothing.

Having read so much about Jhamlu Devta, a god who supposedly controlled and administered the Kullu Valley, I thought it was rather immature of him to boycott the festival because he felt too good for it. His refusal to attend, the old man said, also meant that the villagers of Malana couldn't participate in the celebrations. This seemed unfair, and I was deeply disappointed with Jhamlu Devta—after all, he was one of the main reasons I had come all the way to Kullu.

Leaving the old man to toast in the sun, I took my griping over to the nearby fairground, which was the nonreligious highlight of the event. I watched people buying handfuls of persimmons and plums, moving from stall to stall as they haggled good-naturedly. *Lugri*, the traditional Kullu drink, was flowing freely. Everybody was having fun.

After a while I'd had enough of being pushed around in the crowd and decided to return to my hotel. I spent the next few days exploring Kullu, and I returned to the festival ground only to watch the closing ceremony. I made it in time to see Raghunathji's chariot hurtling at great speed down an incline toward the Beas River. The crowd hurtled along with the chariot, and with them, me. I knew we reached the bank when the moving mass of people stopped suddenly and I banged my nose against the hard shoulder of the person in front.

To signal the closing of ceremonies, the Maharaja of Kullu sacrificed a buffalo and carried its bloody head over to the chariot to present it to Raghunathji. Then the village gods began to arrive one by one on the shoulders of men to say farewell and take their leave. As the palanquins started their slow journeys back home over the mountains, people began to disperse in the direction of the fairground, to look for final discounts before the stalls were dismantled.

I felt that I was the only one who would go back home from the festival without having got what he wanted. A whole week had passed and yet Jhamlu Devta's no-show still rankled. I took one last lingering look at the Beas River and was about to turn away to walk to the fairground, when a small movement across the water caught my eye. I can't say for certain, but I just might have seen a glint of a golden mask among the bushes.

Getting to the Kullu Valley

Ten kilometers from Kullu and Manali, Bhuntar is a small airport that services both towns. Luxury buses to Kullu are also available from Delhi, Shimla, Chandigarh, and other North India cities. To assure accommodation, you may want to make arrangements with a tour company if you are coming for the Dussehra Festival, which takes place during the first week of October.

DHARAMSHALA

Emma Louise Christie is shocked by arguing monks in Dharamshala

I was out on an Indian adventure with two trusted guides: a Tibetan friend and the moonlight. As I stumbled down the pebbled road, I held on to the former's hand, not sure why we were making our way to the Dalai Lama's temple in the dead of night. When I had asked, my friend only smiled mysteriously and said that it was a surprise.

The temple loomed ahead of us, a charcoal silhouette against the dark sky. I had spent plenty of time there, spinning the prayer wheels and listening to the Dalai Lama speak, but the way we were creeping up to it while the rest of the town of Dharamshala slept made me feel slightly uncomfortable.

I detected a murmur in the air, which intensified into clearly audible shouts and derisive laughter as we climbed the stairs up to the main hall. I looked questioningly at my young friend, but he only motioned with his head for me to continue. When loud slapping sounds floated down to us, I started to regret the impulse to accompany him here. I hadn't encountered any religious activity that could produce such noises in this temple before, and the darkness of the night made them seem all the more ominous. My imagination conjured crazy possibilities of what was going on inside, but I willed myself to move toward the source of the commotion.

As we stepped into the main hall, I saw scores of Buddhist monks milling about. Some were huddled on the ground while the others walked agitatedly around them. A ritual was clearly in progress—maybe this was a meeting of a secret brotherhood of monks—and I felt like an interloper. I was the only one not wearing burgundy robes, and whose head didn't shine in the moonlight. I was a white foreign woman on top of that, and I had walked into this midnight scene quite uninvited. My companion attempted to reassure me by explaining what was going on. This was a traditional debate, he said, an integral part of the Tibetan monastic education. Really, none of the monks cared that I was there.

I watched as monks bore down aggressively on fellow monks on the ground, raising their arms behind them and then slapping the air over and over again, jeering all the while. Those on the ground were trying to defend themselves with counterarguments. While I couldn't understand what they were saying, as they spoke in Tibetan, I could see that the points the lowered monks were making had no impact on their tormentors, who continued to stamp their feet and slap the air,

shouting all the time. This could have seemed comical in a different set of circumstances, but at that time I was more concerned than amused.

My Tibetan friend tried again to help me understand. After much gesticulating and shouting back and forth in order to be heard over the arguing monks, I finally understood that nobody was being abused here. Because the questions raised in the debates used to train novice monks were so complex at times, it was difficult to thrash them out with much enthusiasm, so the process was livened up. This also gave the trainee monks a lesson in the art of quick thinking. Apparently, Tibetan scholars loved the energetic physical gestures for the excitement they created and missed debating in this manner once their training period was over. What I was witnessing was nothing more than a common Tibetan Buddhist debate practice. The crazy madman-like gestures of the questioners were just part of a routine.

We wandered from group to group, listening to the exchanges. The monks were so involved in their heated discussions they scarcely noticed us. They wrung the strings of prayer beads in their hands and just went on screaming at each other. One monk, I noticed, was getting a little physical with his opponent while he made his assertions. Every time he walked up to the monk sitting on the ground, he rapped him lightly on the side of the face. It was annoying to watch, and I wondered why the recipient of these blows was not protesting. As we got closer to the pair, however, I saw that the aggressor laughed each time he did it, and his opponent shook his head ruefully. Obviously, the monk on the ground was making a poor show of it and didn't mind being chastised in this way for his lack of good arguments.

Later, I learnt that these debates could disintegrate into open fights. The questioner sometimes became vicious, rubbing in his victory by shouting, "The root thesis is finished! The root thesis is finished!"—the stock phrase winners use to close a debate. In the face of intense public humiliation, some respondents suffered from bouts of depression. On rare occasions, a debate even led to blows and lifetime enmity. On the whole, however, the trainee monks approached the exercise in a positive spirit, and as the session I attended came to an end, the monks closed their debates by congratulating each other, looking happily exhausted and satisfied.

As my friend and I returned from the night's adventure, my mind kept replaying scenes from the debates. Tibetan monks, in my experience thus far, were peaceful people, and I was still having trouble reconciling that image with the aggressive scene I had just witnessed. While it was some-what disconcerting to watch, I have to admit that it was also intriguing once I knew the background. And in the end, my exposure to the debates rounded out my experience with the Tibetan monks in Dharamshala, showing me that these seemingly perfect people are human, after all.

Getting to Dharamshala/ McLeodganj

Go to the fact file on page 118.

Monastic debates

The Tibetan name for this one-on-one debate is *rtsod zla*. In Dharamshala, the monks do not mind if visitors watch or even film a *rtsod zla* in progress. Almost every monastery with trainee monks holds these sessions, and you can ask about times once you arrive in town.

TRIKOOT MOUNTAIN

Linda Saleh wishes her way up Trikoot Mountain

It was well past midnight, but after an exhilarating thirteen-kilometer hike up Trikoot Mountain, I was wide-awake and looking forward to the next leg of the pilgrimage. We had reached a point called Bhawan and were now waiting for our turn to enter the cave of Mother god-dess Vaishno Devi. Even that late, thousands of pilgrims were queued up before us, and our entrance ticket belonged to a batch that would be called in two hours.

My friends Lata and Rishi had gone to take a ritual bath to wake themselves up and wash away the dirt of the journey before standing in Mother's presence. I had bathed with them in a mountain stream at the start of the hike and decided not to join them this time for fear of bringing on a cold. It was April, and pleasantly warm when we started out, but now at such a high altitude, the mountain air was decidedly chilly. I pulled my shawl closer around myself and settled down on a marble staircase to read about Vaishno Devi from a booklet I had bought while waiting.

According to legend, the Mother goddess fled up the mountain, pursued by an insistent demigod who had become enamored of her. Confronted outside the cave at Bhawan, she had no other choice but to kill him. Rather than return to her ashram at the bottom of the mountain, she decided to remain at the cave, shedding her human form and becoming a part of the rock face. Her spirit now lingered in the cave, blessing the thousands of devotees who came every day. The cave was never closed, and it was said that nobody returned empty-handed from Vaishno Devi. If you prayed at her feet, she would certainly grant your wish.

I am one of those tiresome people who insist on material proof before giving credence to any belief. But in this instance, for some mysterious reason, Vaishno Devi silenced all my "whys" and "hows" and held

me in her spell from the moment we started the hike. With the tying of a red and gold Vaishno Devi scarf on my forehead, I became her child, and like the Hindu pilgrims who were climbing with me, I too was going to see my Mother.

Our pilgrimage up Trikoot Mountain had begun in a little town called Katra. After an early dinner, we bought wooden walking sticks and set off. We could have hired a helicopter service, or even horses and palanquins, but we wanted to go on foot for the experience. The path was paved and well maintained, but the inclines were so steep that we had to stop several times to rest and get a drink from one of the food stalls that lined the way.

Many of our fellow pilgrims were climbing barefoot as a mark of respect for the Mother. One of them gave us the scarves in Vaishno Devi's signature colors and taught me to shout "Jai Mata Di!"—"Glory to our Mother." The cry kept up all our spirits, and when our legs were almost buckling under us with tiredness, it gave us the will and the strength to push on. The sound of beating drums and devotional songs celebrating Vaishno Devi ricocheted off the mountainsides. We were still miles away from the main shrine, but my mind already felt illuminated.

We hiked farther up, helping each other along the way, until after several hours we finally reached Bhawan. So here I was, sitting on a staircase near the main shrine, waiting for my friends to return from their baths. Our turn to enter the cave was called soon after, and we joined the fast-moving queue in a long tunnel, walking in freezing water, which was flowing through the cave. As we entered, we had been told to concentrate our thoughts on Vaishno Devi because we wouldn't get more than a few seconds to stand in front of her. I bowed my head and made my wish to her, over and over hoping that my prayer wouldn't be lost among the thousands she must hear every day.

The queue moved forward, and at last, I was standing in front of the shrine of Vaishno Devi. There wasn't an idol, as I had expected, but three natural rock formations that stuck out like knobs. Vaishno Devi was represented here as three powerful female goddesses in the Hindu pantheon—Kali, Lakshmi, and Saraswati. A crown sat near the head of each knob, and a thick necklace of gold was twined around them. The base on which the stones lay was dressed in red and gold cloth. Quickly, I crouched down and tapped my head at Vaishno Devi's feet, the way I had seen the others do. Then I was ushered out of the cave through another tunnel. I wished I had a little more time with the Mother goddess, but there were so many pilgrims each day that the authorities had no option but to move the queue quickly on.

After a short rest, Lata, Rishi, and I started our downhill journey, this time on horseback. The night was growing light with the approaching dawn, and I could make out the contours of the Himalayan range around us. The horses kept a steady pace, and we reached our base town of Katra in a remarkably short time.

It was seven in the morning when we returned to our hotel. My friends went to bed immediately, but I knew I wouldn't get a wink of sleep until I understood the profound impact of this soul-cleansing pilgrimage. The power in the cry Jai Mata Di was still ringing in my ears. The red and gold scarf tied around my head was still connecting my spirit to the Mother goddess. I may have met her only briefly in her cave temple high up on Trikoot Mountain, but I could clearly feel her presence in my tiny hotel room.

Making your wish

The base town of Katra for a Vaishno Devi piligrimage is about fifty kilometers away from the city of Jammu. Make your hotel bookings as early as possible as accommodation is always at a premium here. There are also resting rooms available in Bhawan, but again, you have to book well in advance. At Katra, you must get permits from the Vaishno Devi registration office. For a wealth of information on the legends and history of the goddess, as well as details on planning your visit, go to the Shri Mata Vaishno Devi Shrine Board website.

www.maavaishnodevi.org

JAMMU & KASHMIR

KHAJURAHO

*Frank Goodman
ponders the temple
pornography of Khajuraho*

Temple pornography? In India? The country, I concede, gave the *Kama Sutra* to the world, but carving the walls of a sacred temple with explicit coital positions suggested a kind of sexual permissiveness that, in my opinion, was completely un-Hindu. I felt I had to find out more about this relationship between sex and Hinduism. So I decided to go to the Khajuraho temple and see the sculptures for myself.

Getting to Khajuraho in northeast Madhya Pradesh, however, was easier said than done. For an average traveler like myself, the town is located rather inconveniently in the middle of nowhere. The nearest railway station is well over one hundred kilometers away, and unless I was willing to buy an overpriced air ticket, I had to bus it or take a cab from Jhansi. Five hours, either way.

I overlooked this hardship and made the journey, just like so many others. Photographs in travel brochures of the outer panels of the Khajuraho temples provided sufficient inducement. The panels are lined with sculptures of men and women, sometimes in pairs but more often in groups, executing copulatory feats with such a jumbling of arms and legs that it is difficult to immediately work out which appendage belongs to whom.

Once I arrived at the Khajuraho temple site, I found a guide who gravely introduced himself as "Mr. Buggilal. Call me Bugsy." This small, mustachioed man in a beige safari suit, I thought, would explain the relevance of the erotic in Hinduism in simple layman terms and solve my theological quandary. In short, he would tell me why this temple looks like an ode to Hugh Hefner.

After we negotiated his fee, he took me on an extended tour of the tenth-century temple complex, giving detailed descriptions of the deviant sexual positions carved on its outer walls with too straight a face. Then he struggled to come up with a couple of plausible theories about why they happened to be here.

Maybe, these erotic sculptures depict tantric rituals of ancient times, he said, fiddling unconsciously with an epaulette on his eighties-style safari jacket. Or perhaps, since some panels also show people getting on with their everyday lives, the sexual content is nothing more than a record of the nocturnal activity of Indians at a time when there was no television.

I was hoping to hear more about a melding of yoga's spiritual approach to exercise and *bhoga* (sensory pleasure), the two different paths that led to *moksha* (deliverance of the soul), but Bugsy was more interested in holding up the sculptures as proof of the virility of Indian men than undertaking a discussion on Hindu philosophy.

"What you Westerners do in the name of sexual freedom, we already finish doing a thousand years ago," he announced with a been-there-done-that expression that left me feeling very inadequate. I paid Bugsy his fee and an extra tip and sent him on his way. A few minutes later, I fell into conversation with a retired army brigadier who was willing to sit awhile and answer some questions for me.

I gathered, from what he said, that monastic Buddhism was holding sway over India around the time when the Khajuraho temple was built. More and more people were opting for the Buddhist hermit life, ignoring their social obligations of marriage and reproduction. It was imperative that the men be brought back into the family fold if society was to survive. One way of doing that was to revive their interest in sex. Temples were an obvious place for social congregation, and so their outer walls were used to illustrate the pleasures that men were missing out on by becoming Buddhists.

But orgies with multiple partners? Wasn't that as detrimental to the happy growth of Hindu family life as the spread of Buddhism?

"The sculptures were trying to rekindle an interest in sex by promoting sexual fantasies," the brigadier reasoned. "Fantasy is rarely bound to the marital bed. Though I do think the sculptures of lovemaking with bulls and horses are a bit excessive." He hastened to add that this was just one of many theories about Khajuraho's pornography, but his explanation made a lot of sense.

I was still curious to know how Hindus tolerated this material in the holy temple of their gods. For the life of me, I couldn't imagine any Western church allowing bacchanalian scenes of orgies to be sculpted on its walls.

"It goes to show our broadmindedness," said the brigadier with a smile. "We Hindus make no judgments on Khajuraho from a religious point of view. Our goddesses are often depicted in scant clothing, but we only see them as Mother. Prurient thoughts don't occur to us in the religious context."

I was mulling over this when I heard a burst of raucous laughter. Our attention was drawn to an approaching group of college boys who were clearly enjoying their study tour of the Khajuraho temple. They gathered around a sculpture of a saddled horse that was pleasuring two men. Pointing at the tableau, one of boys said, "Now isn't that disrespectful. These guys haven't even bothered to undress the poor horse first!"

In spite of himself, my old, retired friend began to laugh. I laughed along with him, thinking how wrong I sometimes was when I labeled Indians as conservative. The Khajuraho temple proves, as do many other instances, that the Indian mindscape

PUNJAB

can be an impressive place where conflicting ideas can coexist without intruding on each other. It made what I had thought to be my liberal Western outlook on religion and life seem narrow in comparison.

Getting to Khajuraho

Khajuraho is well connected by air, rail, and road to Delhi, Varanasi, and other major cities. Once you arrive, we recommend exploring the town on a bicycle. You can rent one for a reasonable sum from the stands opposite the western group of temples.

Dining in Khajuraho

Dining options are limited in this small town, but you might want to try the Blue Sky restaurant on Main Road for a fun, treehouse experience. Diners sit among the branches and share food with sparrows and other birds that come here looking for handouts. The restaurant also affords nice views of Khajuraho's western temples.

AMRITSAR

Jorden Leighton savors Sikh generosity in Amritsar

I stumbled off the bus into the sweltering streets of Amritsar around nine at night. Fifteen hours earlier, my journey had begun in the cool, misty dawn of Srinagar, the summer capital of Kashmir, but here, it was beyond hot. The overwhelming heat was only slightly eased by the breeze supplied courtesy of my rickshaw ride.

My destination was the famous Golden Temple, arguably the most unique and beautiful temple in India. Deposited just outside of it, I located the guesthouse provided free of charge for foreigners—and *only* for foreigners. I felt rather callous entering a place where no payment was required while countless local pilgrims snoozed outside in any free space available.

It was just too warm to sleep, and around four thirty that following morning I peeled myself out of bed and plodded toward the temple entrance. Once there, I was gently rebuffed by a spear-toting Sikh guard who communicated, via charades, that I was blundering terribly on two counts: I had nothing covering my head, and I was wearing shoes. Embarrassed but undaunted, I returned in short order, appropriately behatted and deshoed. I was ready for my first glimpse of the Golden Temple.

Photographs of this *gurdwara* do it no justice. The temple is an island of golden architecture surrounded by a holy pool—filled with goldfish, for good measure. It's a small but magnificently designed structure and must be visited to be appreciated. Encircling the pool is a walkway and ivory-white buildings, and on the walkway—day and night—you will find people. The vast majority are Sikhs, and for them the Golden Temple is their Mecca. Most Sikhs attempt to make this pilgrimage at least once in their lifetimes, and the significance they place on the journey is substantial.

Joining the contemplative throng, I spent the next two hours attempting to pick my jaw up off the floor as the sun rose, setting the golden rooftop aflame. Trying to avoid being affected by countless people who are in a state of worship was pointless. Instead, I reveled in it. Time and again over the next three days, I would sit on the edge of the pool and just absorb. Serenity. Connection. Completion. It was all there and impossible to ignore.

More than once, I wandered out of the temple in a fuzzy, contemplative state, making it only as far as the nearby mess hall. Here I joined the thirty thousand others who had come for the *langar*—a free daily meal of gingery dal and chapatti (lentil broth

and flat wheat bread). This dining experience is just one more example of the Sikh philosophy. Sikhs are taught to embrace everyone, offering a bed, a meal, and an open heart. Their religion teaches to avoid an ostentatious lifestyle, do good work, and be of service to humanity.

The Golden Temple was the epitome of all these virtues. It was the site of immense tranquility, where a visitor could sit awhile and meditate in a clean, quiet environment. It healed the spirit with its beauty and revived the body with nutritious meals. There was no pressure here to do anything or pay anything. Visitors could come and go as they pleased. To my mind, this was exactly what religion should be.

Visiting the Golden Temple

While the Golden Temple authorities try to provide resting rooms for every visitor, do not count on this when planning your stay. The sheer number of pilgrims often makes it impossible to offer space to everyone, so we advise making arrangements at a local hotel or guesthouse. To learn more about the history and architecture of the Golden Temple, go to the following website.

www.sacred-destinations.com

Vegetarian dining at the Golden Temple

Volunteers at the Golden Temple prepare free meals for thousands of people every day—basic vegetarian fare called *langar*. This food is served at the *langar ghar*, or community kitchen. Piles of metal plates and bowls are laid out at the entrance, and diners pick up what dishes they need as they enter. There are no tables, so everyone eats sitting on the ground. The dal served here is famous for its flavor, and the food is generally quite delicious. Although meals are free, donations are accepted and appreciated.

DESHNOK

Jennifer Smith wades through Deshnok's sea of rats

Colorful, hand-painted cards outside the marble white facade of the Karni Mata temple put forward this question: "Is this the Eighth Wonder of the World?"

I had no idea. All I could see were towering silver doors. I should have paid more attention to the carvings of rats on the marble arches perhaps, but even if I had, I don't think I would have guessed that I was walking into a den of twenty thousand rodents.

The Karni Mata temple was alive with scurrying creatures. They scuttled this way and that, knocking into each other, dodging human feet, and going around in circles until they confused us and themselves, and nobody knew which way to go next. Our guide, who hadn't bothered to give us any advance notice about the overwhelming rodent population inside the temple, was now suddenly full of warnings. "These rats are much respected," he said, as we bent down to take off our shoes. "If you kill one, you must buy its life-size statue in gold for the temple."

For a passing tourist, fresh from a culture where rats aren't considered a pleasant thing, the idea of worshiping these critters seemed completely bizarre, let alone taking off our shoes in order to walk among them. But these were no ordinary rodents, my group was told. There was a story behind their godlike status, and like all stories in India, it had many versions.

Apparently, according to one version, these rats carried the souls of the descendants of the goddess Karni Mata, who, following the death of one of her sons, appealed to Yama, the god of death, to bring the son back to life. Yama refused, and furious, the goddess swore that none of the members of her clan would ever enter Yama's kingdom. In other words, they would not die. Denied death, Karni Mata's kin turned into rats instead. And here I was among them in their spiritual mansion.

As I was cautiously putting one bare foot before the other to reach the central temple, where the idol of Karni Mata stood, a big brown rat ran over my left foot. I felt the sharpness of its claws and let out a screech of fright, which made the woman next to me laugh loudly under the veil that was covering her face. An ascetic in orange prayer garb scowled at such childish conduct in a place of worship, and his censorious look left me feeling foolish.

"Oh, it's too bad," the woman said, lifting her veil slightly to whisper in my ear. "Next time, pray that you run into a white one. They bring a whole lifetime of good luck, because they are manifestations of Karni Mata herself." Then she added that it wasn't often that one got to see a white rat.

I smiled weakly as I took another step on the sticky floor. I tried to tell myself that the gluey paste under my feet was just the offerings of milk and sweets, which the rats had spread over the tiles, that it had nothing to do with the putrid smell emanating from the yellow-stained corners. As I made my way into the main temple in search of some good luck, I looked up in envy at the pigeons perched high on the protective mesh.

It was dark as a cave inside, and my eyes took some time to adjust to the next rodent spectacle the Karni Mata temple had in store for me: Innumerable rats gathered around metal dishes filled with milk. The worshippers had laid out other goodies for them as well—candies, curds, fruits, and nuts—and the rats were whisking from one plate to another, feasting on whatever took their fancy. The priest of the temple raised a bowl of sacred fire high in the air as he chanted prayers to Karni Mata, and I saw her idol at last, shining in the flickering light. The fire illuminated the feeding rats as well, and I was amazed to see that a few pilgrims were actually eating some of the food the rats had been gnawing at!

The woman behind the veil pointed at a man who was sharing a piece of banana with a rat and said, "The saliva of the rats is holy, and people eat their leftovers in the belief that they will imbibe the rat's resistance to disease. Never has there been an incident of plague or any other rodent-related disease in this temple in the six hundred years of its existence."

I was impressed with this claim. With twenty thousand rats in residence, I could easily imagine the temple spreading all kinds of sickness among the people of Deshnok. Encouraged by the look of surprise on my face, the woman told me of other peculiarities associated with the Karni Mata rats. For example, they never stepped beyond the temple boundaries, although there were no barriers of any sort to keep them in. Even stranger was the fact that they didn't seem to produce babies. No one had ever seen a baby rat inside the temple; it was almost as if the rodents were born as adults.

"Look around you," the woman said. "Even if you spend the whole day searching inside the temple, you will only see full-grown rats."

I stared at the sea of busy brown bodies, not really expecting to be the first one to spy a baby in their midst.

RAJASTHAN

But, as I was about to turn away, I did catch a glimpse of something white. Yes, it was indeed a white rat—small and furry, with its tail curled around a silver rail.

My heart filled with joy at this lucky coincidence. Despite my initial disgust, I suddenly felt very blessed. It had to be pure chance, I knew, but still, I could not help fancy that the cute white rat had chosen me from all others in the crowd to show itself.

Karni Mata temple

The temple is located in Deshnok, about thirty kilometers from the city of Bikaner. If you are staying in Bikaner, you can easily make a day trip of it.

ALLAHABAD

Prem Panicker
feels a spiritual chill
in Allahabad

It was a chilly, blustery morning in January, when I found myself waiting for transport on the main road outside my hotel in Allahabad. An ice-cold breeze was blowing steadily, defying the shirt, jeans, and jacket I had put on as protection against the elements. I had come to this city to attend the Kumbh Mela, the most sacred of all Hindu pilgrimages, which involves a soul-cleansing bath at the confluence of the holy Ganga and Yamuna rivers. The Kumbh Mela takes place in this spot only once every twelve years and is the biggest spiritual gathering of people in the world. This year, I was going to be part of that record-breaking crowd.

As I stood waiting, an autorickshaw came along and stopped to pick me up. Inside, I was happy to find warmth, albeit warmth transmitted by my fellow passengers with all the expected accompanying bodily smells. A short ride brought us to the entrance to Kumbh Nagri, the site where the Kumbh Mela is held, and beyond which vehicles were not allowed. From there to the *sangam ghat*, the point where the two holy rivers meet, is about a kilometer and a half as the crow flies. For non-crows, who needed to take a winding road, the walk in the intensifying chill was over half an hour.

The going was slow as thousands of people were ahead of me, every single one of us on our way to the *sangam ghat*. Although the rivers were broad enough for the entire city of Allahabad to bathe in at one time, and still have enough room left over for the rest of the state of Uttar Pradesh, the point of this religious pilgrimage was to bathe in that one spot where the waters of the Yamuna meet the waters of the Ganga and are joined, so legend says, by the waters of the subterranean Saraswati River.

As I neared the bathing ghat, I waited patiently. I did a lot of things while I waited: I meditated on Hinduism, recalled stories I had heard about the Kumbh Mela, eavesdropped on conversations around me ... anything that took my mind off the fact that the cold had now gone past the outer fortress of my clothes and taken up permanent residence in my bones.

Finally, by a process of attrition—not to mention judicious use of arms, elbows, and the soles of my shoes-I reached the front ranks of the assembled pilgrims at the *sangam* ghat. Confronting me was a barricade made of casuarina poles that opened in only one place to create a narrow walkway extending from the riverbank into the water. A posse of police blocked me at this point, until those who had gone before had completed their ablutions. I was then allowed in a batch of twenty through the barricaded walkway. This in turn led to a row of boats placed sideways to form a makeshift ramp.

I walked along this improvised bridge for about one hundred meters and hopped onto one in a series of little platforms erected on stilts set into the riverbed. Ignoring the crowds around me, I did a complicated striptease that involved wrapping a towel around my middle and peeling off my clothes from under it. I slipped gingerly into the water, which was a little less than waist deep, and promptly lost my ability to breathe. The water was so cold that the lower half of my body seemed to freeze immediately.

Before I could recover, I was exhorted by those waiting behind me to get a move on. So I took a painful breath, bent at the knees, and performed the spiritual ritual of Kumbh Mela, ducking my head into the water three times while facing the rising sun. As I rose after the third immersion, a man accosted me, holding out a glass of watery milk. How considerate, I thought, and I took the glass and raised it to my lips.

The man was irritated. "No, no sir, the milk is not for you. Feed it to Mother Ganga." He gestured urgently at the river.

I poured the milk into the water. Another gent then sidled up to me, this time holding out a bowl of marigold flowers, which I was directed to throw into the rivers. Done. As I clambered back out, there was a tap on my shoulder. "Sir, pay for our services first. The milk and the marigolds cost us half a dollar."

I then performed another ritual, this time a temporal one. I used the soaking wet towel to wipe myself dry. But the towel, bought on the banks of the ghat, seemed to transfer more water to my body than vice versa. Still soggy, I pulled on my clothes and wended my way back along the bridge of boats to the shore. I had officially bathed at the Kumbh Mela, and as the legends had it, that "bath," which took all of sixty seconds, had absolved me of all sins ever committed during my lifetime.

Next morning, after I had time to reflect, I realized that the experience had not left me feeling spiritually fulfilled. From a tourist point of view, of course, there was enough going on at the Kumbh Mela to keep me entertained for days. During this auspicious period, the site of the Mela metamorphosed into a self-sufficient city, and as such was a great place to watch people.

Pilgrims gathered to attend plays and musical recitals, buying trinkets at the Kumbh Mela shops, eating hot, crispy snacks at the makeshift food shacks, or dozing in front of bonfires. I saw Hindu ascetics of every order, doing yoga, saying prayers, and distributing blessings among the pilgrims. Alm seekers dressed up as Hanuman, the monkey god, roamed among the crowd, swinging their tails. Naga *sanyasis* with matted hair and naked bodies covered in ash smoked hashish and sat outside their tents with tridents in their hands, not caring that people were staring at them. There were a good number of foreign tourists too, wearing dots of sandalwood paste and vermilion on their foreheads and going excitedly from tent to tent, spending time with the Naga *sanyasis*, photographing them, and trying to get a firsthand feel of the Hindu religion.

But I was disappointed. For me, at least, the purpose of my journey, the holy dip, had passed too quickly to establish any spiritual contact with my Hindu gods. Could I, at the point of immersion, make out the two distinct streams of the Ganga and the Yamuna? I don't know. Did I have time to meditate? To pray? To think about God? No. Did I feel cleansed, purified?

No. There had been no time for any of that—to absorb, to assimilate, to feel. In the icy waters of the *sangam* ghat, all I did was dunk myself in the water for a little under a minute, time enough for just one thing: to feel the cold.

Attending a Kumbh Mela

Kumbh Mela is held four times in a twelve-year cycle and rotates between four holy Indian cities: Allahabad, Haridwar, Ujjain, and Nashik. The Kumbh Mela can be a once-in-a-lifetime experience—provided you're up to the challenge. Kumbh Mela "camps" are completely lacking in creature comforts. If you want to stay on-site, for example, all you will have to shield you from the elements is a basic tent.

If the proposition of a few days of hard living does not faze you, you can take part in the largest spiritual congregation in the world. You don't even have to join the pilgrims in a ritual dip in ice-cold holy waters. Residents of the Kumbh Mela camp welcome everybody in their midst and are happy to share their food and fire. Some sadhus and tantra practitioners even let you photograph them during their rituals.

You will want to make all arrangements for travel and accommodation before you reach the Kumbh Mela site. You can rent a tent in the Kumbh Mela campground, or you can get a hotel room in the town. Book as early as possible to ensure a place to stay. For more on Kumbh Mela, go to the following website.

www.kumbhamela.net

Short Cut to Nirvana

If you are unable to make the journey to Allahabad for Kumbh Mela, this film will take you inside the experience and includes an address by the Dalai Lama.

http://melafilms.com

The Naga sanyasis of Kumbh Mela

Sadhus, yogis, and other men of religion gather at the Kumbh Mela, the forty-two-day event that hosts over seventy million people every twelve years. Astrologically, it is a very powerful period, and these god-men pray and meditate in unison to attain *moksha*—freedom from the cycle of birth and death.

The event is of particular importance to a group of *sanyasis* known as Nagas, whose ascetic traditions date back at least two thousand years. They are the chief attraction at the Kumbh Mela, as that's about the only time you get to see them in public. The fact that they face the world without wearing any clothes engenders curiosity and awe among the Hindu pilgrims who come here for their ritual bath.

The Naga *sanyasis* are ardent followers of Lord Shiva and emulate the God's form by donning ash instead of clothes. Spiritually, they have risen above the material world, which is why they remain unconcerned and unembarrassed about their physical form. Under the guidance of a guru, the Naga *sanyasis* tread an extremely difficult path to enlightenment and spend most of their time in deep meditation in forests, caves, ashrams, and other secluded places where the temporal world does not intrude.

The Naga *sanyasis* are also known as "warrior ascetics" because of their militant past. Fearless fighters, they have battled with rivaling sects, Muslim invaders, and even the British. Today, the Nagas have lost their martial brief, of course, but you will still see them carrying sticks, spears, and tridents, which further intensifies their mysterious image in the mind of Indians.

FATEHPUR SIKRI

Cynthia Chesterfield makes a wish in Fatehpur Sikri

Forty kilometers away from Agra's famed Taj Mahal is another jewel from the Mughal era: the ghost city of Fatehpur Sikri. I had only one day in Agra, but I was determined to make the time to visit this sixteenth-century site. As soon as I got off the train, I rushed off to see the Taj, and then, ignoring all the nearby monuments recommended by my guidebook, I hired a taxi and set off for Fatehpur Sikri.

The Mughal Emperor Akbar had chosen this lonely spot to build his dream capital—an architectural marvel comprising grand mosques, palaces, audience halls, *hamams* (communal baths) and harems that had no rival in the world. Fatehpur Sikri was going to be the crowning achievement of the Mughal dynasty, but, alas, the city wasn't destined to thrive. Water shortage, a perennial problem in the region, derailed the emperor's ambitions, and the city was populated for only ten short years before being abandoned as a lost cause.

It wasn't touring, however, that drew me to Akbar's red sandstone dream city. I was on a pilgrimage. I wanted to pray at the *dargah* (mausoleum) of Salim Chisti. Convinced that his much-longed-for son and heir had been born after he prayed to Salim Chisti, Akbar erected the *dargah* as a token of his gratitude. According to popular Indian belief, the *dargah* still reverberates with Salim Chisti's powers, and thousands of pilgrims visit the sacred site every day.

I had heard about Salim Chisti from Usha, a Hindu girl who lived next door to me in England. Her family had great faith in the saint's powers to work miracles. In fact, Usha herself was supposedly born only after her mother, who had been childless for eighteen years, prayed at his mosque in Fatehpur Sikri. Every month, Usha's aunt sent her an envelope from India, filled with blessed flowers from Salim Chisti's tomb, and over the years I had gotten used to the sight of Usha placing the flowers respectfully in front of a grainy, black-and-white photograph of the *dargah* on an altar in her home.

Usha, who was England born, had never been to India, and as I stood in front of Salim Chisti's *dargah* that day, I felt I had come to worship here in her stead. The *dargah* was a compact domed structure built of beige marble. Set against the dark background of Fatehpur Sikri's red sandstone, it shone like a pearl under the brilliant afternoon sun. The open marble courtyard in front was too hot to walk barefoot on, and I balanced alternately on my heels and toes as I tried to reach the front steps as quickly as I could. The entranceway was elaborately inlaid and carved, but what caught my attention were the huge latticed windows that took up most of the outer walls. Pilgrims wrote down their wishes on pieces of paper before tying them to the lattices with red strings. As I stepped inside, I could see thousands of written prayers hanging in huge bundles.

Salim Chisti's tomb was installed in the center of the building under a canopy of mother-of-pearl. Pilgrims laid colorful *chaddars* on it, and I realized, too late, that I should have also bought one to offer to the saint. I had flowers though, and I laid them down before the tomb and stood meditating for a few minutes. A group of Sufi musicians sang near the courtyard, and the sonorous notes of their music guided my thoughts inward. The emotional rendition of their religious songs touched my heart, and even though I couldn't follow the lyrics, I found my mind relaxing and turning toward God.

It was fifteen minutes before I finally finished my prayers to Salim Chisti and emerged from his tomb. I sat down on the front staircase with a pen and paper and took some time visualizing my deepest desire before writing it down in two short sentences in English. A couple of young women were sitting below me on the staircase, also writing down their wishes. They kept consulting each

other and scratching out what they had written before starting again. Their eyes met mine, and sensing my amusement at their communal style of wish making, they burst out laughing.

The big vermilion dots on their foreheads and the streaks of vermilion in their hair identified them as newly married Hindu women. I had always found it interesting that Usha, a devout Hindu, had no problem praying to Salim Chisti, a Muslim saint, but looking around me I could see that there were many Hindu pilgrims here. In India, the Hindu and Muslim religions not only coexist, but on some occasions overlap as well, and in this sharply divided world, this religious congeniality was a hopeful thing to see.

I had brought no string with me to tie the paper, but the two women had a few extra, and they lent me one with the warning that I would have to return to India to untie the string after Salim Chisti granted my wish. Of course, it would be impossible to recognize my own string from the hundred others that are tied here every day, so I could untie any one from the jumble as a symbol of thanks. I assured them that I would gladly return to the mosque if my wish was fulfilled.

When I finally got up to leave the *dargah*, the sun had crept behind dark rain clouds. The marble looked magical in the subdued gray light, and I took a few photographs of it from different angles. Once I returned to Delhi, I planned to print and frame the best one and take it back with me as a present for Usha. Replacing the grainy old photo she had on her altar with a nice new one would be my way of sharing my spiritual experience at Salim Chisti's *dargah* with her.

Getting to Fatehpur Sikri

Fatehpur Sikri is a convenient stopover on the Delhi-Agra route. The historic city is located just forty kilometers from Agra, and there are plenty of bus services and taxis that ply between these two tourist hotspots.

Tying a string

Along with fulfilling your wish, tying a string at the *dargah* gives hope and the strength to persevere with whatever your difficulty may be. Because you believe Salim Chisti has heard your *mannat*, everything will come out right—as it is meant to be—in the end.

Sufism

Sufism came to India from the Middle East and flourished during Muslim rule in India. Members are usually associated with Islam, but Sufis can seek to make a spiritual union with God—which is their primary goal—without adhering strictly to any faith in particular. They induce mystic trances and altered states of consciousness with dervishlike dances and a

genre of music that is enjoying a revival of sorts in India since Bollywood has taken it mainstream.

Sufi music

Following are some suggestions to introduce you to Sufism's soul-stirring music.

Rumi: Voice of Longing

A poet with a loyal international following, Rumi is considered the most prolific of the Sufi saints. This two-CD set contains nearly one hundred of Rumi's memorable quatrains, translated by Coleman Barks.

Devotional and Love Songs

Performed by the *qawali* singer Nusrat Fateh Ali Khan, this is a surprisingly accessible and captivating set of Sufi songs, whose subtle instrumentation includes the mandolin and traditional tabla.

Varanasi

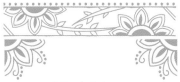

Mark Moxon witnesses life and death in Varanasi

I challenge anybody to come to Varanasi and not be captivated. Yes, there's squalor and suffering, probably more than you've encountered anywhere else in India. There's sickness and death, and the air you breathe is thick with the miasma of cow dung that hangs over this holy town night and day. Despite all this, a strangely seductive mood permeates the ancient lanes. If I had to select one place to represent everything that is truly Indian, I would choose Varanasi.

Life in Varanasi revolves around the ghats—the flights of steps leading into the holy Ganga River. There are more than one hundred, some crumbling and not in use, while others thrive as religious centers, laundries, and the Indian equivalent of the local pub. As far as traditional tourism goes, Varanasi is not a haven in terms of monuments and historical sites. Its appeal is in sitting and just observing the ghats. I spent many hours on the ghat steps, enjoying the sight of scruffy-looking kids splashing more water out of the Ganga than the monsoon put in; men wading in deep and raising their hands in prayer to the sun; others lying on sheets of cloth and enjoying a preablution massage; and women bathing in full attire, expertly slipping soap under the layers of their saris. Watching the ghats throughout the day is indeed instructive.

The most notable ghats, though, at least as far as Westerners are concerned, are those that function as crematoriums. Varanasi isn't just a town with lots of ghats and temples, it's also one of the most auspicious places for Hindus to come to die. Being cremated in Varanasi and scattered in the Ganga is the Hindu equivalent of an Englishman being buried in Westminster Abbey.

The bodies are laid upon a neat pile of logs, which are stacked by "untouchables," or members of society's lowest caste. As I sat overlooking the river, I could see three bodies burning steadily in the breeze, giving off a disturbing smell that I soon began to associate with the holy city. I was rather paranoid about approaching the burning ghats, as I felt the rituals were private, and I satisfied myself with views of the pyres from afar.

When I could wrest myself away from the ghats, I spent time wandering around the old city. With streets seldom wider than three meters—which meant no cars, no rickshaws, and not very many people—this part of town proved to be a lot of fun to wander. It took me a while to figure out that the worst possible way of exploring this area was to try to use my map: some places are impossible to depict on paper, and Varanasi is one of them, right up there with the jungle paths of Malaysia's Taman Negara and Caen in France, where we would always get lost on family holidays. In fact, the best thing to do in Varanasi is ditch the map in the cow dung and fish out a compass: the Ganga is always east. And if you get really stuck, you can always follow your nose back to the ghats on the holy river.

Dawn at the ghats

Days begin early in Varanasi. By four in the morning, people are thronging the ghats, praying to the rising sun and bathing in the holy Ganga River. Buy a glass of tea and some freshly made breakfast sweets from the nearby shops and settle down to watch the various morning rituals that take place here. For a treat, call a passing masseuse over for a famous Varanasi *maalish* (oil massage) right on one of the ghats. For more about the ghats and other Varanasi attractions, visit the following website.

www.varanasicity.com

A shrine in New Delhi

Ganesha image with marigold garland

INTO THE WILD

Outdoor experiences for adventurous travelers

Every year, wildlife buffs from all over the world visit India to answer the siren call of one gloriously beautiful creature: the tiger. The prospect of meeting this beast in its natural habitat, face-to-face, can be irresistible. When you take all the elephants, one-horned rhinos, Asiatic lions, black bucks, and thousands of other mammals and birds into account, this biodiverse country does seem to be the ultimate destination for memorable outdoor adventures.

Though North India is dotted with many national parks and sanctuaries, I chose only two tiger-spotting essays for this chapter. And instead of giving you the well-documented hotspots like Jim Corbett National Park and Ranthambore, I let David Cook and Dan Free take you tiger watching in the more intimate Kanha and Bandhavgarh parks. Dan's safari resulted in some close calls, like when Link 7, a twelve-year-old tigress, stood a mere hair's breadth away from his jeep. As for David, he experienced a lucky first sighting, when he had the chance to observe a prowling orange and black beauty for a good half hour. Their exciting encounters, followed by the bonhomie of evenings spent around cozy forest campfires, are sure to leave you aching for a tiger adventure of your own.

Animals aren't the only way to experience North India's wild-at-heart spirit. Simply getting there can be part of the adventure. Jorden Leighton's journey through the picturesque Suru Valley promises a glimpse of nirvana—if your bones are strong enough to withstand the bumpiest bus ride of your life and your nerves can tolerate hundreds of worms crawling over your skin. Or you might travel up to the Himalayan valley of Nubra, where Kate Wiseman experiences a surreal bus trip on the Khardung La pass, one of the highest motorable roads in the world.

Andrew Soleimany's high-altitude trek left him open to being stranded by nomads without even a tent over his head, while

Partha De Sarkar experienced two crowning achievements in his long trekking career. One took him 4,255 meters above sea level to find the trickling source of the mighty Ganga River, and the other culminated at the eerie Roopkund Lake, in which the bones of hundreds of humans are still lying submerged after thousands of years. If you're not up for such hearty endeavors, follow in Nancy Wong's footsteps, on an invigorating five-hour walking trip to the isolated mountain destination of Triund.

Reading the essays in this chapter, you will find that you can go the challenge in the Himalayas, explore wildlife sanctuaries and national parks, or even stay in the cities and still interact with a variety of animals. To give you an idea of India's urban menagerie, I have to mention a friend's photos from his recent trip. He has images of himself feeding cookies to a band of bearded monkeys, riding an elephant down a high-traffic road, being chased by a bad-tempered piglet, and searching for teeth in the mouth of a somnolent camel. But the most interesting thing about these animal photos was this: they were *all* taken on my friend's *first* day in the city of Delhi.

Now that's pretty wild, isn't it?

McLeodganj

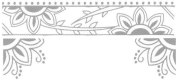

*Nancy Wong
meets man's best friend
outside McLeodganj*

Not long after arriving in McLeodganj, I joined up with a group of walking tour enthusiasts and made plans to go trekking to Triund, a ridge located at an altitude of 2,827 meters in the Dhauladhar mountain range. It would be a nine-kilometer hike up from McLeodganj, and the trip would take at least five hours each way. But the isolated haven was well off the beaten track, and it rewarded the handful of visitors it received with impossibly beautiful scenes of rolling meadows shrouded in swirling mist and snowy peaks at almost touching distance. A small party of travelers we met in town had just visited Triund, and they couldn't stop raving about the soul-expanding experience.

As we started for Triund early the next day, we talked about our concerns regarding the possibility of getting lost, whether we'd be able to get back before dark, and safety on the secluded trail. Apparently, there used to be vicious snow leopards and aggressive monkeys ruling this route until the Dalai Lama came to live in McLeodganj. The locals believed that the Dalai Lama's influence cleared up this menace, and we prayed there was some truth to this legend. We feared being attacked at some point where there was nobody to call out to for help.

Perhaps the Dalai Lama heard our prayers because, before we had even reached the edge of town, a companion was sent to us in the form of a stray dog. The dog appointed himself as our guide and protector and led the way, barking at the groups of monkeys we passed on the road. Even though we had left McLeodganj behind, climbing higher and higher, the dog would not leave our side. If we stopped at a tea stall for refreshments, he quietly waited for us to finish, before taking up the lead again. He didn't like photo breaks and barked his impatience at our dawdling over the gorgeous views, but other than that, he was the best escort we could have hoped for on this lonely trail.

After four or five hours of climbing, we stopped to rest our aching muscles one final time before we hiked the last few hundred yards to Triund. We talked little and concentrated on catching our breath while the dog lay down on his back and kept a lazy eye on us as he licked at his tired paws.

Suddenly, a low-pitched droning floated down from the top of Triund, breaking the quietness of our surroundings. Someone was playing a didgeridoo, an Australian aboriginal wind instrument. Who would bring such an obscure and unwieldy musical instrument to India and then lug it all this way? I wondered. But as the strains of the didgeridoo gathered in strength and then dispersed in revereberating echoes in the air, I understood why the owner of the instrument felt compelled to play it here. The queer lack of melody seemed to underscore the remoteness of Triund and heighten the sense of aloneness we had all come to experience.

Invigorated by the music, we resumed climbing, and in a few short minutes we found ourselves standing in Triund, with the magic of the Himalayas all around us. The snowline was another hour's walk up, the trees were all farther down, and Triund was a vista of rolling grass and rocks with herds of goats grazing everywhere. On one side was the towering face of the snow-clad Dhauladhar range. It was a clear day, and we had a spellbinding view of the hills and the Kangra Valley below. The slopes were abloom with flame of the forest, hollyhock, gladioli, and hydrangea. It was one of those moments to linger in my memory forever afterward.

Meanwhile, our four-legged companion, satisfied with our safe arrival, decided he needed a break. He picked up some scent on the ground and enjoyed a few doggy moments of wild digging before giving up and flopping down in the grass. The rest of us thought this was a great idea and flopped down next to him with the lunch boxes we had packed. While we ate and took in our surroundings, someone from the group went to investigate a lone building we could see up ahead. He came back with the news that the structure was a rest hut where visitors could spend the night.

Unfortunately, none of us had come prepared to overnight in Triund; we hadn't brought our sleeping bags or extra food and provisions, which was a great pity as we would have loved to enjoy a couple of days here if we had known in advance. A man who ran a tea stall nearby also pointed out some unused shepherd huts and caves where people often stayed. He rented out bedrolls and other camping equipment, he said, so we wouldn't have to bring up anything other than our personal belongings. The only problem was of course toilets. There was no place to have a wash, and you had to answer nature's call in any secluded spot you found among the rocks.

Since we had already set up tours in McLeodganj for the next day, we couldn't change our plans and spend the night in Triund this time round. But on our way back to town, we discussed the possibility of making the hike again and getting a booking at the rest hut. The Dhauladhar range apparently changes color with the position of the sun, and that would certainly be a treat to watch if we had the luxury of spending a whole day there. We wondered if the dog would agree to accompany us on another visit and decided that he probably would if we sweetened the deal with more of the delicious salami and ham sandwiches he had enjoyed at lunch.

Getting to Dharamshala/ McLeodganj

Go to the fact file on page 118.

Trekking to Triund

The Triund trek is about nine kilometers and moderately uphill. Trekking at an average pace, you can do the distance in about five hours. The route is well marked, and usually there are other trekkers going up and down, so you're unlikely to get lost. Tea shops along the way offer pleasant opportunities to take a break every now and then. Porters can he hired to carry your bags, especially if you're planning to camp at Triund overnight. For booking the rest hut in Triund, contact the Divisional Forest Office in lower Dharamshala.

LADAKH

Andrew Soleimany breaks camp with nomads in Ladakh

At over four thousand meters, it was freezing cold. Bajirao, our guide, had gone to organize some hot drinks for our party, and I couldn't wait for a steaming cup of the green tea leaf, butter, and salt concoction they favored in those parts. It warmed the blood, and right then I could do with anything short of automobile antifreeze to kick-start my circulation.

We were making a day trip to see Tso Moriri Lake, but a wind had picked up on the way, and Bajirao reckoned there would be some rain. As our jeep turned a bend, a group of six odd tents came into view, and he instructed the driver to park to the side of them. The tents belonged to local Changpa nomads, and Bajirao was certain that they'd be glad to rent us one for a couple of hours. "We will buy some refreshments and wait until the weather clears up a little and visibility improves," he said.

So, there we were, five of us trying to find a comfortable way in which to sit cross-legged on a threadbare rug, hoping our tea would be accompanied by something edible if not remotely palatable. In due course, the tea was brought in by a couple of women, and I was surprised to find milk and sugar in it. "These Changpa nomad people trek down to the towns to sell the goods they make all summer," Bajirao explained. "There they deal with tourists and see and learn town ways." This wasn't a good thing, I gathered from his expression. Nonetheless, I had missed my tea with normal milk and sugar on this trip and was glad for this small corruption.

The women who were now serving us bowls of Rara instant noodle soup (something you had better get used to if you're traveling in these parts) were the first nomad women I encountered in my Ladakh trip. I studied their features and clothes with interest. Set with blue stones that I assumed were turquoise, a sort of half veil covered the center of their heads. Their hair seemed purposely matted into large knots, but I couldn't be sure because of the wide fur wings they wore to cover their ears from the cold wind. The layers of robes they had on were dark and dusty from daily use, which reminded me it was several days since I'd had a wash and a change of clothes myself.

The women smelled peculiar too— a thick, buttery odor that must come from a diet of yak milk products. Then again, my party could hardly smell much better, especially Zorro, a rambunctious American who had joined us on this trip. Poor Zorro had had a small accident on the way. As agile as the swashbuckler of the same name, he hung precariously from a ledge to photograph some ordinary-looking wild ox. More Don Quixote, though, than Don Diego, he slipped on a pile of dung on his way back to the jeep. The seat of his pants still bore his distinctive Mark of Zorro, and none of us wanted to be very close to him.

As Bajirao drew our attention to the ceiling, explaining how the Changpas made these tents out of yak hair, the sound of loud voices and excited chatter broke the silence of our surroundings. We clearly heard a child being dragged forward and smacked, and we surmised the no-

mads were in a bit of a tizzy because of our unexpected arrival. "Why are these people so excited at the sight of people with golden hair?" Zorro, a bodacious blond, enquired of our guide. "Have they never seen Westerners in these parts before?"

"They do not make commotion to see golden hair on white-skinned people at all, sahib," Bajirao answered tersely. "They make commotion because they break camp."

From his gestures we understood he would like us to step out of the tent, and we trooped out obediently to watch the Changpa nomads prepare to leave for warmer climes and business in the plains. A small group of men were busily tying what looked like woolen fabrics into bales and loading them on the back of six or seven yaks. One yak in particular refused his load, and it took two men to coax and cajole until the animal relented moodily.

There was no sign of the four or five other tents we had seen on our way in, and when I turned around, to my great surprise, our own tent was nowhere in sight either! While we were watching the animals, somebody had dismantled it and packed it away. Our backpacks had been placed in neat piles, and seeing that our belongings were safe, I turned my attention back to the camp activities.

A few young Changpa children came up shyly and let us inspect strands of necklaces and an armload of jewelry they had made. One piece caught my attention, but I hastily put it back when on closer inspection the pretty white beads on its surface turned out to be animal teeth. Then it was the turn of a girl of fifteen or sixteen years, who—with her eyes staring matter-of-factly into mine—raised her arms to my neck and wound a string of iridescent brown stones around it. Obviously, the poor girl had been put up to it by her friends, and she blushed prettily and stood hiding her face in her hands when the pranksters began to stamp on the ground and howl with laughter. It was the sweetest and most innocent compliment I'd ever received from a woman.

The first loose formation of yaks laden with goods had meanwhile started its journey with a few minders and a flock of snowy white sheep following in its wake. After more yaks had been loaded, we watched the women leave, and then the stragglers. My young admirer went with the last of them. In the space of fifteen minutes, the site, which had been home to twenty nomads and their livestock for an entire season, was abandoned forever. According to Bajirao, when summer returned, the nomads would return, with money they had made in the towns from selling their pashmina shawls. But they never came back to the same site.

The clouds had cleared, the Changpas had gone, and we made preparations to leave as well. This chance meeting with a group of nomads had pushed Lake Moriri right out of our heads. But Bajirao had given Zorro a "good photo guarantee," and our guidebook did mention it was one of the most splendid lakes in the Ladakh region—a pearl-shaped water body with a thirty-six-kilometer circumference. Not to be missed.

Our jeep took us a short distance farther, and then we elected to walk the rest of the way. The barren beauty of Ladakh was all around us. We seemed to be drowning in an ochre world. The ground under our feet, the steep slopes of the peaks in front of us—everything was painted a bright golden yellow. We trekked half a kilometer or so until we reached an obelisk on which tourists had drawn hearts and scribbled love messages. At Bajirao's urging we turned left from there and walked a hundred yards or so. There it was: a wall of mountain face in the far distance with Lake Moriri spilt and spread like melted emerald in front of it.

It was not just the beauty but the clarity of Lake Moriri and its surroundings that stunned us into silence. The deep blue of its waters is often talked about, but on that day the lake was a luminous green. Flocks of birds of different species hung around the shores. "Great crested grebe, Brahminy ducks, and bar-headed geese," Bajirao counted off loudly, breaking the silence that hung over the group.

Quite unaware of the impact the first sight of Lake Moriri had on his clients, he whistled and waved his hands at a flock of speckled gray birds until they took flight. Zorro howled with glee and raced after them with his camera. Bajirao smiled in acknowledgment of his own capacity to create photo opportunities. "Wait some while here," he said, as if the spectacle of Lake Moriri were of as much consequence as a puddle on a city street, "and Bajirao will next arrange for you the sighting of some Tibetan wild ass!"

Getting to Lake Moriri

Lake Moriri is fewer than 250 kilometers from the Ladakh capital of Leh. Travelers can only visit with a permit. Organized tours are the most convenient option since they provide all camping equipment and a cook, but you can do the trip by hiring your own jeep. There is a bus service that will also take you there, but it is available only in the summer. If you want to stay overnight, Nomadic Life Camp at the nearby village of Korzok offers campsites and tents. For more information contact the Leh Tourist Office.

Main Bazar Road
Leh

leh@nic.in

NUBRA VALLEY

Kate Wiseman
buses through the
surreal Nubra Valley

If you cross the Khardung La, one of the highest motorable roads in the world, and journey as far north in India as a tourist is permitted, you will find yourself in the Nubra Valley, whose mostly fertile landscape is famous for its mini cold desert and two-humped Bactrian camels. By Himalayan standards, a mere six- to eight-hour hop, skip, and a jump from the Ladakh region's hub city of Leh.

What will you need for this trip? A special permit, without which a tourist cannot travel through the area. A strong stomach. And a steady head to avoid motion sickness during the dizzying climbs and descents on the Khardung La. And better camel-hunting abilities than mine.

The group I was traveling with from Leh decided to avoid the expensive and fixed itinerary of the standard jeep tours and do the Nubra Valley on local buses instead. We found an agent in the city who agreed to arrange the permits for us, and we bought tickets for the Saturday bus. But when Saturday arrived, we discovered we had been sold two seats that didn't exist and joined the throng of locals squeezed into the gangway. I managed to bag a proper seat, but my behind still bumped and jumped painfully, as the threadbare tires wound their way up to an altitude of over five thousand meters. The bus lurched into potholes, which bounced us back out dangerously close to the edge of the road. With some trepidation, I noted a heavily loaded truck lying upside down on a slope, but the locals were unperturbed.

Having successfully made it to the top of Khardung La without incident, I was relieved as we began our bone-shaking descent. We passed gangs of men, women, and children on the way. Pickaxes in hand or huddling over steaming black vats of boiling tar, these people were engaged in a constant war against the elements to keep the road open so that soldiers might protect India's sensitive border with Pakistan. Many died every year doing this work, and the sides of the road were littered with small stones marking their passing. Someone told me that most came from the poorest parts of Southern India and the eastern state of Bihar. I wondered what kind of hell for a life could possibly make this one preferable. Unfazed by their circumstances, however, these friendly people often raised a smile and a waving hand as we passed.

The bus finally dumped us into a thin desert valley surrounded by a series of never-ending brown mountains. Unlike in Leh, the mountains here were so close I could almost reach out and touch them. They were immense and almost claustrophobic in their continuity. Two rivers ran through the forked valley at this point, watering the pockets of green and fertile land that supported the communities that lived in it. There was nothing else. No other distraction to cut the heavy silence and lighten the stark, surreal mood. The remoteness of Nubra made it incredibly beautiful. It was also very peaceful, so we decided to make a five-day well-earned escape of it, from the crowds and car horns of Leh.

We spent a day and a night in the village of Diskit, the Nubra Valley's administrative headquarters. A steep morning climb took us up to the monastery overlooking the village, where we relaxed in the company of monks and admired the view. The next day, we headed over to the other side of the valley to stay in a tranquil little village called Sumur. We found lodgings in a wonderful family-run guesthouse and were presented with a huge room with windows on all sides to let in the magic of the mountains. Our evening meal was a feast of fresh vegetables from the kitchen garden, dal, rice, and chapatti.

Getting up early the following morning, I sat outside and watched our hosts bake a fresh batch of local Ladakhi bread that would be our breakfast. And after a day of exploring, we were treated to a cultural show of local music and dance. If you have never heard of Ladakhi accomplishments in these fields, it is no surprise. The performance was as weird and unfamiliar as the cold desert terrain. A wind instrument sounded like a balloon being strangled, and dancing was more like an attempt to get everybody to shuffle about in unison. I stayed as long as was polite and was happy to give my 100 rupees to help fund the education of young local girls in distant colleges outside the valley.

Our luck with the buses ran out on the next leg of our journey, from Sumur to the village of Hundar, as the service proved to be as laid-back as life in Nubra Valley. We waited, a small crowd of locals and tourists, at the appointed time. Several buses sped to a festival happening in the opposite direction. One hour later ... still waiting ... two ... three ... There were now no locals left. They had all given up, gone to the festival, or hitched rides. We had to find a jeep.

Hundar was our last stop in the valley, and I looked forward to riding a Bactrian camel. Their incongruous presence here harked back to the valley's importance as a staging post on the Silk Route of old. Full of enthusiasm, I set off in what I had thought was a vaguely camel-related direction. The village was tiny. Surely, a herd of camels would not be hard to find? Think again. After an hour of walking and several false starts, I was frustrated in my search for the beasts. Later in the afternoon, armed with a proper set of directions and an eager accomplice, I again failed and walked for hours around the outskirts of the village. Finally, as the day drew to an end, I ran into a full hunting party, but it was too late to ask the minders for a ride. Instead, I watched the camels settle into their evening rest.

One by one they all sat down at the urging of their minders and blinked placidly around them as everything was tied, tethered, and made secure for the night. Once the minders left, they sat there looking big and friendly and totally at home in their surroundings. Who would guess from looking at them that their ancestors had been brought here as beasts of burden from Central Asia and then left to die? Against all the odds, these gentle creatures adapted and become an important part of the local economy.

They had star status among all the domesticated animals of Nubra and were probably quite used to being photographed and chased around by mad tourists like myself.

Getting to Nubra Valley

Kate traveled like a local from Leh to the Nubra Valley—by bus. But the five-hour journey is a lot more comfortable if you choose a jeep or taxi service. They are available on a share basis, as well, for those on a budget. Tourists require permits, which are easily available in Leh. Make several photocopies of the permit. Most checkpoints you pass through will want to keep one.

Bactrian camels

The Bactrian first entered the Nubra Valley in 1890 or thereabouts on the ancient trade route from Kashgar. Once over the treacherous mountain passes, the traders abandoned them after their goods had been sold. To protect themselves from the harsh conditions, the camels have bushy eyebrows, a double row of long eyelashes, and hair inside their ears. They can tightly seal their nostrils and lips to keep out sand. The two humps on their back store fat, which is converted into water, and Bactrian camels can go without food or water for long periods of time.

SURU VALLEY

*Jorden Leighton
braves a rooftop ride
through the Suru Valley*

On the remote western edge of the Ladakh region lies the Suru Valley, an astonishingly verdant tract of land for its average altitude of three thousand meters. The valley takes its name from the Suru, a little-known tributary of the mighty Indus River. The rich alluvial soil on Suru's lower banks is intensively cultivated by a hardworking peasantry to produce most of the region's grain and vegetables. Not many tourists venture this way, and the beautiful fields of wispy wheat and rugged mountains mostly remain unappreciated by outsiders.

I was trying to get from the small Suru Valley village of Panikhar to another called Rangdum, but I was having no luck. The "scheduled" bus was nowhere to be seen, so along with two Israelis, I did what all seasoned travelers do under the circumstances: kill time in the best of spirits. We whiled away three hours eating cheap chocolate and playing cards until a private transport truck rolled in, full to overflowing with passengers. We struck a deal with

the driver, who then went on to say, "On top you are riding," gesturing impatiently at the roof of the truck.

It took us a few seconds to realize that the driver was dead serious, and the three of us quickly debated the pros and cons of this alarming prospect. A private vehicle such as this was different from a bus, and the driver took no responsibility for the hitchhikers. Add to that the risk of navigating precarious mountain passes without protection or seat belts, medical help days away should something go wrong, and God knows what type of driver—all in the isolated Indian Himalayas. Smart? No. Adventurous? Definitely.

We opted for the ride. Our incredibly tight space atop the cab was shared with a schoolteacher who had an unsolicited opinion on everything: how narrow the road was, how dilapidated the approaching bridge looked, and how fatal our situation could turn out to be. To top it off, he somehow managed to squeeze himself into the only spot on the roof that seemed half-secure, while constantly reminding me how dangerous my "choice" of seating was. I resisted the urge to toss him off.

Shortly after leaving Panikhar, the bus was forced to pass a line of trees with branches hanging low over the road. Normally, I wouldn't have cared about the occasional whack from a passing twig, but these were no ordinary branches. They were covered in tiny worms! Millions of slippery, gray, sluglike creatures that could fit into almost any crevice imaginable. Soon, worms were crawling all over our heads and arms. Forced to sit in a position with my back to the approaching trees, I couldn't dodge as well as the others and caught the brunt. We shifted, laughed, cursed, and lay as flat as possible on our backs, but there was scant relief from the wormy onslaught. The attack continued for about ten minutes, after which the trees were left behind, and we attempted to pick ourselves clean as best we could.

Because the Suru Valley is not frequently traveled, we met only a handful of other vehicles. This mattered little as the landscape captivated our attention—we were driving into glacier country. Glacier virgins, my two Israeli friends gawked and pointed as we began to pass humongous stacks of ice. Being a resident of the mountainous western region of Canada and no stranger to glaciers, I was interested to watch their awed reactions. I wondered how they would respond to the spectacular sight of great slabs of ice peeling off the glaciers' high front walls and crashing into the Suru River raging below.

Then the scenery changed dramatically again, and we were face-to-face with the towering peaks of Nun and Kun, lording over the valley from a height of over seven thousand meters. What a way to experience the Himalayas! My Israeli friends were spellbound. The breathtaking views distracted us from the constant jostling we endured all the way to Rangdum. When it was finally time to get off, our bottoms were so tender that hauling our large bags away was painfully awkward. The driver of the truck chuckled in amusement at our discomfort, but we hurt too much to care.

In this way, we managed to arrive in Rangdum in a very isolated part of the Suru Valley, barely able to stand on our feet, but we agreed that the trip had been worth it. While our adventure wasn't the most intelligent group decision ever made, it was one that will live on in my memory for many years to come.

Getting to Rangdum

Scheduled bus services from places like Leh, Kargil, and Padum make several stops along the Suru Valley, and Rangdum is on the route. Alternately, you can hire a taxi or just buy a seat in one. Motorcycle enthusiasts can rent a bike for the journey. Exercise extreme caution though, as the climbs are incredibly steep and the journey is fraught with difficulties.

In and around Rangdum

Rangdum (3,657 meters) is an isolated little village in the Suru Valley, surrounded by steep mountains, pastures, and streams. Tourists doing the Suru Valley trail stop at Rangdum to visit the famous Rangdum Monastery, which contains many ancient Buddhist relics. Government-run guesthouses, tourist bungalows, and tents are available for overnight stays. Rangdum offers incredible scenic views and trekking opportunities, but no luxury of any sort. Be prepared to eat whatever's available at the few tea stalls there and be glad to have some sort of roof over your head.

BANDHAVGARH NATIONAL PARK

David Cook tells tiger tales from Bandhavgarh

Bandhavgarh is not India's largest national park by any stretch, but it boasts the highest density of tigers in the country. Of course, density of population does not always guarantee a sighting. One summer on Admiralty Island in Alaska, which claims to be home to the world's greatest concentration of grizzly bears, I saw only some shredded salmon carcasses and steaming piles of bear droppings. So in India I was careful not to get my hopes up.

I was staying at Kum Kum House, a small guesthouse in the village of Tala in the park, and I was the only Westerner in residence. On the afternoon of my arrival, I joined up with the family occupying an adjacent room, and we shared the open-air jeep for a visit to the park. Though I knew there was greater likelihood of

a tiger sighting during morning visits, I just couldn't wait, and off we went.

Our guide Ahmed was entertaining, full of tiger anecdotes, and very experienced at tracking tiger prints and listening for warning calls from other animal species in the brush. Just minutes into the park, we had our first wildlife sighting: a sambar deer. It was close in size to the elk, but still it was only a deer, so it didn't look very different from the kinds I see in my hometown of Indianapolis.

Next, we saw a herd of spotted deer, and it was with this sighting that the drama started. The animals were behaving oddly, making loud whimpering noises, which was out of character. Then it hit me—our guide and driver were already on top of it: a tiger was coming!

We were scanning the forest when we heard a sound. Not quite a growl, but a loud catlike rumble, coming from our left. The leaves on the thick brush began to rustle and shake, and there she was. It was incredible. I was face-to-face with a tiger. I watched, holding my breath, as the two-year-old female walked nonchalantly past the family of deer, ignoring our jeep, which was only thirty feet away, and made her way down the sandy road.

My first tiger sighting (zoos don't count)—the first wild cat I'd seen in my entire life—must have lasted twenty to thirty minutes. I was mesmerized as the orange-and-black-striped beauty strolled along, marking a few trees as her territory with spray. At one point, she reared up on her hind legs, grabbed hold of a tree trunk in the curve of her foreleg, and rubbed her face against the bark. It was just like watching a domestic cat rubbing against a scratching post.

She settled down on a shady piece of ground, bathed herself a little in the dust, and then rolled on her back and kicked her legs up in the air. I lived with seven different cats throughout my childhood—KC, Sinatra, Xena WP, Kendall, Sierra, Stinson, and Nero—and it was so much fun seeing their large, predatory cousin behaving as they did. She kept a lazy eye out for us until the big yawns kicked in and she lost interest. By this time, another jeep or two had also rolled up, and we drove off to explore more of the park.

After this first tiger, my imagination went into overdrive, and I began to see tigers jumping out from all over the place. I saw orange and black stripes and announced I had spotted a tiger's head. It turned out to be the light and shadow of ferns next to a tree stump. Then, in a rather embarrassing display of overenthusiasm, I insisted to the group that I had spotted two pointy ears in the grass. I forced the driver to back up quite a way, so convinced was I, but when the animal raised its head, it showed itself to be only a sambar deer whose afternoon siesta we had disturbed. Thereafter, I submitted to our guide's expertise.

The park's surroundings—mainly forests of *sal* and bamboo trees with a few large prairies and some mountains (though I'd call them mesas)—were the perfect backdrop for a nature holiday. In the three rounds I made through it during my short stay, I came across more

deer and various other species of animals, such as black-faced langur monkeys, peacocks, and boars. Although our guide pointed out many tracks and we heard a number of alarmed warning calls from the deer and monkeys, I didn't see any more tigers.

Bandhavgarh was a magical break from India's busy towns and cities. I had a great time enjoying the sunrises and the open spaces, meeting with an Indian family on each safari, and learning more about tigers. Every evening when I went to town, I ran into my first guide, Ahmed, and we had dinner and exchanged tales about life as a park ranger. He told some great tiger stories from Bandhavgarh, and I shared my experiences from working in the Olympic National Park in America. Bandhavgarh was a great cap to my first six weeks in India and turned out to be my favorite destination in the north of the country.

Getting to Bandhavgarh National Park

The nearest airports to the park are in Khajuraho and Jabalpur—both are a six- to eight-hour drive away, depending on road conditions. If you're up for the adventure, you can rent a car. Otherwise, most foreigners travel such distances by taxi. The following website offers a wealth of information about Bandhavgarh, from a checklist of mammals found in the park to nonsafari attractions both in and near the park.

www.bandhavgarh.net

Mahua Kothi

If you want luxury in a jungle environment, this is the place to stay. Rooms here have been built like *kutiyas* (huts with mud floors), but they contain every modern amenity. Each room leads into a private garden space, which duplicates the look and feel of an ethnic courtyard with traditional swing seats and water bodies. The hotel has an elaborate ayurvedic massage menu and arranges unique meal experiences like a bullock-cart breakfast or a picnic under the shade of *mahua* trees. The hotel staff can make all the arrangements for your national park safaris.

www.tajhotels.com
mahua.kothi@tajhotels.com

KANHA NATIONAL PARK

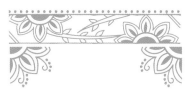

Dan Free
basks in comaraderie at
Kanha National Park

We arrived at Kanha National Park in the most unique fashion. Sensible people would have taken a train from Nagpur or Jabalpur, but we chose to do the seven hundred kilometers from Varanasi by road. Our vehicle of choice: a 1960s Ambassador car with a top speed of sixty kilometers per hour. Slow by any standard, but the hours we spent in it made for a hair-raising, gut-wrenching journey to say the least.

We started late, so it soon got dark. The road was punctured with enormous potholes, and the passing traffic did not bother with headlights. We dodged dangerously, outwitting pedestrians and scaring off cows/dogs/goats to establish our right of way. Despite our best efforts to get our driver to take a break, he stopped for just five minutes during the whole journey. We could only assume that he was in fact a machine ... Robo-Driver. To put it simply, we were hailed as heroes when we finally arrived at Kipling Camp, a comfortable forest lodge where my partner, Dani, and I had made a booking for the duration of our stay.

My first impression of the tiger reserve was that of a dramatically beautiful piece of wooded grassland. With a core area of 940 square kilometers and a buffer zone of 1,005 square kilometers, the sanctuary spread quite a ways. *Sal* and bamboo trees grew profusely everywhere, although the downside of all this excessive vegetation was that it could make for difficult tiger spotting. But on our first safari the following morning, we had some lucky company: Johan, the Crazy Dutchman, and Charlie and Hannah, who had come from London. This group had seen just about every animal possible on their expedition the day before, and we were hoping that some of their good fortune would rub off on us.

The trio came through. About half an hour into the safari, we spotted a tiger—a twelve-year-old female that our guide told us was named Link 7. She stood watching from about one hundred yards away and then began to head straight for us. When she was no more than six feet from our jeep, Charlie lost his nerve and gave in to a bout of panic. I cannot say the rest of us were faring very well either, especially when Link 7 decided to hang around for a good ten minutes or so before she got bored and walked away. We caught up with her about an hour later and once again had an awesome view, this time from a more comfortable distance. Our first safari at Kanha and we had two sightings!

Our second day proved to be even better than the first—not only did we see another tiger, from atop an elephant's back and later from the jeep, but we also spotted a sloth bear, especially requested by Hannah. The male lion she had also wished for wasn't so quick to materialize, but we reckoned we had a pretty successful outing overall.

On our third day, we didn't spot a tiger, but we did see an absolutely brilliant sloth bear. It came so close to the jeep that we could hear him huffing and puffing as he sucked up ants while rummaging around in the undergrowth. Our fourth and final trip into the Kanha forest had two female tigers in store, both busy with a spotted deer kill. All in all, we couldn't be happier with the way this trip turned out for us.

Evenings at Kipling Camp were spent lazing around a campfire with lots of beer and spicy snacks and all sorts of wildlife and conservation gossip floating around us. Along with Johan, Charlie, and Hannah, there was James, a professional wildlife photographer, and his partner, Laria, who ran a safari ranch in Kenya. This made for a good mix of nationalities, and everybody seemed to rub along really well. We were all at Kanha—one of Asia's finest protected areas and probably the best place in the world to see tigers in the wild—hoping we'd be the lucky group to get a sighting. That was good enough reason to feel some sort of kinship toward each other.

Besides our daily tiger treks, the other big delight at Kanha was Tara, the sweetest elephant you're ever likely to meet and undoubtedly the star of the Kipling Camp. Fifteen years earlier, she was rescued from gypsies by Mark Shand (brother of Camilla Parker Bowles), who then rode her across India to an elephant fair. Later, Shand passed her on to the people who set up Kipling Camp and wrote at length about her in his best-selling *Travels on My Elephant*.

Everybody took turns to bathe Tara, as she had to be scrubbed down with bricks so that she remained looking young and beautiful, but she was unstintingly impartial in her affections for us. She did some of her own grooming as well—cleaned her own toenails with a stick, much to our amusement—and happily accepted all the biscuits we forced on her.

It was a sad parting when it was time to say goodbye to Tara and all the friends Dani and I had made at Kanha. When I look at my collection of Kanha photos now, I realize that while the tigers were impressive, they were only part of what made the trip so marvelous. It was sharing our safaris with our fellow guests at Kipling Camp that made our stay such an unforgettable experience.

Getting to Kanha National Park

The nearest big city with rail and air connections to the park is Jabalpur. A taxi ride will get you to Kanha in approximately three hours. Another option for your starting point is the city of Nagpur, which is a driving distance of about five hours. The following travel company websites offer a variety of information about the wildlife at the park.

www.kanhanationalpark.com
www.kanha-national-park.com

Kipling Camp

Dan adds: When we weren't on safari, we were back at Kipling Camp, which was excellent in every way. We had a lovely room with an en suite bath, hot water, mozzie nets, and heater. It was still pretty cold at night, so there were hot water bottles in the beds, which I thought was a nice touch.

www.kiplingcamp.com
info@kiplingcamp.com

KEOLADEO GHANA NATIONAL PARK

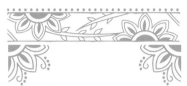

Robin Searle mourns the death of Keoladeo Ghana National Park

RAJASTHAN

Bharatpur was a dream destination for me. It is the home of Keoladeo Ghana National Park—one of Asia's most important wetlands—and just the thought of visiting there helped to keep me motivated whenever the going got tough during my travels.

I had made plans to spend Christmas among the park's flourishing birds and wildlife, and I reached Bharatpur just before the holidays. It was already afternoon, and as a day ticket into the park was quite pricey, I banked my enthusiasm for the time being and did a recce of the area around the edges, instead. Then, the next morning, I set out to enjoy my first sightings of the herons, storks, cranes, ducks, geese, eagles, and other birds that inhabited the marshes.

What I found inside Keoladeo was a tinder-dry landscape with cracked, dry mud for lake beds, and no birds. This was because there was no water. The park, famous for its enormous avian population, was a

RAJASTHAN

vast scrubland with hardly any signs of life. It was a dreadful shock.

It made no sense. In the height of summer, before the monsoon rains, this would be normal, but it was now midwinter. The water levels should have been high, and there should have been literally millions of birds in residence. As I spent hours cycling through the park, what I saw instead were herds of domestic cows grazing on dry grass and locals blatantly cutting down firewood and plucking fruit from trees.

I was convinced there had to be water somewhere, and after much searching I eventually found two tiny, shallow pools. The water for these pools was being pumped out of the ground, which explained their pathetically low levels. Instead of hundreds of waterfowl, there were only six ducks, two herons, and a couple of greylag geese that had flown all the way from arctic Siberia to spend the winter. They must have felt as depressed as I did.

The appalling condition of the park was casually explained away by the park staff, who told me that the monsoon had been poor this year. They didn't add that the monsoon had been poor for a long time and got worse with each passing season. More alarmingly, other tourists seemed to have been told that it was normal for the park to be dry during this season, even though all the free leaflets and information boards claimed otherwise.

Poor monsoons were only part of the problem, though. There was no shortage of water outside the park, where miles and miles of irrigated crops were thriving. The problem— as is so often the case—was one of politics. The water levels in Keoladeo are controlled artificially, and sluices and dams have to be opened to allow water to flow in from storage reservoirs after the monsoons have filled them. But local farmers demand that the water should all be reserved for the irrigation of farmland. No wonder, then, that the park was dying.

The following day, I went to the visitors' center and saw pictures in the displays of what the park used to look like. But there was no information about the severe water crisis at hand or what the management was doing to save the wetlands and its wildlife. Outside, I managed to corner the information officer, who at first tried to gloss over the situation. When he realized I wasn't buying the temporary-drought-due-to-bad-monsoon argument, he became belligerent. Did I want to make a complaint? he asked.

No, I replied, I was merely concerned, and as an ecologist I wanted to know what was being done to save the park.

"What would you like us to do?" he responded, sarcastically. "You tell me what you want and I will do it!"

Sadly, there is no quick fix for the problems at Keoladeo. It seems a lot of the damage has already been done. The park may yet survive as a dry grassland habitat, but the obvious presence of local people cutting down trees for wood and grazing their cattle endangers even this. Park authorities are unconcerned—the keepers themselves cut wood to build bonfires during cold winter mornings. Without the will of the government to first acknowledge the problem and then do something about it, Bharatpur's wetlands will most likely soon be a thing of the past.

On my second afternoon, inside the park I met two local botany students, who asked me if there was any water in the direction from which I had come. They were the only people I met who seemed concerned at the way Keoladeo was slowly turning into a desert. More depressed than ever, I decided not to hang around any longer, and my hotel owner didn't seem surprised when I told him I wouldn't be staying the four nights I had booked.

It was two days before Christmas, and my big plan had been to spend it in a "wildlife paradise." Since that was no longer likely, I set out on my bike for Jaipur. I intended to hook up with some other travelers, find a party, and try to cheer myself up.

Agra alternative

Despite the park's water issues, it is still an interesting place to visit, and by staying there, you can help bring awareness to the situation. As well, the park can make a tranquil base for doing the Taj Mahal and Fatehpur Sikri. Many travelers hate staying over in Agra, as the city is so crowded, touristy, and—frankly—quite filthy. So they take a train from Delhi in the morning and come back after seeing the Taj in the evening. But this is disappointing for people who want to spend more time at the Taj, exploring its many architectural details and seeing how beautifully it changes in different lights. If this is your goal, Bharatpur is a great alternative. Right at the park, it is only fifty kilometers or so away from Agra—about an hour's drive. Staying in Bharatpur, you can enjoy a wilderness setting while going back and forth to Agra and Fatehpur Sikri as often as you like.

GANGOTRI GLACIER

Partha De Sarkar dreams his way up the Ganga River

Like every child in India, I grew up on a diet of legends and mythology. My favorite story was from the epic *Ramayana*, the tale about the origins of the Ganga.

Once there was a time when the holy river flowed in heaven, but a grave situation arose on earth that made it necessary for her to descend. Now, Ganga was a massive river, and the impact of her fall would certainly cause terrible floods and death. The situation on earth grew progressively worse, and the problem remained unsolved until Lord Shiva came to the rescue. He offered to break Ganga's fall with his *jata*, or roll of matted hair. In short, that was how Ganga came to reside in India, and growing up, every time I saw posters and calendar pictures of Lord Shiva with a rivulet of blue water flowing out from his hair, I relived the drama of Ganga's fall from heaven with relish.

As I entered my adolescent years, my fascination with Ganga continued. The river became more than just an exciting character from a storybook. I visited many religious sites around India with my family—Rishikesh, Hardwar, Varanasi, Allahabad—and in each of these places I saw how the Hindu religion had flourished on the Ganga's banks. In her 2,510-kilometer course, Ganga often changed her name. At her source, she was called Bhagirathi, and by the time she reached my native city of Kolkata she was Hooghly. But wherever she went, she cleansed people of their sins, gave them a source of livelihood, and was worshipped as Mother.

When I began trekking, this fixation with Ganga took yet another turn. I became obsessed with the idea of seeing her source. The river was born out of the mighty Gangotri glacier, which stands at 4,255 meters above sea level, and the exact point from which the Ganga emerges is known as Gaumukh (Cow's Mouth), because the shape of the ice formation here resembles the snout of a cow. For years I dreamed of going to Gaumukh,

and when I was twenty-eight I finally managed to make the trip.

My journey began in Hardwar, where a twelve-hour bus ride carried me up to the little village of Gangotri, sitting at an altitude of more than three thousand meters. Once upon a time, the village had only a temple and the most basic accommodation for the few pilgrims who came this way. With the building of a bridge, however, the facilities improved, and Gangotri was a busier place, overrun with sadhus, pilgrims, and trekkers.

The constant cry of "Hara Hara Mahadev"—"Hail Lord Shiva"— echoed down the streets of Gangotri. As a military man, I had heard it often enough in a different context: it was the battle cry of the brave Gurkha regiment of the Indian army. But Lord Shiva wasn't being called upon to assist in war in Gangotri. By crying out "Hara Hara Mahadev," pilgrims were expressing their devotion. The passion and fervor in the refrain beat into my brain, stirring the Hindu inside me. My mind responded by slipping into a trancelike state.

I had rented a room at the local GMVN guesthouse, so I could stay in Gangotri an extra day and acclimatize before continuing with my journey. At the guesthouse, I joined up with a British couple, John and Martha Blake, and together we set off on the first leg of our trek, to the village of Bhojbasa. Although we could have hired horses for the journey, we chose to walk. The trail was easy and the surroundings, astoundingly beautiful with forests of blue pine and silver birch set against a backdrop of pristine white snow peaks. By the time we reached Bhojbasa, dusk had fallen and the cold was moving into our bones. The guesthouse we checked into was very basic with an outdoor bathroom facility. Somehow, we managed to freshen up a bit, and after a quick make-do dinner, we huddled under our blankets for the night.

When we woke the next morning, thick clouds filled the sky, and rain threatened. The guesthouse manager was of the opinion that it was fool-hardy to try and make it to Gaumukh in this weather, but the Blakes, who had the experience of climbing the Alps behind them, were determined to carry on. Disregarding the advice of the manager, I decided to go with them.

The last leg of our journey proved to be quite lonely. Not too many pilgrims passed us on the way. The trail was full of rocks, and the walking tired us, but we kept telling each other that we were almost there. When we finally we made it to the glacier head, we saw a boulder that had the words "snout position 1935" painted on it. We didn't know what to make of it until a pilgrim on his return journey explained that the snout through which the Ganga emerged had shifted many positions with the passage of time. Sure enough, we came across more boulders with dates on them until finally we could see the present Gaumukh. The river trickled out from a little dark hole in the glacier. I couldn't believe that the mighty Ganga could possibly melt into life from such a small aperture.

I stared at the source, trying to imagine the dribble of water making its way down to the plains, meeting tributaries, swelling with great volumes of water, and building a powerful current. I thought of the great gift of fertility the Ganga gave to the land it passed through, of Hindus using its water to purify their homes, of the songs sung in its praise and poems written in its glory, of its role as India's spiritual guide and guru. It all began here, with this thin stream of melted ice.

The miracle of nature, and the mysterious workings of God, held me spellbound in those long minutes. The transformation was difficult to as-similate, as I realized there was more drama in Ganga's course on earth than there was in all the mythological stories I had read about it as a child.

Getting to Gangotri glacier

From Dehradun, the nearest air-port, taxis or shared jeeps can be hired to cover the 226-kilometer distance to the village of Gan-gotri. You can also take transport from the nearest railway station in Rishikesh.

GMVN guesthouses

If you are traveling through the mountains of Uttaranchal, you will find decent accommodations at the GMVN guesthouses. There are several on the Gaumukh route—in Hardwar, Gangotri, and Bhojbasa. Among the many GMVN reservation offices (which are listed on the GMVN website) is a branch in New Delhi.

102, Indraprakash Building
Barakhamba Road
New Delhi

www.gmvnl.com

PINDARI GLACIER

David Cook
communes with the
"god-man" of Zero Point

The swift sound of footsteps along the rocky path outside my tent woke me from a deep slumber. I breathed in the icy air, feeling the earliness of the hour in my throat. It had to be Baba Ji out there, starting his day as usual at the break of dawn. My grogginess cleared, and I jumped out of the sleeping bag and quickly got dressed. This was my last day at Zero Point, Baba Ji's humble abode in the Himalayas, and I wanted to spend these final hours with him.

Baba Ji, as his name suggests, is a man of God—*Baba* means "god-man." He is also the sole occupant of Zero Point, an otherwise arbitrary spot were it not for its name, which sits

next to the receding Pindari glacier, a gargantuan mass of ice gradually melting into streams and rivers that merge with the Ganga River below. For nineteen years, Baba Ji has made Zero Point his home, coming down to the plains in December only for three months when the winter is at its worst. One year, though, he decided to brave the elements and not come down at all. His friends were certain he had perished in the cold, but in April, when trekkers could finally venture his way, they found Baba Ji's hut buried under fifteen feet of snow, but the man—quite miraculously— still alive and well!

For the past three nights, I had been camping just outside Baba Ji's temple—a loosely packed pile of gray stones he has shaped into a hut at the mouth of a natural mountain cave. He also built a garden, a tiny kitchen, and a guest room for trekkers who follow an ancient trading route between India and Tibet high up in the Kumaon region to come to visit him. They make the trip for the thrill of the trek up to Zero Point, and to spend time in the company of this remarkable man.

A bony-framed individual with a long, flowing sadhu's beard, Baba Ji is a strange mix of god-man, naturalist, and carefree mountain goat. He wears his sadhu's saffron garb lightly, making no great show of his spiritual accomplishments. Nobody cares to call him by his high-sounding religious name, Swami Dharmanand, and he is happy to be known by the more accessible and informal Baba Ji.

It was difficult to believe that Baba Ji was any sort of spiritual being when I first saw him squatting low on the ground, giggling and tending to the kitchen fire on which he had cooked a huge meal of puri and *sabji* (fried bread and vegetable curry). Watching him boil up hot cups of sugary chai for his guests to drink after an arduous day of high-altitude trekking, it was easy to mistake him for nothing more than a generous host, trying to make his guests as comfortable as possible in an inhospitable environment.

On my first evening at Zero Point, however, I witnessed the transformation as Baba Ji's thoughts turned to God. He blew on his conch shell to clear negative vibes from the air and declare to the heavens that he was beginning his *puja*. His guests—among whom I was one—took this audible cue to file silently into his temple. A set of roughly hewn stairs took us into the bowels of the actual cave behind the temple walls, inside which Baba Ji had set up his altar to the goddess Durga, Mother of the universe and the female embodiment of power.

In the dim light of candles, we watched as Baba Ji began to recite his Hindu chants in a monotonous singsong. He rang bells whose sound ricocheted back and forth in the tiny, cramped quarters. He lit handfuls of incense, whose smoke stung my eyes and imbued the proceedings with a strong spiritual atmosphere. He threw clarified butter into the altar fire to raise its flames in salute to the goddess, and he offered her flowers and food as tokens of his devotion.

The minutes disappeared down in the cave, but Baba Ji's *puja* held us in such a spell that none of us even thought to move. We didn't understand his words or his worship, but the power of his impassioned call to the goddess was so raw and pure, our own souls awakened in response and joined in. I remember the sense of ease I felt when the *puja* was finally concluded, as if the great weight of the world had suddenly been lifted from my shoulders. No wonder Baba Ji was such a contented man in his corporeal life, going about his duties with a spring in his steps and a smile on his face. He cleansed and regenerated his spirit every evening during his unity with the goddess.

After the evening worship, we all sat around Baba Ji and discussed philosophy, meditation, Hinduism, and yoga in India and the West. He listened to our views and arguments, and then conveyed his own interpretations with simple, colorful imageries that immediately uncomplicated issues and helped us gain a deeper perspective on the Hindu way of life. These discussions went on until late into the night, and his guests were welcome to stay as long as they wished before wandering back to their tents.

Like any traveler to India, I had done my fair share of temple touring all over the north of the country, but through coming to this no man's land called Zero Point and being in the company of Baba Ji I had really felt the spirituality of Hinduism for the first time. Shorn of all the attending grandeur and rituals, it was as it should be, a direct one-on-one communion with God.

Getting to Pindari glacier and Zero Point

Easily accessible from the starting point of Song (Saung) village, Pindari glacier is in the Kumaon region of the Himalayas in the state of Uttarakhand. You do not have to be a serious trekker to make this hike, which ends at Zero Point. To book a trek, visit the Kumaon Himalayas website.

www.kmvn.org

National Outdoor Leadership School (NOLS)

For another option, this American organization has an India branch offering extended wilderness expeditions in the Kumaon Himalayas. Expeditions focus on backpacking, mountaineering, and white water rafting. Most of the expeditions visit Baba Ji at Zero Point, ever since he extended an invitation in the early 1990s for a group of NOLS students to join him in taking shelter from a passing storm.

www.nols.edu

ROOPKUND

Partha De Sarkar treks to Roopkund's skeleton lake

The scene is utter desolation. At an altitude of 5,029 meters, nothing grows, nothing breathes, nothing survives. As if nature has deliberately thinned the air and laid down a cover of ice and snow to discourage trespassers. And hide a terrible secret.

Roopkund—a small, shallow lake with a depth of only two meters—would have been just another Himalayan water body at extreme altitude, unseen and unnamed, had it not been for what has been lying at its bottom for thousands of years: more than three hundred human skeletons, some with bits of flesh still intact on the bones. For most of the year, Roopkund freezes over and the skeletons lie undisturbed. They are entombed in ice except for one month in the summer when the lake melts.

Who were these people, I wondered, whose remains have survived a water burial for more than a millennium? What were they doing so high above the highest inhabitable point in the Himalayas? And why did they die en masse in the Roopkund?

Scientists have studied the bones and reached various conclusions from their conditions: the people were of Indian descent, and of tall and heavy build; the group comprised men, women, and children; many revealed the distinguishing feature of an extra bone in their skull ... But the circumstance of their sudden death remains a matter of conjecture. There are many theories. Nothing has been conclusively proved.

I had chosen September as a good time to trek to the Roopkund. My enthusiastic party of five knew that the going would be tough—the weather at the lake was unpredictable, and there was every chance of an avalanche or two hitting the trail— but we were determined to press ahead. In Delhi, we procured ration, fuel, medicine, and a proper 4x4 vehicle, and then, after we had carefully charted our route, we set off on our eight-day journey to see the Roopkund skeletons for ourselves.

On day three, our truck reached Lohajung, our trek head at 2,133 meters, from which point we would begin to negotiate deep Himalayan valleys, alpine meadows, dense forests, and steep rock faces on foot. Getting to Roopkund itself was an adventure, and the lore and legends we heard along the way added mystery to every sight and reinforced the this-must-be-a-dream sensation that comes with such high altitudes. The lack of sufficient oxygen plays tricks on the mind, and we were ready to believe anything.

The fright we got at 3,558 meters at Patthar Nachani, for instance, may sound a little foolish in the retelling, but I dare anybody to enjoy a peaceful night in the creepy atmosphere of that campground after hearing the legend of how the place came to get its name. Patthar Nachani, or Stone Courtesans, was where an ancient king and his party once set up a rest camp during a pilgrimage. A troupe of nubile, dancing girls accompanied the party, and the king was so excited by their sensuous performance that he cancelled the pilgrimage and gave himself up to the pleasure of wine and women. Now, Nanda Devi, the goddess of the mountains in these parts, wasn't happy with the king at all, and she turned the courtesans to statues of stone to teach him a lesson. The statues do not exist anymore, but the ghosts of the courtesans came to dance in our dreams, driving off any chances of a good night's rest.

The highlight of the trek to Roopkund was the viewing of the most sacred and rare of Indian flowers: the Divine Lotus, or Brahma Kamal. We were told that the flower, with its ethereal, translucent white petals, typically blooms only once in fourteen years, and that too at midnight. It was a pure stroke of luck that we happened to be there at just the right time. The viewing of the Divine Lotus was supposed to bring good fortune, and we were grateful for that—given the unpredictability of the weather at this altitude, we needed all the hallowed help we could get. A group of French backpackers returning from the lake had just given us some bad news. The weather had turned inclement with wind, rain, and sleet. We prayed for improved weather on this last leg and hoped the Divine Lotus would live up to its promise and see us through.

The final bit of the trek up to Roopkund was terribly steep. A howling wind threatened to unbalance us every step of the way, so the going was slow. But by early afternoon, we had made it. The mysterious Roopkund was finally before us.

I stopped for a long minute, looking across at the lake in the distance, trying to imprint this first glimpse forever in my mind. It lay in a shallow sort of a crater, a murky pool of green water, with gray stones rising a few feet around it. From that distance, the skeletons were not visible, but as we ventured closer, we could identify frozen bits and pieces of long-dead humans. A yellowed hand balanced against a rock, its fingers black and twisted with time. A collection of human skulls and thigh bones. Rib cages. Teeth. Scraps of clothing, sandals, and tufts of hair, swept, by a traveler or a researcher perhaps, into neat little piles.

We walked around the lakeside silently, looking in awe at the grizzly display, not daring to touch or even get very close to the skeletons. We didn't want to disturb their peace. There have been reports of people carrying away bones and skulls from here as trophies of their trip, and I

couldn't imagine how anyone could do such a thing.

By late afternoon, the bitterly cold wind had picked up again. It would be foolhardy to push our luck and hang around much longer, so we regrouped and turned to look at Roopkund one last time. Curiosity had brought us this far up, and we had now seen the skeletons for ourselves. But the questions remained, and Roopkund maintained its silence. As we left, it was with the uncomfortable feeling that the lake was willing us to go, so the atmosphere could be still again, the snow could cover all evidence of our interruption, and Roopkund could return to guarding its secret once more.

Trekking to Roopkund

It is advisable to let expert tour operators handle all arrangements if you are planning a trek to the Roopkund. Knowledge of the terrain is crucial, and you'll be a lot safer in their hands. The tour operators will organize everything from equipment to accommodation. To learn more about Roopkund, seek out *Riddles of the Dead: Skeleton Lake*, a documentary that has been shown on the National Geographic channel.

GENERAL NORTH INDIA

The grounds surrounding India Gate are full of lawns and fountains

The Qutab Minar complex is one of three UNESCO World Heritage Sites in Delhi

When in Rome

Lessons on living local and making yourself at home

"**W**e are like this only."

Indians love using this phrase to describe themselves, and really, nothing explains the Indian way of life quite as accurately as these five words do. I'll even go so far as to say that understanding this phrase, in all its fullness, is key to your enjoyment of the Indian experience.

Note, for instance, the insouciance in the casual construction of this sentence. We are like this only—in other words, we are laid-back, unperturbed, and untroubled by all the inconveniences that are so much a part of our daily lives. While in India, you had better renounce your tidy way of thinking and be that way too, or you won't have any fun at all.

When David Cook writes about the lawlessness of the traffic here, he adopts the perfect attitude of a seasoned traveler to India—he cannot avoid it, he cannot change it, so he simply laughs at it. When Adrian Murray goes for a round of golf in Jaipur and is amazed by the strange, homegrown practices that rule the greens, he still plays the game sportingly and then recounts the experience with a great sense of humor. A lighthearted approach is always handy when you are on the road, but it is especially useful in idiosyncratic India, where public toilets often turn out to be unusable, trains don't arrive on time, and scheduled buses sometimes disappear off the timetable altogether.

There is also in this phrase—"we are like this only"—a suggestion of the informality that marks all social interactions here. There is no code of etiquette for a visitor to follow, and Indians rarely take offense if a traveler makes a cultural or religious faux pas. The average man on the street is extremely curious about your background, and by the same token, he sees no impropriety in your being inquisitive about his. Moreover, Indians take great pride in their hospitality—there's a Hindu

perception of guests being gods—and throw open their homes and hearts to visitors.

India may be financially poor, but its spirit is generous, and there's always a welcome waiting wherever you go. Alexandra Nassau-Brownstone discovered this to be true when she abandoned herself to the spirit of Holi and rubbed color on complete strangers during the spring festival. For days after that, she went around Jaipur with pink-stained hair, but the embarrassment she felt about her appearance soon dissipated when she realized she looked very much part of the community, where everybody else also had traces of the festival on their faces and bodies. Cynthia Chesterfield found herself dancing on the streets of Amritsar in the middle of the night, buoyed by the friendliness of the locals who egged on her enthusiasm for bhangra dance, and Margaret Rees joined the patriotic crowd at the Wagah Border between India and Pakistan and cheered as hard for India as everyone around her, forgetting in the moment that she wasn't a citizen of this country.

Finally, in "We are like this only," there's bad grammar. The phrase is a fine example of the way Indians speak what we call "Hinglish," picking up nuances from Hindi and imposing them on English. If you believe the experts, then Hinglish will soon emerge as the most commonly spoken form of English in the world (largely because there are so many of us Indians), so keep your ears open for amusing and peculiarly Indian usages. You'll enjoy peppering your sentences with them, and—who knows—maybe you'll even end up learning the English language of the future. Pair your new vocabulary with the lessons on local customs in this chapter, and you'll soon be on your way to discovering that you, too, are like this only.

NEW DELHI

*Michael Roberts
puffs away with Delhi's
young intellectuals*

I don't know if recommending that you smoke local Indian cigarettes is entirely responsible, but I'm going to do it anyway ... after acquitting myself of any blame with the warning that this essay is not for nonsmoking readers.

I was hanging out with a bunch of guys at JNU (Jawaharlal Nehru University), a top-rung university and a favorite haunt of young intellectuals in Delhi. Every evening at around six, this group gathered at their favorite spot on the campus grounds and launched into lively debates on all kinds of issues over endless cups of tea and *beedi* cigarettes. On at least half a dozen occasions, I joined them to argue about world politics and hone my skill at smoking these quaint, handmade tobacco treats.

Instead of using paper, *beedi* makers roll small quantities of tobacco in dried *tendu* leaves and tie them up with string to make low-cost cigarettes for the masses. When an autorickshaw driver smokes a *beedi*, it is because he can't afford the real

thing. When a JNU student puffs on one, it is mostly to look cool.

There is, I have to admit, a nice feeling about holding a small *beedi* between my thumb and forefinger. Pinching firmly down on the tip, I had to take quick puffs, to keep the fire burning at the end. Three or four puffs, and the *beedi* was gone, leaving a pleasant woody taste in my mouth. The flavor of the *tendu* leaf reminded me of the autumn days of my childhood, when my dad used to sweep dead leaves into a pile in the yard and light a bonfire. It was strong, unrefined, and also slightly cinnamony.

On those balmy summer evenings in Delhi, I had fun sitting cross-legged in the JNU greens, with half my attention on the heated conversation going on around me, and the other half concentrating on getting as many puffs out of a single *beedi* as I could. Jonathan, an Australian friend of mine who studied politics at JNU and had introduced me to this group, said that an experienced *beedi* smoker effortlessly got an average of seven puffs from one. As much as I tried, my *beedi* burnt out before I could progress beyond four.

Jonathan also informed me that the *beedis* would add a swagger to my walk, and others in the group assured me that I'd be a huge hit with the ladies if I tied a handkerchief around my neck and approached them with a *beedi* clamped between my teeth. Of course, I didn't put this kerchiefed playboy persona to test—I had been in India long enough to know that the mischief makers were describing the sidekicks who typically hung around the villain in bad Bollywood movies, and I had no desire to either go courting in such a ridiculous manner or risk a black eye and broken bones. I was content to just sit on the grass with my back against a rock, enjoying my *beedi* in four inexpert puffs.

Buying beedis

Michael recommends looking for the Azad brand, which includes regular as well as flavored *beedis* in gaily colored packets. *Beedis* are sold in all *paan* and cigarette stalls.

www.azadbidi.com

Jawaharlal Nehru University

If you are interested in meeting some of Delhi's young intellectuals for yourself, take a stroll around the university grounds. You can find directions and a campus map at the following website.

www.jnu.ac.in

Jason Staring finds faith at a Delhi bloodletting

My $300 Nike Air Rhyolites failed the India challenge just as I was walking out of the Jama Masjid in Old Delhi. For eight long weeks I had subjected these "high-performance" boots to daily stress tests in the Himalayan foothills, and finally one of the soles came apart on the Masjid's staircase. Bad timing. I had planned to spend the rest of the afternoon exploring other historical pockets of Old Delhi, but now I'd have to find an autorickshaw and go back to the hotel to change my shoes instead.

I was standing on the stairs of the ancient mosque, balancing on one foot and cursing my expensive shoes, when a young lad of about nineteen came up to ask if I needed a cobbler. This is one of the reasons why I so love India. The amenities are to die for. You don't throw out a pair of Nikes here just because the sole has come off. You take them to a roadside cobbler who fixes the problem for less than $1. Gratefully, I followed the boy to a nearby shoe repairman, and after depositing my Nike, invited him to share a cup of tea with me while I waited. The boy, Ahmed, was a local. His family had lived near the Jama Masjid for six generations, and he knew the area like the back of his hand.

I asked the friendly young man if he could suggest something unusual for me to see around the neighborhood, something that only a local would know about. Ahmed scratched his head for a moment, and then said, "Are you queasy?" I had no idea what he was talking about. He added, "I mean, can you stand the sight of blood?"

Good Lord, did he want to show me how they slaughter meat in the

Muslim Halal style? "No, no, please, I don't want to visit an abattoir," I protested in horror, sending him into amused laughter.

"Don't worry, sir," he said. "I only wanted to take you to the Rahat Open Surgery. A very old man there has an open-air clinic where he bleeds his patients back to health. Really, sir, and he is very good too. Last year, he cured my grandmother of arthritis."

Centuries ago it was a common practice among men of medicine to use leeches to bleed patients, but who in their right mind would do such a thing now? However, if somebody was indeed doing it, then the experience junkie in me certainly wanted to see it. I paid the cobbler 100 rupees for my shoe, which looked perfectly good now, and followed Ahmed into an open park, where a group of about a dozen men and women had gathered around a water tank.

"Ghayas *miyan!*"Ahmed called out, using the word that is a mixture of *mister*, *friend*, and *brother* to catch the attention of an old man with a floating white beard. He was bending over the exposed knee of a middle-aged woman, but he straightened up as we approached and raised his hand in welcome. This was Mohammad Ghayas, the *hakeem* (doctor) himself. "Have you come for treatment?" he asked me.

"Mr. Staring here needs treatment, but today he has only come to say hello and ask about the procedure," Ahmed replied with a straight face on my behalf.

I nodded nervously and prayed that nobody would drag me off and bleed me afterward. The old man, unaware of my discomfort, began to talk of his "miracle" work. It appeared that Dr. Ghayas's grandfather had taught him how to locate "bad blood" in the body. Problems like lumbago, gout, rheumatism, paralysis, polio, and diabetes could all be cured, if you removed this bad blood. Since 1980, he had helped over three hundred thousand patients, and many of them had written glowing testimonies in his notebook. Flipping through the pages, I found names and addresses of several patients from Europe, Africa, and Far East Asia.

The doctor then introduced me to his son, who now did most of the bloodletting work. The young man was tying a narrow strip of cloth around a woman's arm. The woman was complaining that the binding was too tight, but Dr. Ghayas's son said it was necessary to cut off the blood circulation. After giving the binding one final jerk, he tied the ends around her chest and left her alone. "Standing in the sun for half an hour will heat up her body and make the blood flow smoothly," he explained, before moving on to a row of patients, all men, with similar bindings on their legs.

He reached down to examine the tied-up leg of the first one, pressed at the skin bulging between the binds, and then unwrapped a brand-new razor blade. He worked quickly, making five or six tiny cuts on a vein in the foot. The patient did not even wince. A thin rivulet of blood began to pour out of each cut, and after watching the flow for a few moments, the doctor moved on to the next patient. The platform on which these guys stood was constantly washed down with water from the tank, but I could see ribbons of blood swirling in the drain below. The sight made me feel slightly nauseated, but I pushed the feeling away. I'd never see such a bizarre sight again in my life, and I needed steady hands to shoot pictures.

I spent the next half an hour taking numerous photographs of Dr. Gayas's son administering the treatment. As I was packing away my camera, my eyes fell on a patient who stood slightly apart from the others. From his attire I guessed he did some sort of white collar job. On an impulse, I went and introduced myself. The man, with his leg wound up and bleeding, was happy to spend a few minutes talking to me. He was a bank clerk, he said, and had been coming here for treatment for the past three years. I was searching wildly for the correct words to frame my next question, but the man read my expression and said, "You want to know how I can have faith in this weird kind of quack medicine."

I nodded dumbly.

"It *is* faith, my friend," he said, patting me lightly on the shoulder. "Faith can work miracles if you can only bring yourself to believe." He pulled up his shirt sleeve to show me his arm, dotted with old scars from previous treatments. "I was in

terrible pain until the *hakeem* started to take care of me. His method makes no sense, I know, and yet I believe. Perhaps it is my own will that is working like a cure. But at the end of the day, aren't will and faith one and the same thing?"

Later, when I was looking at the photographs of this experience on my computer, the man's words came back to me. What he had said applied to so many things I had seen in India. Incidents had defied logic and denied science, and yet I couldn't help but marvel at the strength of the beliefs behind them. To my mind, that was a miracle in itself.

Rahat Open Surgery

Near Dargah Hare Bhare Shah
Gate No. 2, Jama Masjid
Delhi

Andrew Soleimany is entertained at a Delhi's intersection

Entertainment never stops in New Delhi—not even at traffic signals. As soon as a vehicle halts at a stoplight anywhere in the city, a variety of performers materialize out of nowhere and hold the attention of commuters until the light turns green again and off they go.

I observed this most frequently at the big intersection on Delhi's Kasturba Gandhi Marg, where I seemed to fall foul of the red light every time I left or returned to my hotel. After two weeks of traveling the same route, I came to know the "entertainers" working this busy intersection very well. They, in turn, noticed my curious white face staring at them out of the passenger window of a hotel car, for some acknowledged me occasionally with a wink or a friendly wave.

According to my driver, they were all part of a syndicate that ran the roads of Delhi like a business. He had no patience with them, often jumping out of the car to shoo them off if they persisted with their knocking on my window. But I was fascinated, categorizing them according to their trade and trying to keep a mental note of their modus operandi until my car drove off. By my estimate, there are four main kinds of businesses that thrive at the Delhi intersections.

The beggars

It may seem strange to call beggars entertainment, but you will understand why I do so as you read on. These people approached the job of begging at traffic signals in a systematic fashion. The younger ones went after the open autorickshaws and laid their heads down on the laps of embarrassed passengers to make them part with a few rupees. The adults used more sophisticated means of raising money, mentionable among which is the sob story with "proof."

I was familiar with one middle-aged man who roamed around the Kasturba Gandhi intersection with a hospital certificate in hand. He said his son had had an accident and was in immediate need of blood. The hospital had given him this document to help raise funds for the transfusion. This evidence of proof often worked for him, and I watched compassionate, unsuspecting commuters contribute several hundred rupees at a time to help save his son.

The pickings, in fact, were quite good when begging was garbed in the disguise of collecting contributions. I myself was duped by a well-dressed woman who claimed her wallet had been picked. She showed me a big rip in her purse, and I gave her enough money to buy a bus ticket. She spoke reasonably good English, and I had no reason to suspect anything until I saw her the next day at the very same spot. She looked into my window, realized I had recognized her, and walked nonchalantly off to the next car without showing a bit of self-consciousness.

I am not a cold person, but I felt no sympathy for the plight of these traffic signal beggars, as none of them looked hungry, desperate, or even troubled. They went about their business mechanically, with the bored expressions of nine-to-fivers who no longer felt excited by their jobs. Because of this I too could adopt the insouciant Indian attitude of "*chalta hai yaar*"—"all kinds of things happen, my friend"—and sit back and marvel at their acting skills without feeling any pinch of conscience.

The contortionists

The true performers in the traffic signal troupes, however, were not the beggars, but the contortionists, whose sparkling costumes made them hard to miss. They sat quietly on the pavement until the traffic stopped, and then they instantly launched into a gymnastic routine performed at lightning speed. Time was of the essence: they had to finish their act and collect money from the waiting cars before the signal changed and the open-mouthed audience dispersed. I was amazed at how quickly they could switch on and off—one moment they would be sitting there scratching an itch, and the next turning cartwheels in the street.

The four-item sellers

The four-item sellers were a peculiar phenomenon I noticed at every traffic signal I stopped at in New Delhi. Where they could have spot-sold all kinds of small goods to commuters, these guys brought along only four. And what very strange items those four were. I often wondered why the sellers thought that people waiting in traffic would feel compelled to buy these particular products.

One was a battery-operated tennis racket with an electrical charge for swatting mosquitoes to death. The second was a plastic mask that partially covered the face with a mustache, a bulbous nose, and cheesy eyeglasses. Third was a web of netting that sprung open into a laundry bag. And as for the final offering: a vial of colorful jelly balls that I know were wet because I touched them once. Even then I couldn't work out what they were used for. For all of my interest in the traffic signal hawkers, I never felt the desire to purchase any of these things.

The booksellers

Of all the choices, I'd rather be entertained by the traffic signal booksellers any day. They carried an unbelievable number of books, magazines, and newspapers in both arms, and still had the ability to point at each one individually and wait for me to say no before pointing to the next. They did this until they had exhausted their entire collection, and then, they just stood there patiently, letting me read the book covers until my car drove on. I managed to catch up on the news by reading a lot of magazine blurbs and newspaper headlines this way, without having to buy anything.

From what I could gauge, members of New Delhi's traffic signal troupe in the above four categories were quite an optimistic bunch. They didn't seem to care if several minutes of banging on my window did not elicit a donation or a purchase. They would casually move on to the next car, as if they fully expected a benevolent millionaire to turn up and sort out their money hassles once and for all.

Kasturba Gandhi Marg

This tree-lined avenue is one of the main access roads to Connaught Place. On it you will find numerous landmarks, including the British Council Library and the American Center.

Traffic Signal

Bollywood filmmaker Madhur Bhandarkar was as intrigued by the people who hang around traffic signals in India as Andrew, for he made a film on the subject in 2007. Watch *Traffic Signal* for its interesting portrayal of the life of a traffic signal "manager" who runs a network of beggars, tricksters, prostitutes, and hawkers at a major city intersection. The film offers two perspectives on the subject—one of those looking out from the comfort of their cars and one of those looking in.

Giving money

Rather than handing out money to beggars on the street, who may or may not need it, seek out a reputable charity. To get started, read through the essays in the "Paying It Forward" chapter of this book.

GWALIOR

Sean Doogan stumbles upon a secret world in Gwalior

I had come to Gwalior from Agra, and after the crowds in the Taj city, I was glad for the slow pace of life I found in this historic capital of Madhya Pradesh. I was looking forward to visiting the famous fort of Gwalior and the royal palace, and I set off early to get my bearings and do a quick recce.

It was thirsty work, walking around in the sun, so I took a break in a nice park I came upon in the middle of town. I sat down next to a huge statue of Mahatma Gandhi and was drinking from a bottle of water I had purchased and leafing through my Lonely Planet guidebook when two lads walked up to me and asked if they could share my bench. "No problem," I replied and shuffled up to make room. Then one of them inquired if he could ask me some questions. I put down the book and braced myself for the familiar small town game of question-and-answer, in which the local asks the foreign tourist about his homeland, culture, and more, and the tourist answers as best as he can.

"What is your name?"

"Sean."

"Do you like this park?"

"Yes, it's very nice."

"Do you like men?"

"Pardon?"

"Are you gay?"

"No."

"We are all gay in this park. This is our park."

"Oh."

"Are you sure you don't like men?"

"Yes."

I looked around the park properly for the first time, and sure enough, there were only men there, sitting in twos and holding hands. I had been so busy catching my breath and planning my next course of action that I had failed to notice these men cuddling all around me.

Once we had definitively verified my sexual orientation, it was my turn to ask questions. I wasn't likely to wander into too many gay parks by mistake, and I was curious to know how homosexuality was viewed in India. Not at all kindly, the boys informed me. Society was still not comfortable with the idea of same-sex relationships, and gays were viewed as perverts. If their secret was found out, their families cut off ties or forced them to marry women.

As a result, the gay underclass in most provincial towns like Gwalior had no place to meet and spend time together, except in parks. Naturally, big cities like Delhi or Mumbai had more sophisticated hangouts, but

even there, parks were the only place where gays with limited means could rendezvous. The police raided them from time to time, arresting some of the men and accepting small bribes from the rest. Other than this, though, they were mostly left alone.

Later, I found out that there was a nearly 150-year-old colonial law in India that criminalized homosexuality and described it as an "unnatural offense." I also came across a newspaper report about an NGO that had lodged a petition at the Supreme Court in Delhi against this law on the grounds that it violated fundamental human rights and hindered HIV/AIDS prevention work. But at the time I found the park, I was unfamiliar with the situation for gays in India, and when I left, I came away feeling a little saddened by the predicament of these men, some of whom didn't even realize that they were not perverts.

It must have been tough, having to meet so clandestinely, away from the judging eyes of families and friends, in a park where only the statue of Mahatma Gandhi shared their secret. Then again, the Father of the Nation had always stood up for the rights of the oppressed, so they were certainly in good company.

Antigay law overturned

As this book was preparing to go to press, the law mentioned in Sean's essay was overturned. While this is a triumph for human rights, it does not mean that opinions and the treatment of homosexuals in India will change overnight. To find out more about India's gay community, and to meet and network with like-minded people, check out the magazine *Bombay Dost*, which also has an online presence.

www.bombaydost.co.in

. . . .

ORCHHA

. . . .

Jenni Wadams cooks a homemade meal in Orchha

The sleepy little town of Orchha is probably not a place one would readily associate with cooking classes. But homemade Indian dishes are best learnt in somebody's home, and that is what Vandana, an enterprising young Orchha housewife, offers travelers: a chance to learn simple yet delicious recipes that have been in her family for generations.

Now, I'm the sort of cook who cannot handle a dish that requires more than five ingredients, but I love Indian food, and this was a splendid opportunity for me to see how it was prepared. I signed up for a class, and after a lovely day spent rafting in the crystal clear waters of the Betwa River, I set off to find Vandana's residence. The address I had for her simply stated, "Near Betwa River, Orchha, Madhya Pradesh." In this small town, it turned out, no further details were required, and soon I found myself seated next to eleven other students in Vandana's cozy living room.

We were going to cook a large vegetarian meal, Vandana told us, and we all had to help her by shelling hundreds of peas. Being a city girl, I had seen only peas that came frozen in a bag from the supermarket, so I had a rough time getting the shells off of them until Linda, a country girl from Australia, whispered to me that I was trying to open them from the wrong side of the pod. Sure enough, the other side "unzipped" easily. I soon caught up with the others and had a respectable pile of peas to contribute to the proceedings.

While we were doing this, Vandana brought a two-ring burner into the living room and arranged ingredients around it. We weren't going to watch her cook in the kitchen, but right here in the living room, where there was enough space for all of us to gather around her. Sitting down on a low plastic stool, Vandana started to cook, quickly and skillfully, explaining each process as she went.

Indian cooking is very different from Western or other Asian styles, I found, and we had to pay close attention to the way she added the *phorni*—the often-used mixture of cumin seeds, mustard seeds, cardamom, and cinnamon that first go into the wok with the heated oil. This step was crucial if a dish was to

MADHYA PRADESH

come out right, and Vandana showed us exactly how long we should allow these things to fry—a few seconds too long and the ingredients would burn, a few seconds too little and the dish would taste raw.

The spiciness of Indian food comes from a combination of cumin, coriander, and turmeric powder, and lots and lots of onions that Vandana cooked for a lengthy period of time to let them mingle with all the spices in the wok and roast. After this, the rest of the process was easy: just add the vegetables and some water for the sauce, and simmer. I particularly enjoyed watching the chapattis being made: wheat flour, kneaded and rolled out like tortillas, and then tossed on the open gas flame for a few seconds to blow them up like balloons.

In little over an hour, Vandana had whipped up a mouthwatering meal for fifteen people: *alu mutter* (a spicy curry of potatoes and peas), vegetable *pulao* (a delicious rice dish with complex flavors), *raita* (a side dish made of yogurt), and a fresh garden salad. All of this was eaten with chapattis that were still warm and puffed up when they were served. For dessert, we ate *gulab jamun* (a kind of dumpling floating in sweet syrup), which was followed by masala *chai* (sweet, milky tea with spices). The food was not laid out on a dining table, but presented on the floor in the traditional Indian style, so that all of us could sit down together on thin cushions and eat. Fortunately, living in Japan had taught me how to sit comfortably on the floor with my legs folded under me.

Rafting down the Betwa River that morning had left me ravenous, and I ate two portions of all the dishes Vandana prepared. This was the first time I was tasting a home-cooked Indian meal, and I have to say that the restaurant Indian food that I have eaten doesn't have quite the same subtlety. Nothing was too rich or overspiced, and the light hand with which Vandana cooked allowed the vegetables to retain their natural flavor.

Even as we ate, our teacher continued with her instructions, explaining various aspects of dining customs that most Indians follow at home—a complex subject since regional influences complicate Indian cuisine so much that there is little or no similarity between how a North Indian or a South Indian cooks and eats. Listening to Vandana talk, I learnt more about Indian food than I ever could have from any cookbook, and the ordinary details she shared of the everyday life of an average Indian made the food we were eating all the more attractive.

I took thorough notes on every tip Vandana passed on to us, and when I returned to Tokyo, I invited some friends over to taste what I had learnt in my Orchha cooking class. But, as I hinted earlier, my culinary skills leave a lot to be desired, and Tokyo's grocery stores also let me down by not having all the ingredients I needed. Even so, I have to say that the meal didn't turn out too bad, and I think my friends were impressed. It's a great thing to be able to cook the food of a country you have visited—the best souvenir you can bring back of any culture—and I have to thank Vandana for making a passable Indian food cook out of a no-hoper like me.

Getting to Orchha

Orchha is a comfortable driving distance from several tourist towns in the vicinity, such as Jhansi (nearest railway station), Gwalior (nearest airport), Khajuraho, and Agra.

Vandana's cooking class

The cost of the demonstration, with all ingredients provided, was about $4 per person. This fee included lunch. Vandana also paints beautiful henna designs on the hands of female guests for about $1. A cooking class with Vandana can be arranged by contacting Candice Sunney.

crsunney@gmail.com

AMRITSAR

Cynthia Chesterfield grooves to bhangra beats in Amritsar

It was April, the month of the Baisakhi harvest festival, and the whole state of Punjab was dancing the bhangra. Manpreet, a friend with whom I had gone to college in Sheffield, was playing host in the city of Amritsar. He had taken me to a Baisakhi fair earlier, where I bought several pairs of slippers, and after a hearty meal of mutton cooked in copious amounts of butter, we came to the city park to bhangra the night away with hundreds of other merrymakers.

A huge tent had been raised in the middle of the park, a live band was playing, and a group of professional dancers was setting the mood with a choreographed performance before the rest of the crowd joined in. The locals, dressed for bhangra in gayly colored clothes, had already tied large handkerchiefs to their wrists and were raring to go.

The catchy beat of the bhangra music, I discovered, simply doesn't let you sit still. The moment I heard the introductory roll of the percussion instrument called *dhol*, I felt compelled to get up and dance. I watched the professionals closely and picked up a few basic bhangra steps that I thought I could pull off with some degree of finesse. I learnt to raise my index fingers and move my shoulders up and down in rhythm with the *dhol*. I figured I could swing my hips and hop on one leg while kicking out with the other. And of course, I could open my mouth wide and shout "*balle balle*" with all my might.

When the choreographed show came to a close, the master of ceremonies called everybody to the dance floor. The band was playing out a jaunty beat, and a male singer had launched into a raunchy bhangra song that had the crowd rolling with laughter. I was jumping up and down in my seat, and seeing my excitement, an elderly Punjabi lady gave me her handkerchiefs and pushed me toward the dance floor. But Manpreet had gone off to get masala tea for us, and there was nobody I could partner with.

The old lady's husband came to my rescue, and I joined the dancing with the jolly, septuagenarian Sikh gentleman holding my hand and leading me through the first few steps. As the tempo of the music increased, so did the frenzied movements of the bhangra dancers, and cries of "*balle balle*" and "*hai hai hai*" filled the air. I too waved my handkerchiefs with abandon and sped up my steps. When the music finally ended with a massive roll of drums, I collapsed on the floor . with the others and tried to catch my breath between bouts of laughter.

I danced the bhangra at least five more times that evening, and I was no longer short of partners. Emboldened by the friendliness of the people, I dragged total strangers to the floor. The singing and dancing continued full steam until two in the morning, and then, to my great disppointment, the party began to wind down. Manpreet announced he was ravenous, so we went to the food stall that supplied sweets, soda, and tea to the exhausted dancers.

We bought some hot snacks and ate them out of newspaper packets while we walked out to the main

road in search of transport. The music was beating in my head, and I was still dancing when Manpreet flagged down an autorickshaw for us. Amused by my exuberance, the driver sang bhangra songs in his loud, booming voice all the way to the hotel, and I won his respect by shouting "*balle balle*" at all the right intervals.

Needless to say, I became a die-hard bhangra fan from that day on. The Baisakhi harvest festival was going on everywhere, and people came out of their homes every evening to dance in celebration of their full granaries. I joined a group of bhangra enthusiasts at another open-air venue in Chandigarh and later made a spectacle of myself in a small farming village near Bhatinda, where the locals applauded my high kicks and taught me a few more steps to add to my repertoire.

When that evening's festivities came to an end, the villagers folded up the hand-painted banner that announced the bhangra event and gave it to me as a keepsake. I hung it my office at home, and whenever I am asked I about it, I say it is a certificate I brought back from Punjab to prove I am a qualified bhangra artiste!

Bhangra in Amritsar

Bhangra dances take place all round the year in Amritsar. They are usually advertised in the events section in the daily newspapers. For more on the Baisakhi festival, visit the following website.

www.baisakhifestival.com

WAGAH BORDER CROSSING

Margaret Rees cheers like a local at the India–Pakistan border

In Amritsar, close to India's border with Pakistan, we heard about the elaborate closing-of-gates ceremony that took place at the Wagah crossing, just thirty kilometers away. At six every evening, the Indian and Pakistani armies paraded in unison, each on its own side, to lower their respective flags and close the gate between the two countries. A huge number of people gathered to watch this spectacle and, naturally, national fervor ran high among the crowd. With just a gate between them, it was as close as the civilian population of India could come to the people of Pakistan, and both wanted to show their strength and their contempt for the other.

When we stepped out of our taxi at the ceremony site at Wagah, we were immediately swallowed up by a sea of people milling around the viewing galleries, waiting for the show to begin. A posse of children attacked us from all sides before we even reached the grandstands, trying to sell Indian flags and CDs of the ceremony. We pushed our way through the crowd, searching for our VIP seats, but it looked as if everybody else had a VIP seat too. Finally, we were directed to stand near the bottom, from where we could get a clear view of the proceedings.

The atmosphere around us was electric. A handful of Indians had been randomly chosen from the crowd, and they were running to the border gates and back holding up Indian flags. A guy encouraged the crowd (as if they needed it!) to chant and cheer, and the grandstands began to shake as five thousand or so Indians stamped their feet and raised the war cry of "*Jai* Hind!"—"Victory to India!" A similar situation was erupting on the Pakistani side, and a master of ceremonies in a green Pakistani cricket jersey was stoking up patriotism among his people, who were shouting out, "Pakistan *zindabad!*"—"Long live Pakistan!" The mayhem resembled that at an India-Pakistan cricket game, where the competition is waged as ferociously among the spectator stands as it is on the playing field.

As the official ceremony began, the Indian army in beige uniforms marched up to its Pakistani counterpart dressed in dark green, and both parties started to threaten each other. They touched the straps of their guns, made thumbs-down gestures, scowled, and looked at their opponents with murderous expressions in their eyes. Despite the ferocity, the goose-stepping was rather comical to watch as the soldiers tried to outdo each other by raising the soles of their boots as high as possible in the face of the enemy. Each action, I suppose, was carefully choreographed, but the menace in their body language couldn't be part of any act.

Eventually, a couple of soldiers from each side broke away from their groups to carefully lower the flag of their countries. As the crescent of Muslim Pakistan came down at precisely the same time as the tricolor of secular India, the cheering crowds went ballistic. The emotions of the Indian people and their pride in their Indianness carried me away until I was cheering wildly with them.

Finally, an Indian and a Pakistani soldier goose-stepped up to the gate, quickly shook hands, and after aiming final kicks at the other's side, pulled the gate closed. The border between India and Pakistan was sealed for yet another night.

Getting to Wagah

It is best to do the thirty-kilometer distance from Amritsar to Wagah by taxi. The other option is to take a bus from Amritsar to a town called Attari and hire an autorickshaw for the last couple kilometers.

JAIPUR

Alexandra Nassau-Brownstone colors Jaipur purple and pink

When I reached Jaipur a few weeks before Holi, anticipation of this annual Festival of Colors was already visible. Shops along the roads were lined with makeshift stalls selling mounds of the gaily colored powders that people would rub on friends, family, and even strangers. Television was full of the event. The daily soaps were written to include a Holi sequence, and advertisers were piggybacking their products on the festival for all it was worth.

On the actual morning of Holi, I was dragged out of bed by the family I was living with. In preparation, I rubbed liberal quantities of Vaseline into my blond hair, hoping to keep it from being stained by the colored pastes and waters I knew I would be subjected to that day. I had barely swallowed two bites of my *paratha* before I was shoved out into the yard to get my first dunking in a tub of blue water.

I had expected only the younger members of the family to take part in the horseplay and was astonished to find people of all ages joining in, especially my host mother, who was probably the most excited participant in our yard. Everybody smeared colored pastes on everybody else, and in a matter of minutes, I was as bright and patchy as the rest, with reds, greens, purples, and pinks smeared all over my clothes and body. A pesky cousin even managed to get some on my teeth!

With nothing left to lose, I responded with equal enthusiasm, drenching everybody within spraying distance with my Holi squirt gun. Round and round we ran—sometimes I was the aggressor and sometimes the victim—raising a massive commotion in the yard with our screams of hysterical laughter. That half hour of abandoned Holi play was like revisiting my carefree childhood days.

As I threw myself into the action with all the zeal of a local, and was treated like a local in return, it dawned on me just how inextricably connected Hinduism is with the simple pleasures of an Indian's life. It allows its followers to celebrate religious events with a spirit of fun, which I think is a wonderful way to incorporate faith into the everyday. When the Hindu religion celebrates, it assumes that everybody—caste, creed, and race notwithstanding—is welcome.

While chasing people around the yard was a lighthearted experience, cleaning up afterward was an arduous job. I used four buckets of water and still had pink and purple patches all over my body. Worse still was the state of my hair: it was horribly streaked, and I was sure I looked like a clown. So much for the Vaseline! The only hair

the petroleum jelly had protected was my eyebrows, and I was thankful for that. Another American friend of mine wound up with pink eyebrows and went about looking like one of Willy Wonka's Oompa Loompas for weeks.

At first I was upset about my strange appearance. The fact that my entire host family was also stained with remnants of the Holi festival didn't make me feel any better. I already stuck out as it was with my fair coloring, and I was sure that I would now be laughed at on the streets. But the people of Jaipur did not treat me like a foreign clown with funny hair. Everyone knew what had happened to me, and it just made them smile. I was no different from the businessmen in suits with pink fingernails and the schoolteachers with blue streaks on their arms and necks.

Rather than making me feel conspicuous, my tinted hair made me feel more accepted into the lives and culture of those around me. The good-natured grins that came my way were no more than a continued sharing of the Holi spirit, long after the event had passed. It took many months for the pink to finally fade out of my hair—I can still find the faintest trace of it if I look carefully. I'm glad I'm back to my normal self, but I'm already eager for next year and the opportunity to participate in another colorful round of Holi.

Celebrating Holi

The festival of Holi is held every year toward the end of February

RAJASTHAN

or early March. For more about Holi, including its legends and how to make natural colors, go to the following website.

www.holifestival.org

Elephants on parade

On the occasion of Holi, a festival of elephants takes place in Jaipur at the Chaugan polo stadium. Beautifully ornamented pachyderms with painted trunks and foreheads are the stars of the event, and they lead a parade with horses, camels, and a bevy of folk dancers following in their wake. A beauty contest of sorts takes place afterward in which the elephants preen and pose for a panel of judges, who then give out prizes in such imaginative categories as "elephant wearing the best anklets." After the parade, the focus shifts to elephant polo. Polo players in saffron and red turbans approach the game in all seriousness, and though the pace is slow compared to a proper game of polo on horseback, the audience loves it. At the very end, tourists are invited to ride the elephants and play Holi.

Adrian Murray overcomes immovable obstructions in Jaipur

When you are traveling for the long term, it is said that you should give yourself a break at times by doing something "normal," something you usually do back home. I thought golf might be one such activity for me—and when I heard about a course in Jaipur, I jumped at the prospect of spending a few relaxing hours smashing a white ball around the fairways. What I ended up doing, however, was playing a unique round that I could not have done anywhere else but in India.

I was met at the entrance of the Rambagh Golf Club by the course manager, who seemed overly excited by my presence. Initially, I assumed his enthusiasm was because he didn't see many foreigners come through the gates. Later, I realized that his joy was simply because I am a left-hander. Lefties are few and far between in India, and the manager happily rushed about trying to organize some spanking new hire clubs for me. He came up with a wonderful set of perimeter-weighted, graphite-shafted sticks, with the plastic wrapping from the factory still around the club heads.

Clubs in hand, I was then introduced to Manu, my caddie. Back home for $3 I couldn't get anyone to point me to the first tee. Here at the Rambagh, for that same amount, I had Manu to tag along with me all day, carrying a set of clubs in a bag and two liters of water. He would even tend the pin, wipe my ball, and help me with club selection.

My game was going as expected until I reached the third hole and the first unusual aspect of Indian golf. Golf courses around the world have "immovable obstructions" within their boundaries, as per the rules of The Royal & Ancient golf club in Scotland. Here in Jaipur, it turned out, anthills and rat holes are considered immovable. I had an apparent lost ball down a rat hole on the third. I was not willing to stick my arm down to search for it. Neither was Manu. No penalty for the drop.

The course was also scattered with local women in bright saris, handing out water to players and acting as greenskeepers by removing weeds. In addition to the obstacle (and spectacle) provided by these colorful women tending the course, I had to contend with innumerable sprinklers. It was really hot, and I was walking within shooting distance of their spray when Manu warned, "Watch out, sir, the water is not fresh ..."

In India I know that the "fresh" water isn't fresh, so water that is "not fresh" basically means sewage. The warning, however, came too late for my shoes. But what could I do? I got on with the game.

The first nine holes were very slow, mainly because the group ahead of

mine had six players, instead of the universally accepted maximum of four. Add the six caddies, and it was like watching the U.S. Open with a full gallery. Noting my confusion, a younger player in my group explained helpfully, "Groups of six are very common in India. Sometimes even seven or eight players ..."

By observing how the game was being played around me, I learned something about Indian golfing etiquette. Golfers here don't necessarily play the course in the order of the holes. If the day is busy, they might jump from the sixth to the ninth without hesitation, even if it means pushing ahead of a group that is about to leave the eighth green. And, unlike everywhere else in the world where you will hear the word "fore!" shouted out if a stray ball from a slicing five-iron heads in your direction, in India, golfers yell "ball!" Bottom line: there's no hesitation in passing another group, and it's not uncommon to be hollered at even if you aren't playing too slowly. Indians tend to play golf like they drive.

The Rambagh Golf Club contains some unusual holes that are worth mentioning to golfers (or adventurers) who'd like to play a game here. Trees are often found in the middle of fairways. Not just the odd one as an obstacle to hit around. Occasionally, there are dozens in the center of the hole for players to negotiate. The 340-yard, par 4, seventeenth hole is called "Star Crazy" for a reason. It is straight, but that is where any regularity ends. There is no fairway—just

RAJASTHAN

hit your ball over the eighteenth green (players there had better duck if they're putting) toward the flag inside a forest. Hope that your ball lands in a bare patch where you can get a swing, and then chip over the remaining trees onto the green, if you are lucky. For the record, I took a five.

The twelfth hole is a unique 160-yard par 3. You will need to take a five-iron from the tee to carry your ball over the road, the overflow of cars from the members' car park, the practice putting green, and the forest of trees to a bunker-protected green. You'd be mad to park your car in the middle of this hole unless all of your windows are already broken.

Winding up the course was the closing eighteenth hole, a par 3 of 180 yards. I made my club selection carefully. I checked to make sure my backswing off the tee wasn't going to cause my club to hit the low-lying power lines, resulting in massive electrocution and certain death. Lucky golfers play this hole during one of India's regular power blackouts. Without that option, they can adjust to a side area on the down-slope for a completely unstable tee shot. Or, they can do what I did: cheat. Tee off from somewhere forward, away from the risk of a zap. I took a four but want to note that the par put lipped out. I was robbed. Still, I was happy to finish with a ninety. Not too bad for a game played amid rat holes, forest obstacles, sprinklers, and sari-wearing greenskeepers ... and that with a pair of unfamiliar lefty clubs.

Rambagh Golf Club

Playable year-round, the Rambagh course is an eighteen-hole, par 72, championship course. Contact the club ahead of time for information on guest and temporary membership.

www.rambaghgolfclub.com

Tipping

For helping to navigate through the Subcontinent's variation on golf in the midday furnace heat of summer, Adrian felt that his caddie, Manu, deserved a hefty tip of several hundred extra rupees. Remember that while it's exciting to find a great deal on luxuries that are expensive back home, the people you meet still need to feed and house themselves and often their families as well. What may be just a few extra rupees to you can go a long way in making someone's life in India a little better.

JAISALMER

Robert Granger
gets a bhang out of Jaisalmer

While I was sitting in a tea-and-bun shop inside the Jaisalmer Fort, someone pushed a flier into my hand. "Do not anticipate or analyze!" it exuberantly instructed me. "Just Enjoy!" At the bottom of the piece of paper, I found the name of the place where I could avail myself of this enjoyment. The Bhang Shop.

I wasn't sure exactly what bhang was, but I had just arrived from the north of Himachal Pradesh, where I had run into a bunch of Israelis who had made the foothills of the Himalayas their temporary home and blew up their savings in great big clouds of marijuana smoke. It was all illegal of course, but policing wasn't strict so high up in the mountains, and foreign tourists could pretty much get what they wanted if they knew who or where to ask.

This flyer, however, wasn't advertising an illegal drug den. The "mild euphoria" it promised could be enjoyed without falling foul of the law. Now, if you've been to Jaisalmer, you already know how heady the atmosphere inside the fort can be. The monochrome of the golden sandstone plays tricks with the mind at times, inducing a slight feeling of light-headedness. For the past couple of days, I had been clattering around the warren of alleyways feeling as if I had just downed a couple of stiff whiskeys. How much more "euphoria" could the bhang add to the one I was already enjoying?

There was only one way to find out.

The flier's guarantee that I wouldn't "see pink elephants, jump off tall buildings, or turn into an orange" was all the assurance I needed to go off in search of this intriguing Bhang Shop. The premises, when I found it, didn't look at all promising. A man with a handlebar mustache, presumably the owner, was sleeping under a huge hand-painted sign that read "Govt. Authorised Bhang Shop." The shop had only some garlanded pictures of Hindu gods strung on the wall and a couple of big earthen pots. Where were all the piles of mood-altering tobaccolike substance I had been expecting to see? Had he gone out of business? I wondered.

An internal alarm system must have notified the man that a customer was about, because he woke up with a start. I wanted to buy some bhang, I told him, offering an expression of apology for having broken into his afternoon siesta. "I only have bhang *lassi* that I can give you right now, sir," he said, quoting half a dollar for a glass of the drug-laced yogurt drink.

"Do you usually sell other things besides *lassi*?" I asked curiously.

"Yes, if you place an order in advance, I can sell you tasty bhang cakes, bhang candies, and bhang cookies," the man offered. "In fact, you should try my cookies, sir," he added as he stood up to prepare my *lassi*. "Tourists tell me they are better than the stuff they buy in Dutchland." He twisted the tips of his mustache to show disdain for his competitors in the narcotic-laced-cookie market in Amsterdam. "Want to place an order?"

I didn't. I was leaving for Bikaner the following day, and no way was

RAJASTHAN

I traveling with contraband in my luggage. The Bhang Shop owner pooh-poohed this needless caution. He pointed to the signboard behind him and said, "See? It is all legal. And not very strong either. We only use the leaves and buds of cannabis to make bhang. The stronger substance comes out of other parts of the plant, but normal people don't smoke that. Hashish is only for some sadhus and tantra practitioners, who use it to induce a trance."

He drew a chilled glass of *lassi* from one of the earthen pots and handed it to me. I took a tentative sip and was surprised at how ordinary it tasted. Like all the *lassis* I had ever had, it was deliciously thick and sour—sweet without any extra kick whatsoever from the bhang. I took a few more sips. A marvelous feeling of well-being began to uncurl inside me. Was it my imagination, or was my body really loosening up and my mind expanding?

Within moments, my thoughts were spiralling away from me as I wondered if inebriation could happen instantly. Inebriation? I was puzzled. Could I use this word to describe a condition induced by a drug? My mind riffled lazily through my thirty-five years of experiences to see if there was any reference in there about inebriation that hadn't been induced by alcohol. Maybe I should ask the bhang shop owner. Then I thought better of it. After all, how would he know? He was only insightful about Dutch cookies. What a handicap! I felt sorry for him.

"Are you alright?" The man broke into my drugged musings and swam into view. "The bhang in your drink was very mild, since this is your first time." I watched him mouth the words, fascinated by the way his mustache danced up and down as he spoke. "Go home and enjoy," he said. "And come back for more."

My memory of the sequence of events becomes hazy after that. I remember going back inside the fort and settling down on a patio. As the bhang spread its tentacles into the deepest recesses of my brain, I felt a heightened sensation of coziness in the sepia world of the fort's warm, golden sandstone. I also recall the decision I made never to step outside the Jaisalmer Fort ever again in my life.

I don't know how I got into bed that night, but when I woke up the next day, I found that the effects of the bhang had flushed completely out of my system. I felt as refreshed and healthy as ever. The flier hadn't been lying when it said I wouldn't turn into an orange, and I was pretty glad for that. My bhang adventure passed off safely and smoothly, except for one minor mishap: when the room service order taker expressed amazement at my asking for breakfast, I realized I had overslept by eleven hours and missed my train to Bikaner.

The Bhang Shop

This Jaisalmer shop is located outside the First Fort Gate (also known as Akhai Pol) on Gopa Chowk. This gate was once used by the royal family to enter the fort.

About bhang

Although this substance has been part of the Indian culture for thousands of years, in general it is hard to find during most of the year. Official bhang shops, like the one mentioned in this essay, are few and far between. During the Holi festival of colors, however, some Hindus like to heighten the pleasures of the celebration by drinking *lassis* laced with bhang, so it may be more available around that time. Keep in mind that bhang is a drug. It induces hallucinations, and some people experience negative reactions.

Margaret Rees lightens up in the Jaisalmer desert

My friend and I did a touristy thing in Jaisalmer. We went on a camel safari and had a local dinner with Rajasthani music and dancing. The excursion had its high points—the nervous excitement of feeling the camel stand up on its wobbly legs with me on board, walking around the wrinkled sand dunes, and marveling at a spectacular crimson sunset. I'd say we got our money's worth on that camel ride, and I was looking forward to the next treat on the cards: a delicious meal and a folk performance to give us a glimpse of Rajasthan's rural heritage.

While we were making our way to the village where the dinner was to be held, it started to rain. Once we arrived, we discovered that we were the only two guests. Because of the downpour the other tour groups had gone back to the city. We wanted to leave as well, but the manager refused to let us go: our food had already been cooked, he explained, and the musicians were waiting.

We allowed ourselves to be frog-marched to the open-air venue where the evening's entertainment would be held. We sat there, feeling and looking utterly ridiculous while a group of five musicians and two costumed dancers performed for just the two of us. The atmosphere was nil, it was rapidly getting dark, and then it started to rain some more. The musicians hurried inside to protect their instruments, but were forced by the manager to come back out and continue playing. The girls went on dancing in the downpour, and the place just got wetter and wetter, until we were finally moved into a small room where the music was too loud and there wasn't enough space for the girls to dance.

Quite oblivious of our discomfiture, our host asked if there was anything we would especially like the musicians to play. He suggested some local songs, but we had never heard of any of them. Then our food arrived. We were the only ones eating, and we were feeling incredibly uncomfortable about being watched by a troupe of damp and cross-looking entertainers. The meal was freshly cooked and would have been wonderful at any other time, but by now we were really worried about the state of the road and hardly noticed the food. The monsoon didn't seem to concern anyone else, however, except the driver, who kept glancing out the door to see how high the water on the ground had risen.

Eventually, we decided we'd had enough and insisted on breaking up the party. The driver looked relieved, and we managed to get back to Jaisalmer before the roads were completely flooded. Once we reached our hotel room, we succumbed to the hysteria that had been threatening us all evening and collapsed on the bed, laughing. Tears rolled down our faces as we remembered the wet musicians scurrying back and forth while the manager asked us what music we'd like to hear in that hot and crowded room. As soon as one of us recovered, the other recalled something else, and we would start off laughing again.

Alas, the rural dinner and dance performance didn't quite go as planned, but the experience taught us something important about traveling through India: Expect the unexpected, and when the moment is upon you, resign yourself to its inevitability. And laugh. A sense of humor is as indispensable as a guidebook when you are negotiating your way through this eccentric country.

That evening in the desert village wasn't the last of our Indian misadventures, but it worked like an inoculation, and by the time the oth-

ers came along, we had lightened up and were willing to go with the flow. In the process, we converted some potentially disturbing incidents into fond, that's-India-for-you memories that still make us giggle when we think back on them.

Staying among the dunes

If you want to enjoy the Thar Desert's most picturesque cluster of sand dunes, spend a few days in the village of Khuri, about forty-five kilometers from Jaisalmer. The village has many homestay options, but several writers in this book have recommended the modest establishment of a man called Badal Singh. He is a storehouse of information on the area, and his property, Badal House, is clean and reasonably priced. He does not advertise, and guests usually hear of him by word of mouth. To call Badal House within India: 3014-274120.

GENERAL NORTH INDIA

Jennifer Smith experiences the essence of rural hospitality

After weeks of fighting sharp-elbowed, pushy crowds at tourist sights; bartering endlessly with rickshaw drivers; politely turning down offers for a new Indian boyfriend; and dodging bullets of *paan*, the sweet betel leaf that many Indians chew and then spit out randomly on the streets, I was extremely grateful when my yoga teacher invited me to accompany him on a visit to meet his family. Hoorah! A chance to escape Jaipur and get a taste of rural India.

Early the next morning, we climbed onto his rusty motorcycle, which was dubiously named "No Problem Bike." On the three-hour journey into the countryside, we zoomed past fields of dust, camels, carts, and naked children doing cartwheels in the sun. We stopped for cups of tea at roadside shacks and climbed up to the highest hill, where we meditated at a temple cut into the rocks with a man whose hair sat like a big Danish pastry upon his gray head and seemed as if it could have spanned the globe.

While my confident, tracksuit-wearing yoga teacher was apparently a modern man, I had noticed that there was something very calm and different about him compared to most of the city dwellers I had met. Only when I saw his children run across a muddy field of groundnuts and launch into his open arms did I realize that his heart had been nurtured by the land. As we sat on a mound of rocks near his house, his veiled wife prepared maize chapatti, using a stone to grind the grain and the packed dirt floor as a chopping board for the vegetables she cooked over a twig fire. The children took the baby buffalo for a walk around the three-hut farm compound, and my friend apologized, "This is all I have to offer you."

The words cut sharply, like the pin through the buffalo's nose. Did he really not understand that he was giving me the most precious and valuable experience of my life? This was the essence of Indian hospitality—their simple acceptance of a stranger and unreserved pleasure at being able to share their meager resources, something that was very foreign to me.

The time we spent in my teacher's village swept by in a series of snapshots that now seem to be just a figment of an imaginary world. Sometimes I have flashbacks, of singing "Silent Night" to a baby cradled in my arms under an open sky, or of being forced to show off my yoga moves at the village well to raucous applause from the women who had come to wash clothes and fetch water. I see myself picking fresh groundnuts for breakfast and firing them at the family's granddad in a playful fight. I watch the screaming laughter of local boys as this weak Western woman boldly takes up a branch and a piece of fruit to stand her own in an improvised cricket match. Those few days were the antidote to every problem, stress, and strain I'd known since coming to India.

Of all my memories, the most vivid is of my first evening in the village, when a group of women dressed me in traditional clothing and took me to a wedding. A veil obscured my expression as a curious crowd from three neighboring villages gathered around me, prodding, poking, peering, and cheering. People rushed over to see this strange white girl who had strayed into their little community, and we communicated through gasps and giggles. I find it hard to describe the experience. I was a freak, a goddess, and a most welcome guest as we danced into the night.

When it was time to go to bed, I was honored at the invitation to sleep with my teacher's youngest daughter. With her tiny, naked body folded into mine, I drifted off to the comforting sound of the family breathing together as one.

A taste of rural India

Lack of infrastructure is one of the main reasons why tourists often miss out on a significant part of India: its villages. But if you're on the tourist trail in Rajasthan, one village within easy reach that environment-concious travelers will find particularly interesting is Guda Bishnoi, just twenty-five kilometers out of the city of Jodhpur. Travel companies advertise tours of the village, but you can easily take a taxi, bus, or autorickshaw on your own, and a visit is well worth the effort.

The inhabitants of this village— the Bishnoi—are among the pioneers of the green movement in India. Their lifestyle is the stuff of legends. They die to save trees, go hungry to provide food for animals and their womenfolk, and think nothing of suckling motherless deer. At Guda Bishnoi village, you can see wild animals such as antelopes, spotted deer, blue bulls, and blackbucks roam freely, confident and safe in the friendly environment they live in.

A peaceful community of milk-men, goldsmiths, and stone and wood carvers, the Bishnois transform into aggressive custodians of nature when news of hunting in their territory reaches them. If you respect animals and nature, however, these tribespeople respect you back, and a day spent among them can be a rewarding experience.

David Cook scratches the surface of India's road rules

Honk, jerk, corner, speed up ... slam on the brakes as another autorickshaw pulls in front of me. Who's backing up? Someone has to! Left, forward, fast, slow, stop, turn, corner—wild dogs!—slow, kick, turn, fast—two cows! one sleeping, one walking—stop in deference of the cows, turn, go fast, quicker, children—honk!—stop ... I'm totally lost ...

This is a snapshot of my traffic experiences in North India. Don't get me wrong—I adored every twist and turn on these roller-coaster rides. The ego clashes, the battle of wills, the space hogging, the heckling, and the hollering. I had nothing but admiration for the men behind the wheel, who negotiated their way through impossible traffic every day. As a fan, I compiled my own set of the unique rules that keep one hundred million people reasonably safe on Indian roads and make surface transport in the country such an adventure.

The Lane Theory

The term *lane* has a different meaning in India than just about anywhere else on earth. You see, a lane is not always as tangible a thing as you might expect. So my Lane Theory is just an abstract construction I came up with to understand the way I observed the traffic move in Delhi, Agra, and Jaipur. In my experience, most drivers all prefer the same lane: the absolute center of the road. Considerate of them, you might think, to leave so much shoulder space for fellow travelers. Don't be misled. These roads don't actually have shoulders. That's why everyone is trying to drive in the middle!

Having acquired this center "lane," the driver would seem to have left both sides free for the slower-moving traffic—pedestrians, bicycles, rickshaws, pushcarts, animals, etc.—that is also sharing the roadway. But there's something else to consider: the oncoming traffic bearing down head-on. From the biggest buses to the fastest cars, you will find all agents of transport coming dead ahead at you, just as you're returning the favor from their point of view. You must be wondering, what happens then?

A common choice is that the driver swerves all the way to the far side of the road to avoid the oncoming vehicle, depending on the situation. Get the picture? Probably not, because up until now I've been drawing it one brushstroke at a time. I still have to add in the motorbikes, which outnumber all the cars, trucks, and buses combined in every city, town, and village. There are also entire communities of immovable objects (or those choosing not to move), which include—on the road—sitting cows, overturned vegetable carts, sleeping dogs, and lounging horses. So how does a driver maneuver through all of this? Read on.

Horning in

Vehicles in India seem to be equipped with horns of all shapes and sizes, and they definitely include all kinds of sounds. Some are quite standard, while others feature amazing volume enhancements. When I first arrived in Delhi, I quite enjoyed the varied pitches, timbres, and tones of the different horns. But a month into my journey, it devolved into a cacophony of noise, and I felt as if I'd never hear silence again.

Indian drivers are as skilled at horn-blowing as they are at swerve-driving. Even the slightest possibility of another object on the road will incite a horn blast so quickly that if Indian drivers were able to square off in duels with the fastest gunslingers from the historic American West, our cowboys wouldn't stand a chance. It's as though there is a special connection of the nerve synapses between a driver's brain and his horn thumb, creating a lightning-fast reflex.

One time, my driver even honked at road kill, and that's no joke. We were out in the desert, returning to the city of Jaisalmer. The highway was deserted, except for our own jeep and the carcass of a dog. It lay on the road, lifeless and bloodied—and the driver still blasted it with three hard squeezes of the horn button. My only guess is that he was so devout a Hindu that he was worried we might be approaching the dog at the precise moment in which its soul was vacating the body to be reincarnated in another form. Naturally, the situation necessitated a honk to warn the departing spirit to get the hell out of our way.

The light side

As with driving in the correct lane and heeding stoplights, using headlights is optional. While headlights are employed sometimes, usually motorists will wait until the twi-est of twilight before turning them on. Night vision is clearly not a problem in India, though I must confess that at first I didn't have much faith in Indians' optical prowess, and when I was visiting Varanasi, I gave up my evening walks to the market through narrow, winding lanes. This was early on in my trip, though, when my confidence in local motorists' skills wasn't fully in place.

Full speed ahead

The last thing I'd like to note in this informal traffic guide is speed. There is only one speed in India: as fast as possible. New Delhi's traffic snarls are sometimes such that a driver is forced to keep his foot on the brake at all times. But the moment there's a clearing, no matter how small, it's pedal to the metal. The full-speed theory is so ingrained in India's driving culture that it would never—and I mean *never*— occur to an Indian driver to wait his turn.

There were many other such interesting idiosyncracies I found that dictated driving in India, but I leave off the rest of my observations for another time. As it is, the account above is sounding a wee bit fantastical. For those of you who have not visited India, I'm sure you think I'm exaggerating. If you have already been here, you know I've barely scratched the surface.

Ride in a bicycle rickshaw

To really immerse yourself in local transport, take a ride in a bicycle rickshaw. This is eco-friendly, fun, and plentiful. Often, it is also the quickest way to get from one place to another if you're not traveling a long distance. Bicycle rickshaw drivers seem to have a detailed mental map of every quiet alleyway and back lane in their neighborhood, and thanks to this, you miss all the traffic jams on the main roads. They are also the best people to consult if you are looking for a particular shop or restaurant. Fares are cheap, but the drivers don't earn much more than $3 or $4 a day, so it's always nice to pay them a little extra.

Kids on a rickshaw

Suggestions for giving back while you're on the road

This chapter makes me think back to a comment a social worker friend once made about tourists and random acts of kindness. "In my experience, they now want to 'give back' rather than 'give away,'" he had said. "Be out there among the needy, get their hands dirty, and treat the whole business of charity as a give-and-take experience." This growing sense of responsibility among travelers and their genuine desire to help makes "Paying It Forward" an integral part of this book.

Some of the writers here have devoted a lot of time and effort—sometimes even their lives—to charities and causes that are close to their hearts. Mark Templer, for example, who tells us about the horrifying circumstances under which leprosy victims live in India, and how tirelessly he and his colleagues have worked to give them a better life through the HOPE foundation. Or Kelly O'Neil, who makes a commitment to little Jitender, a seven-year-old orphan from Delhi, to be his mother.

Other contributors have fulfilled their desire to help in simple, but important, ways. Cassandra Brill's teaching a Tibetan boy in Dharamshala how to imagine is a wonderful case in point. By helping him learn to create worlds of make-believe, she opened up his mind to so much pleasure and possibility that a mere gift of money or clothes would seem foolish in comparison. Then there is Melly Goodman, who just says "no" to the temptation of buying banned animal goods.

Help doesn't always have to come in the form of donations and volunteer work. It can be just a matter of showing the way. Look closely at the teeming life all around you while you are in India, and you will soon see a situation that is calling out to you. Instances of misfortune that can be alleviated with minimum intervention without your having to make a great cause of it. Answer to that call, for what can be a more wonderful feeling than to know your holiday hasn't been all about pleasure? That there is an unfortunate person out there who is saying, "Thank you for having visited"?

A boy on the bank of the Yamuna River, the largest tributary of the Ganges in northern India   223

NEW DELHI

Mark Templer teaches trust at a leprosy colony in Delhi

When I first came to India in 1985, I saw a man afflicted with leprosy in Bangalore. My initial reaction to the sight of his open sores and disfigurement was no different from anybody else's—I wanted to walk away as quickly as possible and pretend that I hadn't seen him. But for some reason, I couldn't do this. Instead, screwing up my courage, I reached out to hold one of his damaged hands in mine. I could feel two stubs where his thumb and index fingers used to be, but I did not loosen my grip. After all, the only way I could show him I was not repelled by his condition was by touching him.

It was only after I was back at my hotel that I had a full-blown panic attack. What if I contracted the disease? I kept washing my hands, over and over again, praying that I would be spared.

I knew nothing about leprosy back then. I was ignorant, and I am ashamed about how I handled my first encounter with it, although I understand how such a reaction can happen. Yes, leprosy is ugly. It starts out as a light patch on the skin, and then it spreads, destroying the nerves, so that the blood system collapses and the tissues die. Victims of leprosy lose their fingers, toes, hands, feet, eyes, and nose. Eventually, the disease burns itself out and leaves its victims grotesquely disfigured. It is fear of this disfigurement that makes people shun leprosy victims. They do not understand that the disease does not spread by touch, and they do not know that leprosy is curable—through drugs that cost just a few dollars.

The information is all out there, but it will be a long time before society finally accepts leprosy victims with a sense of humanity, and leprosy as a manageable disease. Until that happens, patients suffering from this condition will continue to live like outcasts, grouping together in appalling conditions in their shame and poverty, afraid to show themselves for fear of public ridicule and mistreatment.

Through my organization, the HOPE foundation, my colleagues and I had already started working with leprosy patients living on the streets of Delhi when the daughter of the then-president of India, Padma Venkataraman, took us to the city's Tahirpur colony—the largest colony of leprosy patients in India. More than four thousand had collected here after being thrown out by their families. Not all came from uneducated, impoverished backgrounds. Among their numbers, we were surprised to find people who had held responsible professional positions, such as university lecturers and doctors. It turned out that even those who were privileged and living in clean, healthy environments could be susceptible to the disease.

The Tahirpur colony was a mess, with open sewers everywhere. The inhabitants lived in filthy huts without electricity or water and survived by begging on the streets of Delhi. Drug abuse and alcoholism were rampant, and murders were a regular occurrence. Lack of hope for a better future fed the victims' tremendous rage against the society that had abandoned them.

In the early days of our work with Tahirpur, people were very skeptical about what improvements we could possibly bring to this black hole of disease and depravity. We had some funds from the United States that we wanted to use to build proper houses, but no one believed we could complete such a project. It would be foolishness to expect any support from outside. So we fell back on our own courage.

There were roadblocks everywhere we turned. I remember how contractors cheated us, mixing sand with the cement to save money. Before the houses were completed, one of the roofs caved in, breaking the thin thread of trust we had worked so hard to establish with the leprosy victims. After that, it was hard to convince them that the houses we were building would be safe. To prove ourselves, our architect, Joshy Jose; program manager, Ian Correa; and I

decided to be the first to sleep in one of the new homes. In a nearly completed, mosquito-infested structure the three of us spent a night on the floor. The victims' fears were allayed, and they agreed to move in.

It was the small considerations that went a long way in building and maintaining trust. For instance, I would take my children to eat at the homes of leprosy victims—an action that proved my acceptance better than any amount of verbal assurances would have. Over the years, we managed to get the city to provide sewers, electricity, and roads. We housed every victim we had started the project with. We planted trees, helped start a school, and worked hard to show our love for the people of the Tahirpur colony.

Little by little we saw the community change. Drugs disappeared. Health improved. The murders stopped. People quit begging. The colony is now integrated with other neighborhoods in the area. Many leprosy patients have their own businesses. Tahirpur is a happy place. Or, at least, as happy as such a place can conceivably be.

Symptomatic of the turnaround was the colony's response to the tsunami that hit India on December 26, 2004. The patients collected clothes and cash and donated it to the prime minister's tsunami fund. From embittered beggars they had become givers. It was marvelous to see how confidence in their ability to live like human beings again had returned them to their rightful place in society.

NEW DELHI

HOPE foundation

For its City of HOPE in the Tahirpur colony, the HOPE foundation desperately needs funds to keep their bandaging, vocational training, sanitation, and dental care programs running. If you want to volunteer, give money or other necessary items, or just visit (and hopefully spread the word), visit the foundation's website. Information on the colony can be found in the Delhi I VoH listing in the "locations" section.

www.hopefoundation.org.in

About leprosy

Leprosy is a progressive disease that affects skin, limbs, nerves, and eyes. If left untreated the disease spreads. Throughout history lepers (patients with leprosy) have been ostracized by their communities and even their families. Patients were literally thrown out of the house for fear of the whole family being treated as outcasts. Indians believed—and a large section of the population still does—that you can contract leprosy simply by touching a leper. This is not true.

Caused by a bacteria, most types of leprosy do not spread just by touch. What's more, leprosy is now completely curable with an ordinary multidrug therapy. Patients are no longer infectious after the first dose, and they can be completely cured within six months. If the diagnosis happens early then physical damage and disability does not occur. Now that treatment is so easily available, leprosy should not have such a stigma, but the Indian mind-set is such that lepers rarely have a second chance at life, which is why they live in "colonies." NGOs like HOPE are not only working to improve the lot of patients but fighting to get them social acceptance as well.

Kelly O'Neil helps heat up a Delhi orphanage

Having already adopted two older kids, I consider myself a connoisseur of orphanages. I've seen the good, the bad, and the truly terrifying. So how will the ones in Delhi be? Old? Yes. Impoverished? Partly. But also urban and sophisticated.

Having arrived two days ahead of my husband, Chris, I am traveling with Vijay, our social worker. She is a gracious and educated woman, wearing a plum-colored traditional tunic and pants. A matching wispy scarf floats behind her as she leads me up the stairs. To meet my new son.

She tells me that Jitender is her 3,432nd placement and describes the system that her adoption organization tries to use in its city orphanages. A large (by Indian standards) apartment is rented and staffed with poor young widows. The agency hires them to care for the children, and they are given training, clothing, a decent diet, and regular vacations, something they probably never even dreamed existed.

My son's orphanage is a third-floor walk-up. Stray cats and potted plants lounge around the doorways, and the neighbors nod hello as we climb the stairs. Vijay enters, and we're immediately surrounded by smiling, screaming children. "Vijay Didi! Vijay Didi!" Every child uses the nickname for elder sister and has a story to tell or needs a special hug or kind word. All of which she spreads so liberally that the atmosphere becomes celebratory.

I'm given a toddler-sized chair of honor, and the caretakers put on bhangra music. The place begins to rock, as each child is pulled forward for a solo performance and loudly applauded. My new son, barely able to meet my eyes, keeps sneaking to the back corner. Eventually he is presented to me. He stands shaking between my knees. The shaking of my own body provides a countermeasure. Both of us wondering, can we love each other? Will I be acceptable? Will we become family?

Vijay and I take Jitender to a mall for some new clothing. At almost seven, he is the size of an average American four-year-old. We pick out some jeans, a couple of eye-searing polo shirts, some socks, and shoes. He *loves* the bright-colored shirts and the first pair of new pants he's ever had. We bundle up his ragged jeans, which were tied on with an old flannel bathrobe belt; his thousand-year-old men's-size tighty whities held up by the belt from a little girl's dress; brownish socks; and greasy old T-shirt. He will not wear these clothes again, but new orphans are made daily, and the garments will never go unused.

I'm at that wonderful point that comes in adoption, where it's obvious to me that my new son is brighter, more artistic, better mannered, and just all around more perfect than anyone else's child could aspire to be. Bonding is a very egotistical process; it feels great. But Jitender is not ecstatic. He's exhausted. Vijay tells me that I can't expect the vigor of an American kid out of him for several months. He's dealing with years of undernutrition, and I'll have to wait for him to catch up.

Two days later my big, gorgeous, hairy husband arrives, all red bearded and looking about as foreign as can be. Chris meets his new boy, and they are mutually thrilled with each other. After breakfast in our hotel, we visit the orphanage where the younger children stay. We go to the infant room. Old walls, old paint, and old diaper smells, all fused by heat.

It has been suggested by the partnering adoption agency stateside that we purchase something or make a donation to the orphanage. We're only too glad to comply. The gift the director is hoping we can afford is a generator. Delhi experiences many power outages, and they want to buy a generator so they can heat the infant room. Chris and I are boggled.

"*More* heat?" we ask.

"More heat," Vijay says. "It will cost about $500."

"Yes," Chris says, "of course. We would be happy to." We look at each other, silently questioning the sanity of Indians.

While Vijay goes back to a meeting, we snoop around the nursery. There are two rows of cribs. One crib holds two preemies left at the hospital by their parents. Each weighs less than two kilos. Together, they are lighter than my purse. I pick one up. Its little wrinkled face gives no clue as to beauty or gender, just expresses the hard work of survival. Curious, I unwrap layer after layer of blankets. At the bottom is a minuscule, lightly diapered boy. Chris tears up. I lean on his shoulder. Now we understand the request for the generator. The preemies don't have the energy to heat their own bodies. I wrap the little boy up as fast as I can and rock him the way mothers do when they have no other solution.

Later that day, we return to the orphanage one last time, so Jitender can make his farewells. Seven-year-olds don't really know how to do goodbyes, so Jitender plays quietly on the floor with his special friends for a while. Vijay introduces Chris and me to a tiny baby who was abandoned on the streets at birth. She is a sweet little girl, with a name that sounds like rain dripping from wind chimes and a face that proclaims genetic damage.

"Don't take her," Vijay was told by the police who found her. "She won't live out the night."

A week later, the pediatrician said, "Don't take on this heartache, Vijay, she won't make it through the month."

Three months later, she was warned that the baby would never sit up or be aware of her surroundings.

But Vijay had a special therapy in mind. She placed the tiny girl in the big kid's orphanage. The older children clap for her, or gently pinch her cheek, or tell her a joke. She has love, stimulation, nutrition, and if she wants to keep any toy for long, motivation. Now she is six months old. She smiles at her caretakers and watches the other children dance, while sitting erectly on Vijay's lap.

"Next, we'll have her walking," Vijay tells me in a tone of voice that leaves no room for doubt.

Adopting in India

Jitender's adoption was organized by Children's Hope International, which partnered with SOS in New Delhi. At this time, Children's Hope International does not arrange adoptions in India. If you are interested in adopting a child from India, Kelly recommends Journeys of the Heart, which also has established an international relief fund. Even if you are not planning to adopt, you can contribute to help the many children living in orphanages. From clothing to the generator Kelly and her husband donated, the need is great throughout the country. Wherever you plan to help, make sure to ask before giving, so that your gift will meet the most important needs.

www.journeysoftheheart.net

Nabanita Dutt finds hope for a lonely eunuch in Delhi

As I sit down to write about my memories of Tina, I realize I don't know how to refer to my friend. Should I call Tina a man or a woman? In the eight weeks over which our friendship blossomed, I never worried about defining gender. Tina believed he was female, and our conversations were always woman-to-woman. Today, Tina is no more. But I will respect his dearest wish in this essay and describe him as a twenty-four-year-old female. Tina would have loved that. He would probably have underlined every "she" that appears in this essay and used it as a mirror to view a feminized reflection of himself.

Tina was a part-time cleaner in the guesthouse I was renting in Delhi. Every morning, after she swept and cleaned, she would make a pot of tea and come to share it with me. She often brought little presents with her—a garland of sweet-smelling flowers that she would weave into my hair; a face pack of sandalwood paste for my pimples; or maybe, a mango that had dropped from the tree that leaned into her yard. She refused the money I tried to give her. "If I knew how to accept charity, I would have joined the eunuch gangs that beg on the streets," she used to say. Tina was poor, but she took great pride in her self-reliance. During the day, she worked as a part-time maid. At night, she sold her body for 250 rupees ($5). She was a prostitute.

Like many others in her eunuch community, Tina ran away from home at an early age. She found she couldn't live a male life in a male body and had come to Delhi to have her "operation"— the ceremonial castration that every eunuch dreams of. Tina never told me much about the customs and rituals observed for this procedure ("They are secret!"), but she did let on that the castration took place without any anesthesia and it was months before she could walk properly. "You are lucky," she would often joke. "God gifted you with womanhood, whereas I had to butcher myself to attain it."

Pain and poverty, however, didn't appear to have broken the spirit of this remarkable woman. Neither had the physical and mental abuse that society subjected her to every day. "I have been stoned on the streets for my ugly eunuch appearance," she once told me. "People have spat on me and tried to rip the sari off my body. But I don't mind, because I know I am one of God's chosen people. He has put me to a test by sending me into this world without a proper identity." She spoke of herself as Noah. Her womanhood was the ark that she had to negotiate through storms of hatred and cruelty to finally reach the arms of God.

Tina didn't care about the fact that she had to prostitute herself to make a living. There were no decent jobs for eunuchs in this country. "Imagine! A eunuch going to office!" she would exclaim and roll about laughing. But she was proud to be a maid in this guesthouse. The owner was a soft-hearted woman who had offered Tina temporary work as long as no guest felt uncomfortable about her presence.

I didn't ask Tina too many questions about what she did in the evenings. The matter only came up when she fell sick for a few days and returned to work looking tired and listless. Her male clients were making her ill, she said. I begged her to get a health checkup, but she refused to see a doctor. So I took it upon myself to find medical help and got to know of a society called Aradhya that ran a program to assist eunuchs. I called the institution and learnt of their Friday meetings, where eunuchs came to interact with each other and share their problems. Aradhya also offered free doctors' services, medicine, and sex education.

It was no easy task to send Tina there, but I finally managed to get her to register for one Friday meeting. To my surprise and delight, the meeting went off very well. The doctors at Aradhya were kind and helpful, and they treated her just like any ordinary girl. This was a novel experience for Tina, and I mentally blessed the Aradhya staff for making her feel so special. For this, if

for nothing else, she would continue to go there and allow them help her. Plus, she had made many friends. They all danced and sang and swapped stories about families, loves, and relationships.

Over the next month, I watched Tina blossom into a giggly and carefree young girl. The Fridays at Aradhya gave her something to look forward to all week, and when she returned, she told me about all the fun things that happened there. For the first time in her life perhaps, she had a place to go to where she belonged. She was part of an exclusive club. And she was so very happy.

The time came for me to leave Delhi and return home to Kolkata. The day I said goodbye to Tina was a Friday. She hadn't come to work because her Aradhya friends were having a party, and she wanted to go shopping for a new sari, but she dropped by the guesthouse to bid me farewell. She said she was sorry I wouldn't get to see her new clothes. I gave her my address and forced her to take my camera as a gift. "I want to see pictures of you in that sari," I said.

Months passed, but she never sent me those pictures. As time went on, Tina slowly faded in my memory. I hadn't thought of her in a long time when I received a letter from one of her friends at Aradhya. In that letter, I learnt that Tina had died. She had contracted AIDS. She must have known of her condition before I left, but she chose not to tell me. Maybe she thought I would turn my back on her. Maybe she wanted to spare me the painful knowledge.

The letter brought with it a great sense of loss. I knew I would have met her again because I was moving to Delhi permanently. In fact, I had been planning to donate some money to Aradhya and accompany Tina to one of those Friday meetings to see her friends. Now that would never happen. I would still visit Aradhya and thank them for what they did for Tina, but she would not be there to drag me by the hand and excitedly show me around.

You may have noticed that in this entire account, I have not written about how Tina looked. The omission was deliberate. Her appearance was a burden she stoically bore when people abused her and stoned her on the streets. I could not bring myself to humiliate her memory by itemizing it all over again. Instead, she will be remembered in this essay for her great spirit, and I hope a lot of travelers will read this and come forward to help others like Tina find hope in life.

Aradhya

E-97, D.D.A. Colony
Khyala
New Delhi

www.aaradhyaindia.org
aradhya_2004@rediffmail.com

DHARAMSHALA

Cassandra Brill imagines possibilities in Dharamshala

At the Open Sky Café in Dharamshala, where I was working on my journal as usual, a teenage Tibetan boy sat nearby, engrossed in his studies. He was reading aloud, but quietly, to himself. When he felt my eyes on him, he looked up and shyly asked if I would speak some English, so he could practice the language. I happily obliged, and our conversation was the beginning of a deeply fulfilling cultural exchange.

On that first afternoon, I learned the inspiring story of my new seventeen-year-old friend. At the age of twelve, he left his home, family, and friends, because his mother wanted a new life and better education for him in India. Like so many other Tibetans in and around Dharamshala, he arrived after a twenty-one-day trek from Tibet, three of those days walking in chest-deep snow. Upon safely reaching his destination, he poured his heart and soul into his studies, hoping one day to return to Tibet as a teacher or a businessman.

HIMACHAL PRADESH

We met for a few hours over the next four days to exchange language lessons and stories. On our final day, he wanted to practice his writing skills, so I asked him to write me a short story about a monk—where he was coming from, where he was going—to practice verb tenses. The boy looked at me with some confusion. He did not know which monk I was talking about. I encouraged him to imagine. Even if he didn't have a specific monk in mind, he could pretend. At this point, I realized that this boy had never experienced such a thing as make-believe.

By the end of that afternoon spent writing "imagined" stories about the people we saw, he wore the most incredible grin. And when he looked at me wide-eyed and said, "Now I can write about anything. I will never run out of things to write about, because I can write about things that aren't even real," I finally had the feeling that he might take away as much from our exchange as I knew that I was going to.

Before I left, he told me he was sad that I was going. He had learned so much in those few short days. I told him I was sure he would find other people to speak English with, especially if he studied at the cafés near McLeodganj, which were always packed with Westerners. But the boy wasn't so sure. The café owners discouraged locals from interacting with tourists because they felt the tourists wouldn't want to be bothered.

I encourage travelers to change this perception, and to give locals the time and attention they often crave. It is unnecessary to search for a formal volunteer program in India—there are opportunities to share all around. Just open your eyes and your heart, and what you give will be returned in more ways than you can imagine.

Getting to Dharamshala/ McLeodganj
Go to the fact file on page 118.

Favorite cafés in Dharamshala and McLeodganj

As everywhere else in the world, the best places to run into locals in this pair of tourist towns are the cafés. Those recommended here are always packed out starting from nine in the morning. Settle in with a cup of tea, and you're sure to meet an interesting mix of fellow travelers and local Tibetans.

Chuki's

Besides a large selection of teas, this quaint little tearoom in the middle of McLeodganj keeps a lot of reading material. You can even trade in your old books here.

Om Café

Located near the Dip Tse Chok Ling Monastery, this café makes the best fruit pancakes in Dharamshala.

Open Sky Café

On Jogiwara Road in Dharamshala, this café isn't instantly

recognizable from the road, so keep an eye out for a lone building perched on the hill on the right-hand side. A short staircase leads up to it.

Tenyang Café

Located in the main temple area, this place features great coffees—the real thing, not the usual instant variety found in North India—and bakes the best muffins in town.

McLEODGANJ

Paul Garrioch takes refuge at a monastery in McLeodganj

McLeodganj is largely a Tibetan settlement, sitting higher up on a hill from the bigger and more commercial town of Dharamshala. Famous as the headquarters of the Tibetan government in exile and the home of His Holiness the Fourteenth Dalai Lama, this part of the northern state of Himachal Pradesh is overrun with Tibetan monks, nuns, recently arrived refugees, and hundreds of tourists—all with their own spiritual agendas.

Strangely, the pizza places, beer bars, Internet cafés, guesthouses, and other manifestations of a thriving tourist industry do not seem to take anything away from the peaceful and incredibly friendly paradise the Tibetans have created here. There is so much to see that just walking around the narrow streets can keep you occupied for hours: monks engaged in heated debates on Buddhism, pilgrims looking glassy-eyed and mentally detached from the world, and streams of lay residents going about their daily business in a range of traditional, colorful costumes.

For me, McLeodganj was a holiday from the world of worries, unpaid bills, and mortgages. It was an oasis of temporary freedom that made reality seem a million miles away. I was glad to arrive in the midst of all these happy people, who seemed to have found some secret elixir in the Buddhist religion that washed away their cares and made them forever cheerful.

Turned out, I couldn't have been more wrong. During my short stay at the Tsechokling Monastery, I was stunned to learn about the horrifying circumstances that had caused most of the area's refugee population to flee Tibet and come here. Where I had originally delighted in their placid nature and easy friendliness, I now felt humbled by their fortitude and capacity to hide great pain behind broad, open smiles.

The Tsechokling Monastery gave shelter to newly arrived refugees who had escaped from Chinese-occupied Tibet, and I spent several evenings in their company, listening to their stories and trying to come to terms with the magnitude of their losses. A young refugee I remember in particular, no more than twelve or thirteen, had arrived in McLeodganj just a few months earlier.

The boy's father had decided to send his children and their grandparents to live in India. In this country, they could be free to practice Tibetan culture and religion, and they could also be near His Holiness, the Dalai Lama. The whole family made the grueling trip through deep snow and high passes toward Nepal. Sometimes they could travel during the day, but near the larger towns they moved silently at night to avoid the Chinese police and army. They were often helped and given lodgings and food by Tibetan families along the way.

The trip took about a month, but before the end, the boy's grandfather died of exposure on one of the passes. The family buried him there and kept moving, until at last they reached the border. The boy had been told nothing about his parents' intent, and he was devastated when they hugged him and gave him what little money they had and the name of a contact in India. They then handed him, with his brother and grandmother, to a smuggler. Before he could protest he was taken across the border. Once he was safely on Indian soil, he came to McLeodganj and was accepted as a monk at Tsechokling Monastery. In time, he accepted the fact that he would never see his parents again, although, occasionally, he did hear news of them from the other refugees who were constantly arriving.

The boy revealed none of the sorrow he must have carried in his heart while he narrated his story. His eyes clouded over only once, at the mention of his mother, but he recovered quickly and carried on with a dignity that was amazing to see in one so young. He had accepted the Buddhist religion as a replacement for his family and found solace in his proximity to the Dalai Lama whenever the demon from of his lost past returned to haunt him. It was his duty now to apply himself to his studies and fulfill the dreams his parents had for him.

Other monks, newly arrived from Tibet, told similar tales of the sorrow and hardships that had tested their faith during the long, treacherous journey to McLeodganj. Settling in hadn't been easy either—most initially suffered from the warm climate and strange food in India, but they were relieved to have survived and were grateful to be at the Tsechokling Monastery, where they could follow the ideals of a true Tibetan.

The monastery itself was an ode to the Tibetan refugees and their faith. The original Tsechokling, the monks told me, was built in the 1700s and lay a few miles south of the city of Lhasa in Tibet. But the communist Chinese destroyed this place of worship, and with it, hundreds of precious scrolls, paintings, and scripts. An enterprising Lama managed to escape with some of the monastery's treasures and started a new Tsechokling in McLeodganj in a rented hut. With more and more refugees arriving from Tibet, the monastic community grew and increased its resources until finally, in 1984, it could build the yellow-roofed building we were sitting in.

Leaning against the wood railings in front of the whitewashed monk's quarters, I realized that I had learnt one of the most valuable lessons of my life from these refugees: forbearance in the face of adversity. Measured against the experiences of their lives, the disappointments and shortcomings in mine seemed irrelevant and inconsequential. I was glad I had chosen to rent a modest room at the Tsechokling Monastery. If I had checked into a hotel, my holiday in McLeodganj would have been refreshing and peaceful, but my soul would have been poorer for not having come to know the true spirit of the place and the amazing strength of its people.

Staying at Tsechokling Monastery

You can help the monastery carry on its good work by renting a room there. The monks have a block of seventeen accommodations with very basic amenities that they let out to tourists for a nominal charge. A nonmonk Tibetan looks after the needs of guests, and he is a great resource if you want to learn more about the monastery and the situation of the Tibetans in McLeodganj. To make a booking, write in care of "Thubten Pema Lama, Director," at the following address or email.

Tsechokling Monastery
Camel Track Road
PO McLeodganj-176219

Dharamshala
Himachal Pradesh

tpemalama@yahoo.co.in

SPITI

Keya Sen stays home in the remote Spiti Valley

Cut off from the rest of the world for many months of the year, the ten-thousand-odd inhabitants of the remote Spiti Valley have survived thus far on agriculture and barter. But with one crop annually, and that too only if the snow melts enough to provide irrigation, these people are in dire need of new sources of income. Tourism is a good way to supplement their earnings, and groups such as the Snow Leopard Conservancy have started the Himalayan Homestays project with local Buddhist families, for travelers who want to immerse themselves in Himalayan life and culture.

My own Spiti homestay took place in the village of Langza. This settlement was less of a village and more of a hamlet, with only a handful of mud huts and a massive Buddha statue. Millions of years ago, Spiti lay submerged under the Tethys Sea, and fossils of sea life are still scattered around Langza, giving the village a prehistoric atmosphere.

During daylight hours, I enjoyed the solitude of hiking around the Langza village. Hundreds of marine animal fossils, bearing curious marks and surface striations, lay in the valleys and streams. I had no idea what creatures they must have been. It just amazed me that their remnants had survived like this for thousands of years. The presence of the bone-white fossils underscored Langza's timelessness. When I returned to the house of my host family every evening, I felt relaxed and open to their simple lifestyle.

The family I stayed with had two rooms to share with their guests. The larger one was used as a living room, and everybody gathered here in the evenings to chat, sing songs, and share a hot meal. Food was basic Tibetan fare of homemade noodles, dumplings, and buttered tea, all prepared by the lady of the house, who made up for her lack of English with a warm, gap-toothed smile. The hot, delicious meals she cooked were her way of saying that she loved having me as a guest in her home. The accommodation was by no means luxurious, but after a long, tiring day of trekking, it was wonderful to come back to that cozy hut and relax on the warm, threadbare rugs with a cup of tea, watching the sun set behind the mountain peaks that hung like a photograph outside the window.

At night, when the family had gone to sleep, I would retire to my platform bed in the guest room and write poetry by candlelight. The icy winds of Langza had cleared my mind, and the words I struggled to find in the city poured out of me. I wrote simple limericks, too, on little bits of paper that the kids in the house loved to collect.

On the day I left, the children gathered around me and recited some of the limericks they had memorized in secrecy. My hostess stuffed a plastic bag full of dumplings in my rucksack and reminded me to drink enough water. She was always worrying that I never had enough.

I got into the car and waved a final goodbye to my host family, wondering if they had any idea how deeply our short friendship had touched me. I had come for a homestay in Langza expecting to help the people here with the money I paid for room and board. But as the car wound its way back to Spiti's main town of Kaza, I realized how much I was taking away from this trip—a new sense of calm and an appreciation for how rich a modest life can be.

Himalayan homestays

Homestays in the Spiti Valley are available in several villages, such as Langza, Komic, Demul, Dhankar, and Mikkim. Langza, where Keya stayed, is a short one-and-a-half-hour drive from Kaza, the main town in Spiti. Getting to Kaza, how-ever, is only possible by road from Shimla or Manali. The journey time is two days and one day respec-tively. Whether by taxi or bus, both routes are incredibly scenic.

Homestays include all meals. Bathwater is provided in buckets, and there are no laundry facilities, but rooms are extremely clean and cozy. Host families decorate their space with lots of carpets on the floor and local handicraft items. Often the companies that organize the stays—such as the Snow Leopard Conservancy—include trekking and cultural and farming activities as part of the package. For more about homestays and the Spiti Valley, go to the following websites.

www.snowleopardconservancy.org/spiticonservation.htm

www.spitivalley.com
www.spiti.org

JAISALMER

Cynthia Chesterfield encounters courage in a Jaisalmer kitchen

If you are going to visit Jaisalmer, you must eat a Rajasthani *thaali* at Vyas Meal Service. The food is vegetarian and tastes refreshingly homemade, but that isn't why I`m sending you there. The meal is just a pretext to meet and help the elderly woman who relies on tradition and trust to run this operation.

Chanda Vyas doesn't know her own age, but from the looks of her, she must be well over eighty. Her eyes have sunk deep into her face, and the relentless Jaisalmer sun has marked innumerable little grooves around her eyes and mouth. The end of her sari is always wrapped like a veil around her head, and she pulls at it constantly in embarrassment and pleasure when you praise her for her cooking.

Her arthritis is so bad these days that she finds it difficult to get around, and she's grateful if her guests come down to the kitchen and carry their own food to their table. Unable to read and write, she cannot take down your order, so she will memorize which *thaali* you request. Unable to add, she also relies on customers to make their own bills.

Chanda Vyas is an incredible human being. Her husband died, leaving her alone in the world. Her son then threw her out of the house, but she refused to beg or starve to death on the streets. Instead, she chose to keep her husband's little restaurant running and depended on the integrity and goodwill of her customers to make allowances for her old age and continue to give her their custom.

I am so thankful that a local friend of mine took me to lunch at Vyas Meal Service and told me her story. I will always remember the happiness in Chanda Vyas's smile when I told her what a heavenly cook she is. She gestured at the stove and lime-washed walls of her kitchen, as if apologizing for the humbleness of her establishment. I waved away her concerns, and she ran her hands over my chest and head in what I knew was an *aashirvaad* (blessing). She peered at my face with such affectionate, maternal curiosity, I couldn't help but put my arms around her in the only hug I have ever given to a stranger. As her bony chest pressed for a few fleeting moments against mine, I understood why mothers are revered as goddesses in this country.

The example of Chanda Vyas's brave fight for survival helped me deal with the rough patch I was going through emotionally at the time. My problems didn't look smaller in comparison to hers; they just appeared more conquerable. I even cried a little when I returned to my hotel room after meeting her that day. Not tears of pity, but a show of respect for Chanda Vyas's courage to go on, despite the obstacles in her way.

Vyas Meal Service
Chanda Vyas's restaurant is located near the Jain temples inside Jaisalmer Fort.

ANUPSHAHR

Dave Prager shares the story of a teenage bride in Anupshahr

Sam told us Ruksana's story while my wife, Jenny, and I were driving with him to a tiny village near Anup-

shahr in the state of Uttar Pradesh. Sam Singh was the founder of the Pardada Pardadi Educational Society, which runs a school that offers free education to over a thousand girls, along with free meals, uniforms, transportation, and 10 rupees for every day of attendance. The 10 rupees is necessary to convince fathers that educating their daughters is worth more than keeping them home to mind the buffalo.

Ruksana had once been just one of Sam's many students. Anonymous in her green and yellow school uniform until a rumor about her started doing the rounds. Ruksana was getting married. At the age of thirteen.

Her father was a rapist who had disappeared from her life, and her mother was too troubled to take care of her. "She runs around the village naked," as Sam put it. So Ruksana lived with her grandmother.

According to Sam, he had called Ruksana into his office and asked her if the rumor was true. It was. Her grandmother had arranged everything. Ruksana would quit school to become wife to a forty-year-old street barber from a neighboring village.

Sam then went to see Ruksana's grandmother. "Why are you marrying off such a young girl?" he demanded. "Why are you throwing her future away? What can we do to prevent this?"

Nothing. The grandmother was poor and in ill health. She feared that when she died, Ruksana would be forced to become a prostitute. To the grandmother's way of thinking, marriage—even to such an undesirable partner as a man three times her age—was the best choice.

"You want to help?" the grandmother retorted. "You adopt Ruksana, or you marry her."

Sam, of course, could do neither. As Sam was telling us this story, Jenny was unnaturally quiet, staring fixedly out the car window. Later she told me she was thinking about her own life when she was thirteen. An eighth-grader at Madison Middle School in Albuquerque, Jenny had a swimming pool in her backyard and a black poodle named Gypsy. She was on the yearbook committee. To amuse her friends, she crumbled packages of Saltine crackers in her mouth and then showered them with cracker dust when she talked.

Before Ruksana completed her thirteenth year, she had already had her first child.

After he finished Ruksana's story, Sam confided that he hadn't thought of her in a long time. As sad as it was, hers was just one of many sad stories he heard every day. Spurred by our questions though, he made some calls and arranged to meet Ruksana and her grandmother at the home of a prominent lawyer in Anupshahr.

We'd heard about rural Indian girls' problems in the abstract: that they're valued in the family hierarchy behind the boys and then behind the livestock; that they're not considered worth educating; that when you ask a mother how many children she has, she counts only the boys. But sitting before us in her pale blue *salwar* and flowered white veil pulled low over her face, Ruksana was not an abstract problem, an academic depiction of suffering. She was there. She was real. She was heartbreaking.

Four years had gone by since Ruksana ended her schooling. Though she had given him an adorable son, her husband had deserted her. The grandmother, still alive and even more frail, was again terrified for her granddaughter's future. What choice did she have but to arrange another marriage? And so Ruksana, now seventeen and mother of one, was once again engaged to be married.

Sam's school had grown in the intervening years, and his connections had grown as well. This time, he could do more than just protest Ruksana's fate: he could offer an alternative. He knew an organization that gives shelter and jobs to poor, uneducated Muslim girls. It was in Goa in west India—an unimaginable distance by the old lady's reckoning, of course—but Ruksana would be looked after no matter what happened to her grandmother. If only her grandmother could bear the humiliation of cancelling the marriage, and the sad possibly of never seeing her granddaughter and great-grandson again.

Ruksana cast her eyes downward as the adults discussed her fate. Her son squirmed in her lap. Jenny and I listened in silence as Sam and the lawyer berated, cajoled, and pleaded with the grandmother. We didn't understand the language, but we understood the message: Ruksana had missed one chance, but a miraculous second chance had arrived. If only they were brave enough to accept it.

Finally, Sam asked Ruksana what *she* wanted. Ruksana glanced timidly at her grandmother. But a negative twitch of the grandmother's head sealed her future. Ruksana would marry for the second time, and she would meet her fate in Anupshahr.

Pardada Pardadi Educational Society

Dave saw Ruksana pass up her second chance at a better future, but he also witnessed a thousand other students who were actively bettering theirs at the Pardada Pardadi school. These girls were the lucky few to escape a life of unending chores and early marriage—a life that still awaits an estimated fifty thousand girls in the area who qualify as poor enough to study at Pardada Pardadi. If only Pardada Pardadi had room for all of them.

The girls inspired Dave: to volunteer for Pardada Pardadi, to raise money for Pardada Pardadi, to donate to Pardada Pardadi, and even, in his wife's case, to become an employee of Pardada Pardadi. If Dave's story makes you want to do something to help, Pardada Pardadi is always seeking donors, fundraisers, and professionals in its Delhi office. The organization also offers six-month and one-year English-language teaching positions, during which you can live in the village and experience the beauty and challenges of rural India for yourself.

A-47 Lajpat Nagar - 1
New Delhi

www.education4change.org

GENERAL NORTH INDIA

Melly Goodman meets a shady shahtoosh dealer in Srinagar

My husband and I rented a houseboat on idyllic Dal Lake in Srinagar, and every evening at around five, a group of sellers would row up to our boat in *shikaras* (Kashmiri canoes) and show us their merchandise. Among them was a shawl dealer who called himself Akeel. He offered to sell me a *shahtoosh*. "How would you like the most exquisite shawl in the world that is soft enough to pass through a ring?" he said, with the air of someone who was presenting me with an opportunity to buy the Taj Mahal.

I had never heard of *shahtoosh*, but I was hardly going to tell him that and risk raising the price. I was also still in the first flush of my romance with living in India and was in a great hurry to start a collection of beautiful things that would later become precious souvenirs of my time here. So I said yes, I'd like to see one. He promised to come the next evening with an exceptional piece I wouldn't be able to turn down. It was very expensive, of course, but he wouldn't quote any prices until I had held it in my hands.

Akeel did turn up the next night, but very late. I was just finishing dinner when the houseboat butler announced that a *shikara* seller was asking for me by name. I stepped out with half a mind to send him away. But before I could say anything, Akeel motioned for me to keep quiet until the butler had returned to the kitchen. Then he quickly pulled out a small paper package from his pocket. When I tried to switch on the verandah light, he again motioned me to stop and produced a stub of candle instead. In the feeble light of the candle, he unwrapped a diaphanous gray shawl with a white leafy border. The design wasn't immediately appealing, but when I ran my fingers over it, I felt as if I were touching a fluff of cloud. Akeel hadn't brought a ring, but I had no doubt that the wispy wool would easily pass through one.

I knew immediately that I would part with a considerably large sum to own that *shahtoosh*. Seeing that I was hooked, Akeel started discussing prices. Whispering prices, rather, because he dropped his voice to such a low decibel, I had to strain to understand his words. The supply of *shahtoosh* had completely dried up, he informed me, and I would be hard put to find one even if I had contacts.

He, however, knew a source from whom he could get one or two pieces occasionally, and so the price was quite high. Four thousand dollars, and he couldn't climb down from that figure. Naturally, I was startled.

"Come on," he encouraged. "It's a collector's piece that you can sell off one day for ten times more. Look upon it as an investment."

I said no, no, and no, but still Akeel persisted. He tried to push the shawl into my hands. "Keep it tonight," he said. "Tomorrow, I will come back, and then you can return it if you still think it is too expensive."

I was sorely tempted to keep the shawl, but there was something in the man's behavior that struck a suspicious chord. His arrival at such a late hour and then all this urgent whispering was very odd and irritating. I told him to come back in two days, to give me sufficient time to think this over.

Akeel finally left, taking his *shahtoosh* shawl with him. I mulled over the proposition as I lay in bed, and the next day, I went to a big woolen goods store in town and asked about *shahtoosh*. The owner laughed at first, saying that the police would haul me off to jail if I was heard enquiring about it. I thought he was joking, and I told him the price Akeel had quoted for a gray *shahtoosh* the night before. The shop owner sobered up quickly after that. He did not know any Akeel, but he asked for a detailed description of the man and what exactly had transpired between us. Then he asked me if I wanted to report the matter to the police.

Police? My heart dropped a beat.

"It is a police matter, ma'am," the shop owner said. "Buying, selling, and even possessing a *shahtoosh* is a punishable offense." The whole story then slowly came out. Apparently, *shahtoosh* was made with a very special wool that came from a Himalayan antelope called chiru. As many as three chirus had to die to make one *shahtoosh* shawl, and the species, as a result, was on the brink of extinction. With a worldwide ban on *shahtoosh* now in place, it was illegal to even own one of these shawls. Yet in spite of law enforcement's best efforts, the shawls were being smuggled out of India, and wily local manufacturers were selling them clandestinely to foreign tourists.

My fascination with the beautiful gray shawl died right then and there. But what should I do when Akeel showed up? "Don't worry, ma'am, he won't come," the shop owner assured me. "Srinagar is a small town, and it is easy to follow your movements here. He must know that his game is up."

The shop owner was right. Akeel did not return. But it was a long time before I could get past the incident. I did extensive research on chiru antelopes, and from then on, started warning others to watch out for unscrupulous traffickers trying to unload *shahtoosh* shawls on them. I had had a lucky escape, but I didn't want my friends and family to unwittingly become party to the destruction of these beautiful creatures who paid with their lives just for having the finest coats in the world.

Shahtoosh ban

Not only can you not purchase a *shahtoosh*, you cannot own one—even an old one that has been in the family for many years must be surrendered. To learn more about the *shahtoosh* situation, go to the following website.

http://shahtoosh.info

Saving the chiru

You can help the Wildlife Trust of India to protect these endangered antelopes and stop illegal trade in *shahtoosh* by donating money to the organization or getting involved in one of their conservation programs. Along with preserving the animals, they also have a program that offers alternative vocational training to former *shahtoosh* producers.

www.wildlifetrustofindia.org

Socially conscious alternative

Rather than a *shahtoosh*, we suggest you purchase a pashmina. For more on this traditional, chiru-friendly Indian shawl, go to Nabanita Dutt's essay on page 118. Also, to learn more about helping stop the mistreatment of animals in India, continue on to the following essay.

Naomi Naam protests the mistreatment of working animals

My eight-year-old daughter agreed to come to India on two conditions: that we would buy her glass bangles and we would take her to see a monkey dance. She had heard from our Indian neighbor that there were people who had monkeys performing tricks and dancing on the roads, and she simply had to see it for herself.

We kept our promise and found one such man with two monkeys near India Gate in Delhi. But he spoiled it for my daughter when one of the animals disobeyed and he jabbed it with a metal tong. Weary looking, the monkey squealed loudly in pain, and throughout the performance rubbed his thigh where his owner had hurt him.

The crowd that had gathered to watch seemed unaware of—or perhaps unsympathetic to—the monkey's discomfort. Many threw coins into the man's bowl and dispersed. But my daughter refused to allow us to pay the man at the end of the show. Instead, she insisted that we buy ice cream and nuts from nearby hawkers as treats for the monkeys. Their owner kept haranguing us for money, but when we pointedly ignored him, he subsided into a sullen silence and watched impatiently as my daughter fed vanilla ice cream and a bag of peanuts to the miserable simians.

That day, I learned something from my girl: how to stand up and say no to the mistreatment of animals. In all the time we spent in India, we followed our daughter's example and protested against numerous instances of animals being tortured in order to make money for their owners. Camels with open wounds hauled tourists over the desert. Bears were led by ropes through their noses to perform painful, unnatural stunts. Cocks were forced to kill each other in pitched fights with blades attached to their feet.

Each time, we followed my daughter's example and refused to give money to the animals' owners. We bought food for the hungry creatures and fed them instead. In our small way, we made our protest known. And we were gratified to see a few other Western travelers follow suit. So many animals in India are used in the business of entertainment, and it is our duty as tourists to say we do not want to have a good time at their cost. Such practices should be as unacceptable here as they are in the Western world.

Lodging a complaint

In every major city in India you will find organizations upholding animal rights. Local tourist offices will be able to guide you if you want to lodge a complaint about any incident of cruelty you have witnessed. Local passersby will also assist you in cautioning the offender if you ask for help. Following are two groups in New Delhi working against the mistreatment of animals.

GENERAL NORTH INDIA

Friendicoes SECA

Friendicoes Society for the Eradication of Cruelty to Animals includes animal rescue, a shelter, veterinary hospital, ambulance service, and crematorium.

271 & 273 Defence Colony Flyover Market (Jungpura side) New Delhi

www.friendicoes.org

Circle of Animal Lovers

This animal shelter offers a mobile clinic, feeding, spaying, and the vaccination of stray animals.

E-67 D.D.A. Flats
Saket
New Delhi

www.circleofanimallovers.org

Shannon McLaughlin recommends research before lending a helping hand

During our middle school class field trip to the foothills of the Himalayas, we stopped one morning in a village near Dehradun for a cultural exchange assembly. Our American students were to meet and interact with local Indian children, and they were all excited at the prospect: It was a chance for them to see how kids in remote parts of India went to school and what kind of lives they led. Also, we were carrying many gifts for the school, and they were looking forward to the fun of distributing them.

We had spoken to our students beforehand about the kind of reception they could expect. Verbal communication would be difficult because of the language barrier, and it was likely that the Indian children would try to communicate by touching and holding hands instead. American children, on the whole, are very aware of their personal space, and we didn't want them to appear rude or standoffish.

As it turned out, we needn't have worried. Our students took the idea of a cultural exchange in the right spirit and responded enthusiastically to the warmth and friendship the village kids greeted them with. Undeterred by the absence of words, they communicated in the universal children's language of games and laughter, and we were proud of the way they played and held hands with perfect strangers.

From their point of view, the excursion to a Himalayan village school had gone off very well. It was us teachers who returned from the trip squirming with embarrassment at the faux pas we felt we had made. We had arrived at the school with a typical, fumbling, paternalistic attitude, having no clue about the ground realities at all. Bearing down like Santa Claus, we brought many exciting gifts that neither the school nor the village children had any use for. A world map for example, printed in English—a distant third language that none of these elementary-aged students could make sense of. An electric globe that lit up when plugged in—for a school that had no electricity.

Come to think of it, the school had very little of anything. Just one small hall that served as the classroom, and an annex that the teachers used as an office. There were no tables or chairs, and the students had to take their lessons sitting on a freezing concrete floor. There were no chalkboards either, and books were a precious commodity. The school had no running water, and the kids had to hike half a kilometer to fetch buckets of water from the village pump if they wanted to drink.

I thought back to those rare days in the United States when the school where I taught would immediately cancel classes if storms shut down basic amenities like electricity and water. Here in this remote Himalayan village, the school survived every day in such circumstances, and the kids, in spite of all the hardship, didn't miss a day.

We realized—too late—how useful and appreciated some simple gifts of books, paper, and pencils would have been. If only we had a notion of just how poor the conditions were here …

This experience makes me want to tell other travelers not to make the mistake we did. The desire to help is always welcome, but it is important to know the best way to do the most good. Sponsoring a child's education would be a lot more valuable than a school visit such as ours with some misguided but well-intentioned gifts. Children must provide a uniform and supplies to attend school, but most of the kids in these remote, rural pockets of India cannot afford even these basic costs.

Organizations like India's Bighelp collect money from sponsors to cover a child's school expenses. Simply paying for a uniform and necessary supplies means that you are giving a child an education. Your gift won't come gaily packaged in colorful wrapping paper like our electric globe did. But while our globe sits and gathers dust in some corner of a Himalayan village school, your gift will be a much-needed investment in India's future.

Sponsor a child's education

Bighelp is a program that sponsors the education of orphans or financially disadvantaged children who are at risk of discontinuing their studies. Students who receive sponsorship through this program live only in remote Indian villages and towns. With a donation of less than $10 a month, you can help educate one child, who will also receive study materials, food, and two uniforms annually.

www.bighelp.org

Suggestions for paying it forward around North India

If you are interested in ways you can help the locals you meet while traveling the tourist trail, the following organizations offer grassroots—and often unique—solutions to advancing education and alleviating poverty throughout North India.

Lha Charitable Trust
Dharamshala, Himachal Pradesh
www.lhasocialwork.org

This charitable trust was established in 1997 to help Tibetan refugees adjust to life in India. Often, the refugees who escape China's oppressive regime in Tibet arrive in Dharamshala half-dead with fright and exhaustion from the perilous journey. They find themselves in a foreign country where they cannot deal with the sudden change in food, climate, language, and lifestyle.

Through various awareness and assistance programs, Lha makes the transition easier. Lha's services are offered to the local Indian population living in the area and other Himalayan communities as well. The organization is always grateful for any type of volunteer work offered by visitors to Dharamshala, especially doctors, nurses, and other professionals whose expertise can extend Lha's reach.

Friends of Orchha
Orchha, Madhya Pradesh
www.orchha.org

This Swiss nonprofit organization is run by an Indo/Swiss-Dutch couple who has made the village of Orchha their home. Through various programs, they are promoting tourism-linked livelihoods and spreading awareness about environmentalism and conservation. Their determination to make Orchha polythene free, for example, resulted in a major campaign with schoolchildren stopping people at a local market and temple and persuading them to use paper bags instead of plastic. You can buy "Polythene-Free Orchha" cloth bags from the Friends of Orchha to help keep the village clean—as well as keep the cows healthy, since a lot of them die after ingesting plastic bags people throw out with their garbage.

Along with wanting to stop plastic waste in Orchha, the couple want streams of waste water to disappear. They are also working hard for the day when women will have more decision-making powers and the local youth will be constructively engaged in building a better tomorrow. Check out their website for current Friends of Orchha programs if you would like to be of any assistance while you're visiting the tourist town.

Barefoot College
Ajmer, Rajasthan
www.barefootcollege.org

An unusual institution that denounces formal education, Barefoot College strongly believes that undeveloped communities need practical training rather than book learning to pull themselves out of the quagmire of poverty. They do not need the assistance of urban-based professionals with big degrees to improve their quality of life. The solutions—and the solution makers—exist within the community itself. By tapping into these unrecognized resources, Barefoot is endeavoring to create self-sustaining, healthy, and confident societies.

The college has an impressive campus in Ajmer, built by its "Barefoot architects," including an illiterate farmer and the village blacksmith. The empowerment of Barefoot students takes place in an informal atmosphere of mutual sharing of ideas and experiences. Students can depend on the Barefoot support structure until they feel fully equipped to practice their newfound vocations on their own.

Shakti Project of Rajasthan
Pushkar, Rajasthan
www.shakti-streetkids-pushkar.org

The caste system may no longer exist in India, but class bias continues. Especially in rural pockets of the country, where years of repression have stymied the desire to change and grow in certain lower-caste communities. The Shakti Project in Pushkar is working with children born into the local Nath caste of traveling performers to give them a better shot at life. Members of this caste have lived a nomadic existence for generations, doing puppets shows, acrobatic acts, and musical performances for the entertainment of villagers.

The Shakti Project is taking Nath caste kids off the streets and providing food and education six days a week. This task isn't always easy, as their families would rather have them begging or doing street acts than going to school. But the kids are excited by the prospect of moving away from the nomadic lifestyle with the help of a good education.

Visit the school if you're in Pushkar. The children are inspired by travelers from all over the world who care to spare some time for them. The Shakti Project is always looking for helping hands and welcomes temporary teachers.

Umrao Singh Memorial Girls School and Intermediate College
Allahabad, Uttar Pradesh
http://umraosinghschool.org

One woman's effort to educate two underprivileged girls was how this school started in 1967. When money is short, families in India often don't let their female children to go to school. Umrao Singh is fighting this gender discrimination by focusing on educating girls from kindergarten to twelfth grade. Along with health care, the children receive a nutritious meal every day at the school. The poorest students are given uniforms, shoes, and books. If you would like to donate or get involved, visit the school website for more information.

RESOURCES FOR THE ROAD

Practical advice to help you prepare for your travels

If you are a serious reader, then you must already be familiar with some of the literature that has emerged from the Indian subcontinent in the last decade or so: Arundhati Roy's international bestseller *The God of Small Things*; Nobel Prize winner V. S. Naipaul's nonfiction trilogy (*An Area of Darkness*, *India: A Wounded Civilization*, and *India: A Million Mutinies Now*); Salman Rushdie's monumental *Midnight's Children* ... Each of these books captures a different face of India—valid and relevant in its own place because there are so many Indias—and encourages you to explore the country's many layers while you are traveling and experiencing the culture firsthand.

India is unusual among Asian countries in that many of our finest authors write in English. As well, so many of the classics in different Indian languages have been translated that you're in no danger of running out of good reading material that provides plenty of interesting native perspectives on Indian culture, tradition, and people. When it comes to translations, I must recommend a quick read of any abridged version of the epic *Mahabharata* you can get your hands on. Having read *To North India With Love* this far, you have discovered how closely legends are linked with every monument and relic from India's past. Use the *Mahabharata* like a handbook of who's who in Indian mythology when you travel, and you'll find yourself referring to it as often as you do your maps and guidebooks. In this vein you should also consider Amar Chitra Katha. Available in English, this series on Indian mythology, with over five hundred titles, is great for both children and adults. You can buy volumes at any bookstore in India or online at WWW.AMARCHITRAKATHA.COM.

In this chapter you will find unique book lists compiled by avid readers, tailored not only to suit a traveler's interests and needs but also to complement the essays in *To North India With Love*. Contributors have also offered suggestions about specialized travel guides, timetables, and maps they found to be accurate and trustworthy. I have added my own two pennies to their

recommendations by drawing up some special-interest travel itineraries that you may find helpful.

Finally, in rounding out your trip planning, there's Bollywood—the country's booming movie industry, which can give you a colorful and entertaining taste of Indian popular culture. With elaborate costumes and dramatic dance performances, Bollywood films are often parodied in the West, but this is in fact a respected art form, whose nuances are many if you take the time to appreciate them. For my short list, I have compiled recommendations for some of the best Bollywood films of recent times—for their depictions of Indian life and their contemporary outlook—to help you ease into this genre of filmmaking.

Whether it's a novel or map, guidebook or movie, I have tried to ensure that this selective, eclectic chapter contains some useful resource for everybody. But you mustn't limit your preparation just to what is offered here. As mentioned earlier in the introduction to this book, extensive research is something you should always do before embarking on a journey. I know this does sound like a lot of homework, but if you go about it in the right spirit, getting ready for your trip can be just as rewarding as the trip itself.

BOOK RECOMMENDATIONS

Ajit Vikram Singh narrows down his must-read list for foreign visitors

As a longtime bookshop owner in Delhi, I often find myself recommending books on India to travelers. Not wanting to overload them with ponderous, definitive works, I like to suggest a sampler instead, narratives that will satisfy their initial curiosities about India, and at the same time encourage them to want to read more. In my experience, foreigners doing the North India route are most interested in three subjects—a short history of the region, Mughul India, and Rajasthan's royalty. The list below contains my favorite titles within these areas.

Emperors of the Peacock Throne
by Abraham Eraly

Many of my foreign customers become interested in the Mughal dynasty after seeing the Taj Mahal and other awe-inspiring instances of Mughal art and architecture in North India. My best choice of book for them is *Emperors of the Peacock Throne*, a colorful and dramatic account of the lives of the six great Mughal emperors who ruled from 1526 to 1707. I recommend this book not so much for the history or the accounts of conquests, but for the sumptuous background details of the luxurious Mughal times, which explain to a certain extent why India enjoyed its golden age of art, craft, and creativity under these rulers. Take the Peacock Throne mentioned in the title, for example—one of the world's most expensive treasures that the Mughals once sat upon, costing twice as much as the Taj Mahal at the time of its making and valued in recent years at around $804 million! Eraly is a master storyteller who effortlessly plucks the emperors out of the pages of history, fleshes out their characters with extravagant imagery and interesting details, and then traces their amazing lives, both as great rulers and as imperfect human beings. (This book was also published in the United States as *The Mughal Throne: The Saga of India's Great Emperors*.)

India: A History
by John Keays

This is an easy-to-read, one-volume edition of Indian history. Keays begins his narrative from the Harappan civilization in 3,000 BC, traces the growth of subsequent states and kingdoms, and then draws the book to a satisfying close with the India-Pakistan conflict in the late 1990s. The beauty of the book is the manner in which the author has managed to cut India's long story short without once losing his way. Also, this book devotes a good number of pages to ancient India, an impressive period of the country's past that historians often ignore.

A Princess Remembers: The Memoirs of the Maharani of Jaipur
by Gayatri Devi

People buy this autobiography because they are curious about Gayatri Devi, India's most celebrated beauty. Then they discover to their surprise that the book does much more than merely chronicle the triumphs of a beautiful woman—it draws a detailed picture of the lifestyle of Rajasthan's royalty and the political turmoil that took place in the aftermath of British rule in India. With delightful asides and colorful anecdotes, Gayatri Devi takes the reader on an emotionally fraught journey through her life: her childhood years as a cherished princess of the district of Cooch Behar; her adolescent crush on the Maharaja of Jaipur; the circumstances under which she agreed to become his third wife; the joys and jealousies of being married to a Maharaja; the responsibilities of administering a royal household; the tragic loss of her husband in a polo accident in England; and then her first tentative steps into politics, her stunning electoral victories, followed by her humiliating spell in prison. This extremely personal and highly readable narrative is supplemented by many rare and exciting photographs of the Jaipur royalty.

Book shopping

To read more about Ajit Vikram Singh's Fact & Fiction bookshop, go to page 256.

Soumya Bhattacharya immigrates into Indian literature

"Reading," according to the writer Jean Rhys, "makes immigrants of us all. It takes us away from home, but more important, it finds homes for us everywhere."

If you want to make yourself at home in India, I highly recommend that you read about the country first. It is too various and too bewildering a destination, too much of an assault on the senses, for anyone to be able to handle unprepared. The following books will as much help you make sense of your destination as they will help you appreciate it. They are as diverse in their styles as the country they are about, and although none of them are guidebooks, they can easily serve as your guide.

The Argumentative Indian: Writings on Indian History, Culture and Identity
by Amartya Sen

This isn't a travel narrative or a novel, but I recommend it because it reveals more about India—the country as a whole—than any other contemporary work I can think of. It defines "Indianness," and at a time when the cliché about India being the back office of the world has been supplanted by the cliché about India being the next world economic superpower, this is the book to read to find out the truth about a country that is almost impossible to categorize.

Amartya Sen is India's Nobel Prize-winning economist, and in this collection of illuminating, engaging, breathtakingly allusive yet accessible essays, he smashes quite a few stereotypes and places the idea of India and Indianness in its rightful, deserved context. Central to his notion of India is the long tradition of argument, public debate, and orthodoxy, of intellectual pluralism and the generosity that informs India's history. Sen is not a triumphalist, nor does he spare Western influences such James Mills's *The History of British India*, which, in my opinion, have oversimplified and distorted the Indian reality.

City of Djinns: A Year in Delhi
by William Dalrymple

Before William Dalrymple began in earnest his pursuit of becoming a historian, and before his best-selling, award-winning, huge-advance-grabbing Mughal trilogy (*White Mughals, The Last Mughal*, and a third volume on the way), he used to be a travel writer, and a fine one at that. *City of Djinns* found him an appreciative Indian audience to add to the many fans he has in other countries of the world. And rightly so. This witty, funny, superbly researched account

of his year in Delhi is one of the best contemporary books on India's capital. One of Dalrymple's special skills is being able to spot how the past resonates in the present, how the pieces of the jigsaw puzzle of time not merely fit but hold together. This book smells and tastes and breathes of the city. Spellbinding stuff.

In Spite of the Gods: The Strange Rise of Modern India
by Edward Luce

Between 2001 and 2005, Edward Luce was South Asia bureau chief of the *Financial Times*, one of Britain's best-known and most respected financial papers. Using his experience of India during that period—a time of momentous change with a rapidly growing economy as the engine—Luce examines India's dichotomy: how despite its rise as an important global economic force, it has remained "an intensely religious, spiritual, and, in some ways, superstitious society." The euphoria about India's capability in information technology, economic might, and superpower potential has of late been tempered by an awareness of just how much darkness still exists beneath the lamp. Luce explores, without jumping to hasty conclusions and while dovetailing the novelist's sense of narrative with the journalist's eye for detail, the savage inequalities between the country's burgeoning, educated, urban elite and the shockingly poor who live in the vast hinterlands. It is a thoughtful and thorough book, best described in his own words as "an unsentimental evaluation of contemporary India against the backdrop of its widely expected ascent to great power status in the twenty-first century."

A sporting read

You cannot visit India and avoid cricket, the sport that has a peculiar hold on the nation and unifies its people more intensely than the national flag. To understand the madness surrounding this game, read Soumya Bhattacharya's own *You Must Like Cricket? Memoirs of an Indian Cricket Fan*. This is a superbly intimate and beautifully written tale of a lifetime spent watching batsmen, bowlers, and wicket keepers run around on a green field in the company of a billion fellow countrymen. It is part cultural politics, part travel essay, and part reportage, tracing thirty years of highs and lows (mostly the lows) of being an Indian cricket fan.

While the game provides the narrative spine of the book, you don't need to be into cricket to love it. This is a book about India, about its sense of identity and its own notions of its place in the wider world. The book succeeds in holding up a very real picture of Indians and the Indian mind-set, which should be of interest to travelers hoping to get a handle on what makes Indians tick. You can buy the book online or at any leading bookstore in Delhi.

Naomi Naam pictures books about India for young readers

On my second visit to India, I brought along my eight-year-old daughter, Shesha. Like me, she is a born traveler and an avid bookworm, so we ended up spending a lot of time at Oxford Bookstore in New Delhi, browsing through the children's books section. Shesha made a wish list of all the books she liked, and then we sat at the store's tea bar and decided on which ones to buy over a glass of her favorite iced lemon tea. Shesha wanted books not only for herself but also for some of her friends in school. She was having a great time in India, and she wanted to show them what this country was really like. The book recommendations I give below are three of Shesha's all-time favorites. The opinions about each are also mostly hers.

The Birth of the Ganga
by Harish Johari

Geographically, this is a very relevant book for kids traveling in North India, as they will see the Ganga River flowing through many cities and towns. *The Birth of the Ganga* tells the mythological story of how the river dropped from heaven onto this earth, a fascinating tale that also introduces children to many of the Hindu gods and goddesses they will later see in temples and monuments.

Elephant Dance: A Journey to India
by Therese Heine

This book is a particular favorite in our family. Every night while we were in India my wife and I had to read a fresh passage from it for our daughter, who liked to fall asleep listening to the adventures that an anonymous grandfather has while visiting India. When this grandfather goes back home, he tells his grandson about the many amazing things he saw and did. The grandson is fascinated by the descriptions of the Himalayas that look like "ice-cream peaks," monsoon rain that cascades like a waterfall, a scorching Indian sun as ferocious as a tiger, and elephants parading with howdahs on their backs. Inspired by these images, the boy composes his own "elephant song," the sheet music for which comes with the book. We enjoyed the details about Indian culture and people in the endnotes, which answered many questions that Shesha thought up while listening to the story. As we do not have a piano at home, we could not use the sheet music, but Shesha took it to school and was thrilled when her music teacher read the book and taught the song to her class.

I Is for India
by Prodeepta Das

The content of this beautifully designed book has been organized alphabetically, so each page contains a large photo and a paragraph for each letter of the alphabet, showing different aspects of Indian life from a child's point of view. Shesha chose this book as a gift for obvious reasons—it detailed pictures of some of her favorite things in India: bullock carts, *jalebis* (delicious orange whorls of a syrupy sweet dessert), and Diwali (the autumn festival of lights). If you are traveling with children, this book is a great way to excite their curiosity and make them want to find out more about the country they are visiting.

Oxford Bookstore

148, Barakhamba Road
Statesman House
Connaught Place
New Delhi

www.oxfordbookstore.com

Cha Bar

You can enjoy a cup of tea while you read magazines and browse through books at this cozy tea bar inside the Oxford Bookstore. The menu has more than sixty varieties of masala, herbal, and ayurvedic teas, as well as a good selection of sweet and savory small bites.

BOOKSHOPS IN NEW DELHI

Vir Sanghvi frequents his best friend's Delhi bookstore

For years I used to lament the absence of good literary bookshops in India's capital. In such a country of readers, I could never work out why this should be so. Even when India faced a foreign exchange crisis and most imports were banned, the government continued to allow the import of books at a zero tax rate. Sadly, booksellers rarely took advantage of this provision.

Then, in 1982, an old schoolmate of mine decided it was time somebody did something about this lack of access to quality books. Against the advice of his land-owning family, which urged him to go into agriculture or industry, he prepared to open his own bookstore. The only place he could afford was in the then-remote Basant Lok shopping complex. Even that space was not very large. But Ajit Vikram Singh, my closest friend, had decided that somehow he was going to make it work. There must be other people like us who long for good books, he declared, and he paid no attention to his family's objections.

I was never thrilled by the name he chose for his bookshop—Fact & Fiction, how dull is that?—but I was impressed by the dedication with which he took up the challenge of getting literature to the public. Not only did he choose every book himself, but he sat in the store and personally sold each one.

As Ajit is not one of the world's great natural salesmen, this sometimes has comical results. Around half of all his customers demand a discount, and in the beginning, Ajit tried explaining that his margins were simply too small to offer discounts. But over the years, as millionaires drove up in Mercedes-Benzes and asked for markdowns on paperback best sellers, he began to lose patience with their cheapness.

At other times, he is simply rude to people he regards as philistines. Walk into Fact & Fiction and enquire about pornography, and expect to be insulted. Waste his time asking for the latest schmaltzy best seller, and you will be treated to his withering contempt. Still, somehow, against all the odds, he has succeeded.

Today, Fact & Fiction is universally regarded as one of Delhi's best bookstores, and Ajit's curmudgeonly nature has actually added to its legendary appeal. It is one of those rare gems of the twenty-first century: a place for genuine book lovers.

Fact & Fiction

39, Basant Lok (opposite the Priya Cinema Complex)
New Delhi

Basant Lok

Over the last few years, this out-of-the-way shopping and entertainment complex has metamorphosed into a popular hangout for Delhi's young crowd with sporty shops and many upscale restaurants. International chains such as T.G.I. Friday's, Pizza Hut, and Baskin-Robbins have all also opened franchises in Basant Lok, as have trendy Indian coffee bars including Barista, but the action is still centered around Priya, one of the city's first multiplexes. Insider tip: visit the charcuterie run by the Oberoi hotel chain here for some of the best cold cuts in the city.

MAP AND GUIDE RECOMMENDATIONS

Good Earth travel guides
www.eicherworld.com

Some of the best and most visual guidebooks I found in Indian bookstores were by Good Earth Publications. Organized not just by region or city, the books from this press also offer themed itineraries. This was especially useful when I was traveling through Himachal Pradesh. I bought two from the series—one on temples and another about places of Buddhist interest within the state. When I was confronted with unfamiliar religious sites and practices, both books were

of enormous help. The Eicher website includes a list of retail stores in India where the books may be purchased. (Jason Staring)

A Historical Dictionary of Indian Food
compiled by K. T. Achaya

For an Indian food enthusiast like myself who actually knows very little about the cuisine, this dictionary of common food names and terms came in very handy when I was traveling through North India. Wherever I went to eat, my trusty dictionary went with me to explain dishes on the menu that I had never even heard of before. As the title suggests, this book gives more than just descriptions. It puts each food item within its historical context and includes all kinds of additional information that makes it fun and interesting to read. (Maurice Young)

HT City Eating Out
by the *Hindustan Times*
www.hindustantimes.com

There is no Zagat guide to Delhi. Nor, for that matter, is there a Michelin. Fortunately, *HT City Eating Out* is published by the *Hindustan Times* newspaper every year. The book is based on reviewers who visit restaurants anonymously and pay for their own meals. I have found leads to many holes-in-the-wall doing really good food, thanks to this user-friendly guide. My favorite section is "Vir's Choice," in which Vir Sanghvi (www. virsanghvi.com), India's best-known food writer, gives a long, "entirely arbitrary" list of dining venues he enjoys. From the best place for a romantic dinner to a top Sunday brunch, Vir has a suggestion for every mood and occasion. Available in local bookstores, the book may also be ordered from the *Hindustan Times* website. (Anupam Tripathi)

Maps of India
www.mapsofindia.com

For $50 I had the whole of India at my disposal, thanks to a Maps of India CD suggested by a friend. The road maps printed out neatly, and I found everything from train schedules to hotel and restaurant options. The Maps of India website will even customize a map for you, if you have specific needs, or you can do it yourself with an interactive map tool. At the time of my leaving India, another tourist bought mine off me, which meant I got back 40 percent of the money I paid for it. Apparently, maps and travel-related CDs can be bought and sold quite easily in the Paharganj area in Delhi. Ask around at the local coffee shops, and you may just find yourself a discounted Maps of India. Otherwise, you can buy it online. (Frank Goodman)

Tourists at the Taj
by Tim Edensor

"Henceforth, let the inhabitants of the world be divided into two classes—them as has seen the Taj Mahal; and them as hasn't."

I discovered this quote by Edward Lear in *Tourists at the Taj* and

repeated it whenever my friends at home asked me the usual question about my tour of North India: "So, how *was* the Taj Mahal?" In many sections, Edensor's analysis of tourist viewpoints, impressions, and narratives on the Taj became too technical for me to comprehend. But overall the book gave so many insights about exploring the monument that it transformed my Taj visit into a special, individual experience.

For one thing, I was glad I hadn't arrived at the Taj as part of a package tour. By Edensor's reckoning, travelers on group tours get to spend about an hour at the site, and they see only what their guide chooses to show them. There is a pattern, he says, to these time-budgeted guided tours, and Edensor includes a very interesting map that traces their path through the Taj complex. He even marks specific spots that he calls the stereotypical "gazing and photography points." I doubt Edensor meant this book as a guide to the Taj Mahal, but that is exactly how I used it, and I ended up discovering many interesting aspects of the marble wonder that I would have otherwise missed. (Amiya Dasgupta)

Trains at a Glance
by Indian Railways
www.indianrailways.gov.in

One of the most vital travel tools you can pick up at the outset of your North India tour is the *Trains at a Glance* timetable published by Indian

Railways. In this age of specialized "must-have" travel gear (of which I have amassed a fair amount of expensive and unnecessary items), perhaps nothing was more valuable in enabling me to find my way around the Subcontinent. This large, magazine-format publication includes maps and timetables for all the trains on India's railway network.

A foldout map near the inside cover provides a color-coded diagram of routes between the major train stations. The number assigned to each route refers to a timetable, which you can easily find inside this well-produced guide. Once equipped with the relevant information, you can either proceed directly to the railway station to purchase your ticket or hire a travel agent to do so for you. The agent will send a runner to stand in the chaotic queues, which can at times last for hours. However you choose to buy your ticket, by first getting organized with *Trains at a Glance*, you can create a reliable itinerary in the comfort of your hotel room. (David Cook)

SUGGESTED ITINERARIES

Once you have gathered all of your maps and train schedules, it's time to hit the road. The most obvious route through North India is of course the Delhi-Agra-Jaipur tour, known in the travel trade as the Golden Triangle. But all the essays you have read so far in *To North India With Love* must already have told you something that travel agents often don't: there are countless other ways to enjoy this region. Ask yourself what you really want to get out of the area, make a short list of the places that excite you—and there you have it. A tailor-made tour of your own devising. The following itineraries are just three suggestions to get you started, help you incorporate recommendations from this book, and discover a few extra favorites we'd like to recommend.

The Golden Triangle tour

Doing the Golden Triangle doesn't necessarily mean you have to stick faithfully to the Delhi-Agra-Jaipur route. Tinker with your itinerary just a bit, and you'll manage to see a lot more of North India without veering off this popular tourist trail. The trick is not to linger too long in Agra. Spend a couple of days with the Taj Mahal—a lot of people, quite reasonably, want to return to the Taj again and again to enjoy and photograph its various moods—but save half a day at least to drive down to nearby Fatehpur Sikri (page 158), the abandoned city that Emperor Akbar built with elaborate palaces, courts, and harems. Fatehpur Sikri is a prime example of ambitious Mughal architecture, and there's the added attraction of the Sufi saint Salim Chisti's mausoleum housed in the complex, where one can tie a string on the latticed windows and leave a prayer wish behind for the saint to fulfill.

From Agra, move on to Jaipur (page 56), the capital of Rajasthan, which will act as a hub for the rest of your tours. Over the next few days, visit the Amber Fort, the Palace of Winds, the Gaitor crematorium—sights that show off the city's royal heritage. Or spend the bulk of your time in Jaipur's many shopping districts, buying unique art and crafts that are brought here from all over Rajasthan. Enjoy Jaipur however you want to, but do reserve a few hours every day to make short forays out of the city to visit some of the villages that are scattered around it. The hamlet of Abhaneri, for example, where you can see the remains of Rajasthan's gloriously designed stepwells. Or the village of Bagru (page 123), where almost every villager is involved in the production of the signature block-printed Bagru cloth. The craftsmen will gladly demonstrate how they turn bolts of unbleached cotton and silk into beautiful pieces of art. You can even select your own designs and colors and try your hand at block printing as well.

As a final treat, I'd like to suggest a palace hotel stay. I urge you to consider the Deogarh Mahal (page 65). This castle in Rajasthan's Rajsamand district has been converted into accommodation that often finds itself in top-ten lists of boutique hotels around the world. The tariffs are far more reasonable than other high-end properties like the Rambagh Palace in Jaipur and the Taj Lake Palace in Udaipur, and if you want an authentic palace experi-

ence, this is the best value for your money. The food is much better too. Relax here for a couple of days, and let the staff treat you like royalty in true Rajasthani style before you return to the anonymity of city life in New Delhi.

The Himachal Pradesh tour

If surreal scenes of impossibly beautiful mountain terrain and endless cold deserts sound like an attractive proposition, then you must plan a tour of the state of Himachal Pradesh. As you make your way up Himachal, the surroundings get drier, colder, and sparser, culminating finally into a kind of moon surface territory that most of us have never encountered in our lives.

Begin your journey in the town of Dharamshala (page 231), some five hundred kilometers away from New Delhi. This little settlement is now home to a community of displaced Tibetans and their leader, the Dalai Lama, and after a few days here, you will probably agree that there's no place like this for a bit of spiritual cleansing. Dharamshala also exposes travelers to Buddhism, and you can even experience little-known Buddhist training exercises (page 143) during your stay.

Next, retrace the route you took to get to Dharamshala, and turn off at Kalka to visit Shimla. A small train from Kalka makes a slow journey up the mountains to this vacation town, and if you have the time, do book a seat on it. You will enjoy some memorable scenes of lush green highlands before you move on to the Spiti Valley (page 235) at an altitude of over 3,500 meters, where nature compels you to hold your breath and wonder at its alarmingly harsh beauty.

Shimla is worth a day's stopover, but the reason you are here is to take the road that leads on to Spiti. At times, the Shimla-Spiti road is impassable, in which case, you will have to change your plans and go via Manali instead. Some permissions and permits are required, but all that's easily arranged once you are there. Getting to Spiti, whether you take the Shimla or the Manali route, is more exhilarating than any roller-coaster ride. If the thought that you're driving through some of the world's highest passes isn't enough of a thrill, the sharp bends and curves and the constant fear of toppling over the edge will certainly make you sit up and start praying.

As you begin your approach to the Spiti Valley, the tensions caused by the journey will melt away when you see the beauty of the place. Snow peaks at six thousand meters, hanging glaciers, and views of scrubby wasteland that seem to go on for ever and ever, filling your heart with such a heavy sense of aloneness that you will have trouble believing you are still somewhere on planet earth.

There are small hotels and tourist lodges in Kaza, the main town in the Spiti Valley, but you'll have more fun living with a local family in one of the five Spiti villages that offer home-stays to tourists. Kibber, touted as the highest village in the world, gets the maximum number of homestay guests; we strongly recommend the village of Langza as an option.

Until 1993, Spiti was cut off from the rest of the world, and even now, the area sees very few tourists. The locals are a unique people, having developed their community and culture without any outside influence. Traveling from village to village in the Spiti Valley is such a broadening experience, you won't mind the lack of indoor plumbing, gourmet food, and soft beds.

The wildlife tour

Many of the country's major wildlife reserves are located in North India, and if you are a wildlife enthusiast, you can build an entire itinerary around some of the best of them. Two of our recommendations, Bandhavgarh National Park (page 177) and Kanha National Park (page 179) in the state of Madhya Pradesh, are a bit off the beaten path, so we have devised an itinerary for those travelers with limited time who want to stay on the main tourist route. Interspersed with pit stops in a couple of cities, this can make for an exciting two weeks with lots of nature and some of North India's most famous attractions as well.

The legendary Corbett National Park, comfortably connected to New Delhi by both road and rail, is a good place to start. So much has been written about the park that I deliberately omitted it from this book, but you cannot do the North India wildlife tour without stopping here. There are some great books you can read beforehand to get you into the mood: *The Man-eating Leopard of*

Rudraprayag and *Man-eaters of Kumaon,* for example, both Indian jungle classics written by Jim Corbett, the hunter-turned-conservationist who is still worshipped like God in these parts, and whose escapades are the stuff of storybooks. Whenever a man-eater was on the prowl, killing men and livestock, the local people of the Garhwal and Kumaon region would call on Corbett—their beloved "Carpet Sahib"—to save them from the menace with his inexplicable tiger-stalking and tiger-sensing skills.

Tall grass and a thick undergrowth make tiger spotting a little difficult in this park, but hissing rock pythons, packs of wild elephants, and native gharial crocodiles (with their evil grins and ugly, blade-thin snouts) keep the thrill of adventure very much alive. With hundreds of species of flora and fauna, there's altogether too much happening in the forests of Corbett for you to be disappointed if the tigers don't bother to show up or the leopards remain hidden in the upper reaches of the park.

Four days is the minimum time you should devote to the Corbett experience before moving on to Agra, some three hundred kilometers away. After a day or two of sightseeing in the Taj city, it is less than an hour's drive to your next sanctuary: the Keoladeo Ghana National Park (page 181). Formerly, this stretch of marshy land was a rich duck-hunting ground for the Maharajas of Bharatpur, and there are startling records of their royal excesses, such as more than four thousand birds shot in a single day for the amusement of their visiting guests. Today, it is one of the major wintering

areas for some 380 species of aquatic birds that fly in from Afghanistan, Turkmenistan, China, and Siberia. After the excitement of Corbett, this bird reserve may seem a little low-key (severe water shortage is reducing the guest list of migratory birds each year), but the picturesque blend of bogs, woodlands, and scrublands makes Keoladeo a quiet and restful place to enjoy nature at a more leisurely pace.

From Keoladeo it is on to the hub of the princely state of Rajasthan: the colorful city of Jaipur. Sightseeing will take up most of the time you plan to spend here, and you can enjoy delicious Rajasthani food and a bit of luxury living in one of Jaipur's palace hotels before you hit Ranthambore National Park, your last tryst with nature before you return to New Delhi.

Ranthambore is one of the most filmed reserves in the world, and chances are that most of the photographs and footage of tigers you have ever seen have been shot here. The big cats of Ranthambore are said to be "friendly," in that they are not overly concerned about human presence in their environment and go about their business in broad daylight, thereby greatly increasing the likelihood of sightings. It's possible to see several in a single day. Ranthambore National Park used to be a private hunting ground belonging to the Maharajas of Jaipur, and the abandoned Ranthambore Fort standing high on top of a hill harks back to a time when the forestland lost a significant proportion of its wildlife population every time the king had a fancy to head a party of thousands for a spot of game.

The reserve is now beautifully maintained, and human traffic is carefully monitored with not more than two minibuses or open-air jeeps traveling on one of the seven designated routes at any given time. Unless you are extremely unlucky, you will enjoy several tiger sightings in the time you spend here and be able to take some dramatic photographs as well.

MOVIE RECOMMENDATIONS

Devdas

Revolving around the wavering sentiments of a weak-willed man, this film follows the protagonist as he succumbs to family pressure and spurns his lover and then spends the rest of his life in the arms of a courtesan, mourning his lost love and slowly killing himself with drink. The story line is simple, but then, the appeal of this film has nothing to do with the story at all. It is the treatment—the sumptuous sets, the elaborate costumes, the languid lighting, and the unusual frame compositions—that turn this adaptation of an early-twentieth-century novella by Sharat Chandra Chatterji into an extravaganza in the best Bollywood tradition. At the time of its release in 2002, *Devdas* was said to be the most expensive Bollywood film ever produced. (Keya Sen)

Lagaan: Once Upon a Time in India

This major box office hit appealed to Indians' national pride by taking the struggle against British oppression onto the cricket field. The film is set in 1893, in a barren village in Queen Victoria's India. After several years of bad crops, the villagers find that they cannot pay the enormous taxes levied on them by the British government. Their pleas for mercy fail to impress the British officers, and they are resigned to the prospect of the whole village dying of starvation, when a particularly obnoxious government official casually throws a challenge at them. If the villagers beat the British in a game of cricket, there will be no taxes to pay for three years. If they don't, they have to pay thrice the sum. With nothing left to lose, the villagers accept the challenge and put together a straggly team of players who have never held a cricket bat in their lives. This is a taut and remarkably well-made film that received an Oscar nomination for Best Foreign Language Film in 2002. (Amiya Dasgupta)

Rang De Basanti

Sue, a young, British woman, comes to India to make a docudrama about Indian revolutionaries who fought to free the country from British rule. Strapped for cash, she finds her actors in a motley group of University of Delhi students, who scoff at her idealistic vision of patriotic India, but agree to do the project anyway. The first half of the film dwells on these college students, who motorbike their way through life without a serious care in the world, until one of their friends—an Indian air force pilot—dies in a plane crash. The accident occurs because of poor maintenance of the airplanes, but the government tries to hide its own culpability by publicly blaming the pilot for the crash. In an attempt to clear their friend's name, Sue's halfhearted actors become real life revolutionaries. With the tagline "a generation awakens," this film achieved cult status in India, and caused a minirevolution with its unequivocal stop-being-part-of-the-silent-majority message. The youth of the country suddenly saw themselves as agents of change, and public opinion became more vociferous on various issues after the release of *Rang De Basanti* in 2006. (Ananya Basu)

Sholay

The story of *Sholay* revolves around a pair of small-time thieves who are hired by a village overlord to capture a fearsome *dacoit* with whom he has old scores to settle. Although made in 1975, this film deserves mention in any list of Bollywood films as probably the most important movie the Indian industry has ever produced. The tale of two happy outlaws recalls *Butch Cassidy and the Sundance Kid*, and the treatment owes thanks to Sergio Leone's spaghetti westerns. But the plot moves forward so effortlessly, with numerous subplots, tight editing, and some really wonderful photography, that it is without argument a rare Bollywood masterpiece. (Vir Sanghvi)

Swades: We, the People

Mohan is a NASA scientist who returns to India after many years away to look for his former governess. He goes to a small village in North India where the old woman now lives and is shocked to find the villagers making do without basic civic amenities like electricity. He takes it upon himself to teach the villagers to be self-reliant and devises a plan to harness the water of a nearby stream to generate electricity. The project is successful, and Mohan becomes the savior of the village, but soon it is time for him to return to his job in the United States. Through Mohan's ensuing dilemma, the film explores the quandary of many educated, nonresident Indians: should they pursue their successful lives and careers abroad, or should they come back to their home country, where they are sorely needed to spearhead social and economic changes? *Swades* plays out on an even keel without any remarkable highs and lows, but the dispassionate portrayal of India's caste-ridden rural society actually adds poignancy to many thought-provoking moments that lift the film out of the ordinary. (Anupam Tripathi)

Central Park, Connaught Place, New Delhi

GENERAL NORTH INDIA

Young boys in Old Delhi

Epilogue

One writer returns from India with a mosaic of memories

David Cook returns from India with a mosaic of memories

It is the thirty-first of October. I am at the end of my visit to the forested Kumaon region of the state of Uttaranchal, where we had been staying with the Kumaonese tribal people, who sing songs of the soil and trust nature to endow their lives. On the long journey back down the mountainside, the forests are now costumed in the pumpkin colors of autumn. The temperature has dropped during the days since we passed through this valley on the way up, and the trees hail the season's arrival by passing out pale golden leaves to our group of trekkers. The gusts of wind have increased in intensity, raising whorls of fallen leaves from the ground. Turning back to look up the valley from where we've come, I see for the last time the immensity of the Himalayas, the snow-capped peaks alight in the pink glow of sunset. The trek is nearly at an end, and from now on, my time in the mountains will be only a memory.

Autumn has come and gone, yet I still see those Himalayan moments with clarity as I sit here at home in Bainbridge Island, near Seattle, Washington, typing these words up onto my computer screen. I have no photographs of those moments. They are just one small part of what has become my favorite souvenir from my travels—a mosaic, made in India. I didn't buy it from a tout or chance upon it while talking to a street merchant. Not this keepsake. It is my creation, and it exists only as a collage of images in my mind.

Trekking through the Himalayas is just one such memory. There are so many more, and now that I'm home, they come back to me, sometimes drawn forth intentionally, but at other times prompted by the simplest of actions. When a drop of too-hot tea scalds my tongue, I recall drizzly evenings in Bandhavgarh National Park, when I would duck under the eaves of a clay hut that served as a *dhaba* to share a saucer of tea and swap wildlife stories with Ahmed, the national park ranger who led me through the jungle to spy on a two-year-old tigress. Or I feel the comforting warmth of a cup of the spiced brew that a stranger pushed into in my hands on a cold desert evening outside Jaisalmer, while our camels rested their tired legs and my guide Dilboi broke into the melancholy folk songs of the Rohi Desert.

In many cases, these images fill the gaps when my camera was not handy. Sure, I can show you an entire album of photographs from all the sightseeing I did in North India. But it's only my mental mosaic that contains a moment caught fleetingly through the window of a speeding train as I entered Delhi wrapped in early morning smog. A glimpse of hundreds of people living in slums near the railroad tracks. Row upon row upon row of huts built by tacking together pieces of tin, sacking, wood, plastic, and anything else that might provide some shelter from the sun and rain.

Somehow, memories such as this one are more alive in my mind than anything I captured with my camera. They can move. They have sound. Each time I study them, they appear slightly different. They not only help me to reflect on my time in India, they also help to reconcile visions of beauty with darker images of despair. I laugh as I once again see the intricate pattern of an exquisite Kashmiri rug that nobody wants to buy from a funny old barrow woman in Srinagar because she is bad-tempered and swears horribly at passersby. I am captured by the imposing backdrop of the Mehrangar Fort in Jodhpur, against which my tabla teacher accompanies a sitar in a recital of twilight ragas on the terrace of a friend's ancient *haveli*.

At the very same instant, I am also watching a disfigured beggar hobbling on twisted, stunted legs along a station platform before falling down and dragging himself forward on all fours. I observe a bewildered five-year-old who is having his hair shaved off so that he can perform the last rites for a dead father who fell prey to common malaria, because the family couldn't afford nine tablets of quinine. I wait with a row of temporary laborers sitting with their tools, hoping some contractor will hire them for a few hours so they can take a pound of rice back home to feed their wives and children.

This is India. A country where people disown you for the kind of meat you eat, and then join hands with you in prayer when the cricket-crazy nation is poised to win the Cricket World Cup. How on earth could a place so diverse, so eccentric, and so unpredictable be captured in just one image?

If there's a single memory I brought back that I'd like to change, it's the one of my homecoming. When it was time for me to return from India, I found that I simply wasn't ready to leave. In the months and weeks leading up to my great Indian Adventure, I spent so much time thinking about the journey itself that it never occurred to me that I should take pause to consider the return. So when the day of my departure arrived, I was not only unprepared to say goodbye, I was completely malcontent.

Chagrined, I now watch myself retrieving a crumpled airline ticket from the bottom of my backpack, where it has been sitting for months. I reluctantly examine the text printed on its upper left corner. There's no mistake. The date stamped in bold red states clearly that it is time for me to leave. What do I do? Full of emotion, I fall into childishness.

"But I don't want to go home," I whine to myself, as if I am a seven-year-old being dragged onto the plane by my parents. "We still haven't been to Dharamshala or Udaipur. That other family got to stay in the Lake Palace, and we didn't even get to see it. We're already here, it's so close. Come on, let's stay."

Little did I know that I can return any time I like. It just requires a moment to make my way through my mosaic of memories. It's not too far a distance to travel. As it turns out, I never left India, even in coming back home halfway around the world.

Rinoti Amin
(Pg. 67, 140)

Warm climes, vibrant cultures, and spicy foods are some of the attractions that often take San Francisco Bay Area-based Rinoti to distant lands. From being accosted by gypsies in Granada to being chased by bovines in Jaisalmer, she seems to travel the world in search of cultural mis adventures.

Ananya Basu
(Pg. 42, 264)

As an Odissi dance exponent, Ananya frequently finds herself on the road, taking her performances all over Asia and Europe. After her marriage to a German software engineer, Ananya is now based in Pune and concentrating on researching her first book on Indian ragas.

Debasish Bhaduri
(Pg. 29)

This California-based documentary filmmaker has come to India several times to find himself a traditional Indian bride. While his soul mate remains elusive, Debasish has fallen in love with his country of origin and plans to work out of Bangalore six months of the year.

Soumya Bhattacharya
(Pg. 252)

Soumya is a journalist with the *Hindustan Times* and lives in Mumbai. His essays and literary criticism appear in publications across the world—from England's *Guardian* to *The New York*

Times. His first book, a work of narrative nonfiction called *You Must Like Cricket?* was published across the world to critical acclaim in 2006.

Adrianne Bourassa
(Pg. 110)

Adrianne is a graduate of the International and Comparative Studies program at Huron University College in London, Ontario, Canada. She cultivated a strong interest in South Asian development during her studies, and shortly after her graduation, she traveled to India on her own. She hopes to return to South Asia soon.

Cassandra Brill
(Pg. 117, 231)

Cassandra grew up in Southern California and Texas but has spent most of these past few years in Australia and New Zealand. She loves beauty, learning, smiling at strangers, and yoga, and all of those passions brought her to India, ten years after she first began to dream of this trip.

Cynthia Chesterfield
(Pg. 43, 122, 158, 205, 237)

A music teacher from Sheffield, UK, Cynthia has been a fan of Indian classical music since she was twelve. A love for the sitar compelled her to visit India on six occasions in the past four years for short spells of training with the instrument. She dreams of starting an Indian music school in her hometown some day.

Suzie Chiodo
(Pg. 139)

Suzie is a British freelance journalist living in Canada. She has traveled to thirty countries, has probably crossed the Atlantic more times than Richard Branson, and speaks French, Italian, and Turkish. She is a regular contributor to the *Daily Mail* travel section and several Canadian publications.

Emma Louise Christie
(Pg. 143)

Emma Louise is a Scottish lass who doesn't like whiskey, haggis, or snow, but nurses a weak spot for a man in a kilt. One day, she packed her bags and went out into the world to seek adventures. In time, she reached Indian shores and found a warm land and people she instantly fell in love with.

David Cook
(Pg. 177, 186, 219, 259, 267)

David is an environmental educator and avid traveler. At the time of publication, he was working in East Africa with the Jane Goodall Institute's Roots & Shoots program. When not overseas, he can usually be found exploring the mountains, glaciers, waterways, and wildlife of the Pacific Northwest.

Amiya Dasgupta
(Pg. 22, 40, 83, 258, 263)

A travel agent by profession, Amiya has designed hundreds of tours and set up scores of film shoots all over Nepal and India. His innate charm and intimate knowledge of the Subcontinent has won him accolades in the tourism industry, but he brushes all that aside and talks only of his current passion: working with impoverished schoolkids in remote, Mao-infested pockets of Nepal. Currently, Amiya divides his time between Nepal, India, and China.

Dipanwita Deb
(Pg. 26)

Dipanwita was working as an editor at the *Hindustan Times* in Kolkata when she decided to give it all up and marry her school sweetheart. Currently, she is living in the United States and dealing with domesticity and motherhood with a lot of humor.

Lora Defries
(Pg. 39)

Lora spent a year in New Delhi as a Rotary Ambassadorial Scholar before moving back to the United States, where she is running a restaurant called The White House in New Harmony, Indiana.

Partha De Sarkar
(Pg. 183, 188)

When he was young, Partha picked up the travel bug from his father, a renowned Bengali writer who enjoyed driving long distances around India in his car. Later, as an Indian Air Force officer, Partha toured the country, and after retirement, he broadened his horizons and took his journeys overseas. His passion for nature photography and adventure tourism gives him much to write about in his postretirement years.

Sean Doogan
(Pg. 201)

A busy management accountant in London, Sean still tries to get away from the spreadsheets every now and then to explore new countries. He arrived in Delhi at the start of a round-the-world trip and instantly fell in love with the place and its people. Two months in India was simply not enough, and he is already planning to go back.

David Dorkin
(Pg. 32)

A former Fulbright scholar in law and social theory who most recently was a fellow at the European University Institute in Florence, Italy, David is also a professional and immensely talented jazz guitarist. Currently, he lives in Louisville, Kentucky.

Dan Free
(Pg. 179)

Twenty-four-year-old Dan studied biology at the University of London and now looks forward to a career in wildlife conservation. But that's after he has managed to visit as many countries as he can with his partner, Dani Sweet.

Paul Garrioch
(Pg. 233)

Paul was a paratroop officer in the Australian army and then a tour guide in Borneo before he finally based himself in Chiang Rai, Thailand. He now divides his time between working for a Thai NGO, Mirror Foundation, and an Australian volunteer tour company, Antipodeans. His interest in India was sparked by a chance meeting with His Holiness the Dalai Lama.

Frank and Melly Goodman
(Pg. 41, 111, 148, 240, 258)

A career in the hotel business brought Frank and his wife, Melly, to India for two years. They used their time there well, traveling all over the country and making friends wherever they went. Currently, they live in Australia and hope to return to India in a few years to start a handicraft export business.

Robert Granger
(Pg. 34, 212)

A designer of commercial and residential buildings and a volunteer firefighter in Wisconsin, Robert likes to spend much of his life outdoors. In the company of his dog, Diesel, he swims in the pond on his property, goes duck hunting, tries to build airplanes, and takes his boat out on the Mississippi River. To liven up his home life, he got himself some goats, but is worried about finding dependable goat-sitters when he goes traveling again.

Indranil and Mahalakshmi Gupta
(Pg. 48, 87, 103)

Their jobs in a prominent Indian multinational brought Indranil and Mahalakshmi together, as did their passion for eating good food and traveling to new places. Marriage and three daughters later, their gastronomic adventures have ground to a halt. The couple has turned vegetarian, which takes all

CONTRIBUTOR BIOGRAPHIES

273

the pleasure out of the eating, but the Guptas still travel with a passion, loading the kids into the car and driving off to distant locations on a whim.

Jeannine Hohmann
(Pg. 137)

Jeannine's fascination with Asian cultures brought her to India. Traveling solo around the country was not without problems, but the trip left a lasting impression and changed some of her perspectives and priorities. Now she's back home in Michigan, to her job in food retail; her husband, Basant; and her two cats.

Carol Koster
(Pg. 106)

Carol grew up in Canada with various places to call home, such as Terrace, Ladysmith, and Victoria. Now, in her late twenties, she's taking time off to travel, so that ten years down the road, she and her husband, Jarrod, can have some great memories to add flavor to mundane conversations about household matters and mortgage payments.

Jorden Leighton
(Pg. 96, 150, 175)

Jorden is a prairie-born Canadian lad, currently residing in the seaside oasis of Victoria, BC. Having traveled in Asia, the Americas, and Europe, he is always yearning for more journeys to distant lands. Two of his passions (aside from writing) are photography and zigging when others zag.

Shannon McLaughlin
(Pg. 244)

Shannon has spent half her teaching career in South America, the Middle East, and Asia. California is where her heart is, along with her family and her storage unit. She has many other loved ones scattered across the world. Have passport, will travel.

Asha Mallya
(Pg. 42)

Asha is a Pune-based scientist working with hepatitis vaccines. When she's not in the lab, she is furiously making plans for her next long road journey with friends and son, Aniruddha. Wherever she goes, Asha is passionate about tasting all the local delicacies, which is odd because she usually disapproves of most of them.

Beverley Millar
(Pg. 79)

Once she completed her language studies at the University of Brighton in the United Kingdom, Beverley took off for India with her boyfriend. After spending a month in the north and west of the country, she decided that urban India wasn't quite her thing. It was the smaller towns and mountain villages that made her trip memorable, and she plans to return someday to explore more of that.

Mark Moxon
(Pg. 66, 161)

www.moxon.net

Mark is a freelance journalist who can't resist writing about everywhere he visits (much to the bemusement of his partner). This is probably why his website contains over 650 travel articles and 2,500 photographs, and—if you look hard enough—at least one joke.

Nilanjan Mukherjee
(Pg. 28)

A passion for nature photography has taken Nilanjan to sixty-seven countries all around the world. Back home in India, he likes to take time off from his software engineering job to travel through rural India with his camera case, computer, and three-year-old, nonvegetarian monkey, Nripen.

A. Murray
(Pg. 50, 72)

A stand-up comedian and actor, A. Murray traveled to India for business rather than pleasure, in order to break into Bollywood. After one embarrassingly small role where all his lines (and lethargic dance moves) were strewn all over the cutting room floor, he bid the dream goodbye. Returning to his native Australia, he plans to open a Bollywood-themed musical theater restaurant, for which he already has a name: Hello Delhi.

Adrian Murray
(Pg. 59, 210)

By Australian standards, Adrian was a late bloomer to long-term travel, discovering Asia via a two-month journey after many shorter stints. Although dying to scribble "Professional Traveler" in the occupation section of exotic visa applications, he has resigned himself to a music company management job in Melbourne, with the threat of travel always nagging away at him. Don't tell his current employer …

Naomi Naam
(Pg. 13, 41, 80, 108, 243, 254)

India has had the greatest creative influence on the life of this South African architect. Naomi's fascination with the Subcontinent's cultures and religions prompted him to choose an Indian wife, whom he married after converting to Hinduism in an Arya Samaj ceremony in 1995.

Alexandra Nassau-Brownstone
(Pg. 128, 208)

Alexandra began dreaming of faraway adventures as a little girl. She grew up in Boston, spending many afternoons transforming her room into other countries and time periods with pieces of cloth and trinkets. In her final semester of school, she had the opportunity to study and travel through India and Nepal. Currently, Alexandra spends her time in Washington, DC, gardening, photographing, writing, and dreaming of her next adventure.

Kelly O'Neil
(Pg. 226)

Kelly O'Neil lives with her husband and four adopted children in the hills outside of Portland, Oregon. Their household also contains four dogs, two guinea pigs, two gerbils, three hens, one rooster, and a species-identification-confused duck. In her copious free time, she loves to read and sleep.

Prem Panicker
(Pg. 154)
www.indiaabroad.com

After stints in the feature writing departments of *The Indian Post, Mid-Day*, and the *Sunday Observer*, Prem joined a select group of journalists who started Rediff.com, India's first online news portal. He is also editor of *India Abroad*, the New York-based weekly newspaper that caters to the Indian American community.

Jan Polatschek
(Pg. 71)
http://travelwithjan.com

Jan Polatschek, a native New Yorker, now lives in Thailand. Using Bangkok as his hub, he travels in Asia, the Middle East, and beyond and writes about his adventures. His essays appear in several ThingsAsian Press publications. He posts his photos and travel letters on his website, *Travel With Jan*.

William Potter
(Pg. 56)

William is a writer/editor of children's books and magazines. When he's not putting words into the mouths of Rugrats, Shrek, Winnie the Pooh, and Ninja Turtles, he plays bass for reformed UK indie band CUD.

Dave Prager
(Pg. 17, 104, 238)
http://ourdelhistruggle.com

After eight years in New York City, Dave and his wife, Jenny Steeves, moved to New Delhi mostly for the food. They've written about their experiences at *Our Delhi Struggle* to an absurd amount of critical acclaim. Visit their site for more short essays and news about their book about living and working in New Delhi.

Margaret Rees
(Pg. 207, 215)

At the age of forty-eight, Margaret got a degree in psychology and felt she now deserved her twelve-month holiday traveling the world. India was somewhere at the bottom of her itinerary, and when she finally landed in Delhi, she found that the six weeks she had there were too few to venture very far from the capital. So she spent the time doing an extended version of North India's Golden Triangle and took back enough memories of people and places to want to come back again and complete another pocket of the country.

Michael Roberts
(Pg. 40, 195)

A fashion photographer by trade, Michael likes to live life on his own terms—run five miles a day; exercise his aged dogs, who'd sooner rest at home; sleep behind the sofa; and raid the refrigerator at three in the morning. He travels to distant countries whenever the mood seizes him and takes great interest in local cuisines. Homemade Indian food would have been his favorite thing to eat, if only the cooks would leave off the whole spices that keep getting stuck between his teeth. Michael lives in Syracuse, in Upstate New York.

Linda Saleh
(Pg. 43, 44, 120, 145)

From Albany, New York, Linda is a trained nurse who has traveled the world with her Lebanese husband, Ali. After the sudden passing of her husband, Linda moved to Florida and keeps herself busy with her music, needle arts, and listening to Michael Savage's radio talk show.

Vir Sanghvi
(Pg. 64, 256, 264)

Vir is one of India's best-known media celebrities, with magazines, newspapers, books, and several successful TV shows to his credit. Among his many achievements is *Rude Food*, a collection of his food columns that won the Cointreau Award (the culinary equivalent of the Oscars) for world's best literature in Stockholm in 2004.

Deblina Sarkar
(Pg. 40, 54)

Deblina is terribly confused when people ask her where she is from. Kathmandu? Kolkata? Pune? Since childhood, the economics graduate traveled so much, she didn't quite know what to call home. Marriage, however, resolved that conundrum, locating her permanently in Dubai, where she now waits patiently for inspiration to strike for her first romantic novel.

Deepanjana Sarkar
(Pg. 91, 130)

Deepanjana was ready to set the catwalk aflame when a quick brain and family pressure yanked her out of the fashion world and set her on course for a career in architecture. She lived in India for a few years before moving to Kuwait, where she is now designing her dreams in concrete.

Robin Searle
(Pg. 81, 181)

www.mytb.org/Banchory-to-the-Bosphorous-by-Bike

Robin grew up in Scotland, where he trained as an ecologist and gained a love of mountains and all things outdoors. Cycling to work, he would dream of riding past the office and over the horizon. One day, he did just that, heading east toward India and beyond. He is still pedaling.

Avirook Sen
(Pg. 24)

From a trainee journalist who was always bunking office to go play cricket with his old college mates, Avirook has come a long way. After a couple of high-profile positions as newspaper editor, this immensely talented Delhi-based writer is currently on a long hiatus. Maybe he's writing a book.

Keya Sen
(Pg. 235, 263)

Keya is a student of Rabindranath Tagore's famous educational institution in Shantiniketan (West Bengal), and like many other graduates of her alma mater, Keya excels in the creative field. Her exquisite embroidery and sitar playing talents keep her company when she is not traveling to indulge her third great passion: researching Indian flora and fauna.

Helene Shapiro
(Pg. 19, 42, 94, 124)

Helene, from New York City, has worked all her life for the same hospital she was born in and plans to retire shortly from her nursing job there. Her postretirement plans include lots of beach holidays and building on her frog collection.

Suparna Sharma
(Pg. 114)

When this Delhi journalist is not chasing stories around the capital, she can be found in the markets and bazars, rummaging around for interesting clothes and jewelry. Years of compulsive shopping has sharpened her buyer's eye, and Suparna can be depended on to know what treasures can be found in little hole-in-the-wall outlets dotting the city.

Ajit Vikram Singh
(Pg. 251)

Ajit owns Fact & Fiction, one of Delhi's best-known bookshops in Vasant Vihar. He is usually to be found sitting behind the counter, scowling at customers who love him for his eclectic book collection, great book recommendations, and off-the-wall humor.

Jennifer Smith
(Pg. 152, 217)

A nineteen-year-old student of languages at Oxford University in England, Jennifer found her spiritual home in India while traveling and volunteering there for four months. Every spare moment she gets, she likes to spend planning her next visit, writing to friends, checking the price of flights, listening to Hindi music, and reading more in a desperate attempt to try to understand this mysterious country better.

Andrew Soleimany
(Pg. 15, 169, 198)

Airplanes keep this rocket science graduate's head permanently lost in the clouds. He works as a flight test engineer during the week and flies small Cessna and Piper aircraft around America's Pacific Northwest during the weekends. The only thing that can keep Andrew tied to the ground is bad flying weather.

Jason Staring
(Pg. 41, 196, 257)

Jason is a resident of Troy, New York. After working for a while in the health insurance sector, he went back to college to do a course in death and dying. Jason has a passion for Indian language, food, and culture, and is not at all averse to the idea of settling down one day with an Indian wife.

Mark Templer
(Pg. 224)

Mark has spent most of his adult life in social and community service in the Third World. He made India his home in 1987 and has been working tirelessly since then to bring dignity into the lives of leprosy patients through the HOPE Foundation. Mark lives in Delhi with his wife, Nadine, and their four children.

Anupam Tripathi
(Pg. 31, 257, 264)

Anupam is the chairman of a very successful law firm called The Practice in Delhi. When he is not busy settling contractual disputes and personal injury cases, he likes to travel, play golf, and write.

Jeroen van Marle
(Pg. 93)

The bilingual Dutch-English travel writer, currently based in the Netherlands after eight years abroad, has worked for travel guides such as InYourPocket.com, Rough Guides, Thomas Cook, DK Eyewitness, Time Out, Lonely Planet, Compass PopOut map guides, and Berlitz since 1999. He spent six action-packed months in India, traveling from Kerala in the south to Leh in the north, and now considers himself to be a bit of an expert on the country.

Jenni Wadams
(Pg. 52, 126, 203)

A New Zealand-born girl who always wanted to travel, Jenni grabbed a chance to study in Spain and then go on a working holiday to Japan. Drawn back to Asia, she has now lived and worked in Japan for many years, first as an English teacher and now as a yoga instructor. She visits India every year to practice yoga and see more of this fascinating country.

Kate Wiseman
(Pg. 85, 172)

At thirty-two years of age, tired of the stresses of her London life, job, and commute, Kate decided there had to be more to her existence than over-ambitious sales targets and over-crowded trains. Selling everything she owned and blowing savings that could have been put toward buying a house, she swapped handbag for rucksack and bought a plane ticket to one of the most overpopulated countries in the world. India was calling ...

Nancy Wong
(Pg. 167)

Nancy, from Massachusetts, has a Master's in Applied Sociology and has worked in the fields of human and social services as well as educational research. She spent thirteen months traveling, volunteering, and experiencing the world, a part of which time she devoted to India. Nancy is a keen hiker, writer, and photographer.

Paul and Melissa Yeung
(Pg. 61)

Paul and Melissa left their law practices, loaded two backpacks, and took off on a trip around the world for eight months—too short to see it all, but long enough to suffer some serious bouts of diarrhea. Back in Vancouver, BC, they are now planning their next adventure.

Maurice Young
(Pg. 37, 44, 89, 257)

Maurice has spent most of his adult life living and teaching in Asia. After a six-month cultural tour of India, he is now back in his native hometown of Brisbane, working as an advertising copywriter and missing the good old days when he was on the road.

CREDITS

"Dave Prager poses Bollywood-style in New Delhi" reprinted in an edited and updated form from "Dave and Jenny, Bollywood style," originally published at *Our Delhi Struggle* (www.ourdelhistruggle.com). Reprinted by permission of the author. Copyright © 2009 by Dave Prager.

"Dave Prager shares the story of a teenage bride in Anupshahr" reprinted in an edited and updated form from "The Story of Ruksana," originally published at *Our Delhi Struggle* (www.ourdelhistruggle.com). Reprinted by permission of the author. Copyright © 2008 by Dave Prager.

"Dave Prager speaks frankly about tandoori *bakra* in Delhi" reprinted in an edited and updated form from "Karim's," originally published at *Our Delhi Struggle* (www.ourdelhistruggle.com). Reprinted by permission of the author. Copyright © 2008 by Dave Prager.

"Jan Polatschek learns to look up in Shekhawati" reprinted in an edited and updated form from "Nawalgarh: The Haveli and Mundan Sanskar," originally published at *Travel With Jan* (http://travelwithjan.com). Reprinted by permission of the author. Copyright © 2007 by Jan Polatschek.

"Mark Moxon gives in to 'guidebookese' at the temples of Mt. Abu" reprinted in an edited and updated form from "India: Mt Abu," originally published at

INDEX

INDEX

INDEX

INDEX

Nabanita Dutt

A journalist by accident, Nabanita Dutt started her career with a news magazine in order to finance her obsession with clothes. The excitement of running a business desk, however, soon took the edge off her fascination with fashion, and she surprised both herself and her employers by displaying a talent for the job. She went on to edit the weekend feature magazine for one of India's largest-selling newspapers, and her career in journalism continued. Almost every month, she finds herself in a different country, and she uses these trips to explore ethnic cuisines and culture, while also writing travel features for publications in the UK and Asia.

Nana Chen

Nana Chen is an internationally published freelance photographer and writer whose work has appeared in *South China Morning Post*, *Real Travel UK*, *Adbusters*, and major in-flight magazines, including those for Thai Airways, Scandinavian Airlines, and China Airlines. She has made several guest appearances on the Travel Channel's *Bizarre Foods* with Andrew Zimmern and contributed to art columns for the Council for Cultural Affairs Taiwan and *South China Morning Post*'s "WorldBeat." She is the photographer for *Tone Deaf in Bangkok* from ThingsAsian Press. Nana is currently based in Bangkok and continues to travel wherever work takes her.

TO ASIA WITH LOVE SERIES

TO VIETNAM WITH LOVE
A Travel Guide for the Connoisseur
Edited & with contributions by Kim Fay
Photographs by Julie Fay Ashborn

TO THAILAND WITH LOVE
A Travel Guide for the Connoisseur
Edited & with contributions by Joe Cummings
Photographs by Marc Schultz

TO CAMBODIA WITH LOVE
A Travel Guide for the Connoisseur
Edited & with contributions by Andy Brouwer
Photographs by Tewfic El-Sawy

TO MYANMAR WITH LOVE
A Travel Guide for the Connoisseur
Edited & with contributions by Morgan Edwardson
Photographs by Steve Goodman

TO SHANGHAI WITH LOVE
A Travel Guide for the Connoisseur
Edited & with contributions by Crystyl Mo
Photographs by Coca Dai

TO NORTH INDIA WITH LOVE
A Travel Guide for the Connoisseur
Edited & with contributions by Nabanita Dutt
Photographs by Nana Chen

TO JAPAN WITH LOVE
A Travel Guide for the Connoisseur
Edited & with contributions by Celeste Heiter
Photographs by Robert George

TO NEPAL WITH LOVE
A Travel Guide for the Connoisseur
Edited & with contributions by Cristi Hegranes
Photographs by Kraig Lieb

For more information, visit www.toasiawithlove.com